Edmund White

Also by Stephen Barber

Antonin Artaud: Blows and Bombs

Weapons of Liberation

Tokyo Vertigo

Fragments of the European City

Edmund White

The Burning World

STEPHEN BARBER

St. Martin's Press ♏ New York

EDMUND WHITE: THE BURNING WORLD. Copyright © 1999 by Stephen Barber. All rights reserved. Printed in the United States of America. No part of this book may be used or reproduced in any manner whatsoever without written permission except in the case of brief quotations embodied in critical articles or reviews. For information, address St. Martin's Press, 175 Fifth Avenue, New York, N.Y. 10010.

Library of Congress Cataloging-in-Publication Data

Barber, Stephen, 1961–
    Edmund White : the burning world / Stephen Barber.
      p.   cm.
    Includes bibliographical references (p.   ).
    ISBN 0-312-19974-0
    1. White, Edmund, 1940– . 2. Novelists, American—20th century—Biography. 3. Journalists—United States—Biography. 4. Gay men—United States—Biography. I. Title.
    PS3573.H463Z54   1999
    813'.54—dc21
    [B]   98-33116
                                   CIP

First published in Great Britain under the title *Edmund White: The Burning World: A Biography* by Picador, an imprint of Macmillan Publishers Ltd.

First U.S. Edition: December 1999

10 9 8 7 6 5 4 3 2 1

Acknowledgements

I'd like to thank Edmund White for all his generous encouragement, for giving me absolute access to all the memories and materials I needed for this book, and for unlimited interviews in Paris and London over a period of four years between 1993 and 1997.

I'm also grateful to everyone else I interviewed for the book or who discussed it with me or who encouraged and helped me, particularly Jane Giles, Marina Warner, Neil Bartlett, Adam Mars-Jones, John Maybury, Aaron Williamson, Martin Amis, Julian Barnes, Salman Rushdie, Jeremy Reed, Mandy Merck, Barbara Read, Toni Melechi, Catherine Lupton, Jonathan Burnham, Hubert Sorin, Julien Sorin, Michael Carroll, Albert Dichy, Gregory Rowe, Pierre Guyotat, Philippe Sollers, Diane Henneton, Marianne Alphant, Marie-Claude de Brunhoff, Isabelle Blondiaux, Donald Richie, Wolfgang Cilharz, Rainer Fetting, Lynne Tillman, Peter Sellars and Patti Smith; also to my agent, Deborah Rogers, and her assistant Stephen Edwards, and to Peter Straus, Jon Riley and Ursula Doyle at Picador.

I've myself been a close witness to Edmund White's life for

over ten years, and before the project of this book came into existence I had also met a number of the people who appear in it, including Hubert Le Gall, Rachel Stella, Robert Wilson, Robert Coover, Kathy Lette and Leila Shahid. I also met John Purcell, David Stevenson, Paule Thévenin and Gilles Barbedette (who have all since died).

I'd finally like to thank Patricia Willis, who supervises the collection of Edmund White's manuscripts at the Beinecke Rare Book and Manuscript Library at Yale University in the United States, for her help during my time there.

This book is dedicated to Aaron.

Stephen Barber,
Tokyo, 1997

Contents

List of Illustrations

Introduction

Body to Body

This is a book about one of the most extraordinary writers of our time. Edmund White's life and work form an ecstatic and compelling exploration of contemporary life and its essential components. He explores sex and the human body; death and creativity; the city and its sensations; and, most of all, the precarious but exhilarating instant of life which we all inhabit.

It might be argued that nothing is more vital for a contemporary writer than creating a new world of language – extracting the intricacies and contradictions from human existence and assembling them into an arena of language that we can touch and feel. Edmund White is a pre-eminently contemporary writer, and he has created just such a world. It roars and blazes with words and images. It exhales with ecstasy, and delicately burns with joy and with fury. The invention of that world emerged from a life which is one long and astonishing journey, ricocheting from city to city, between the United States and Europe – a journey which finally focuses itself in the most evocative and vivid of all the great European cities: Paris. This book follows White on that journey, with all it has to reveal about our searing culture, our compelling desires, and, finally, about our own lives.

The central fact that propels Edmund White's life and work is being gay. He has been a seminal figure in the trajectory of the gay movement since 1969, when, in his late twenties, he participated in the legendary Stonewall riots against homophobic persecution. From that formative moment in New York City, he has meticulously tracked the course of gay sensibility, its languages, its upheavals and its resistances, through the intervening three decades of raw liberation and brutal calamity. If, as White believes, AIDS has been a futile genocide issuing from some unknowable and void source (lacking even the bogus dignity of a God-given plague), then its witnesses and survivors have an urgent and communal responsibility to themselves – to collect together the traces of lost lives, through writing, through art, and through an excavation of the nature of memory itself.

The deeply felt and determining memories of death and lust which make up those three decades after Stonewall are White's territory of remembering. From the sexual experimentation of the 1960s and 1970s to the endless deaths of the 1980s and 1990s – and the reinvention of the gay experience which those deaths provoked – White has shaped the way in which sensation is translated into language and finally into the configurations of memory. White is a writer about sex, and his work has intensively created the sexual memory of his time. The fragile skin between lust and death is uniquely permeable in that work.

A community immersed simultaneously in both lust and death is necessarily attuned to the vital facts of life. White's books have had to sustain the gay community through multiply difficult times, since it is a community that has often been perilously in conflict with the dominant political, religious and legal arrangements of society. If it is true, as White believes, that whatever is socially dominant seeks only repetition, power and homogeneity, then his work has been a crucial shattering – it has been instrumental in the appearance of a contemporary gay culture that is resistantly multiplicitous and polymorphous, composed of brilliant intersections of creativity and sexuality, of deep penetration and deep analysis. In that sense, White's work has helped to engender a community that is magnificently and eruptively anti-social.

However attuned White's world may be to the teeming contemporary consciousness, its essential substance is still that of the lone human being with its isolated sensations. White's work and his life have sought to throw together glittering individual existences into ambitious amalgams, but finally those human lives are alone with their elemental fears and responses, both to exterior and interior dangers. It is work about overcoming but loving solitude. In White's work, human bodies listen attentively and obsessively to their own internal processes, to their malfunctions and their physical compulsions. It is a world of adrenalized ecstasy which only the excessive human body has access to, but it is also a world of spontaneous combustion into sudden horror, collapse and death. For White, the body turns on a knife-edge, always ready to inflame itself orgasmically, but always subject to its own fatal betrayal and attack.

That threat of attack has transformed itself in the years since the onset of AIDS. At the end of the 1970s, when White was travelling around North America to write *States of Desire*, his eye-witness account of the gay male community in a moment of explosive development, AIDS had never been heard of. The exterior threat came principally from fanatically vocal anti-gay campaigners such as Anita Bryant, who denounced the gay community from her base in Miami. Twenty years on, that threat of attack may be less vocal and visible in some ways, but it is more pervasively present. The impact of the AIDS virus itself has been exacerbated by less strident but no less explicit persecution from governments, fundamentalists and media powers. The years of AIDS have seen a vast metamorphosis in the way in which the ill human body is represented, imagined and experienced. The resulting horror and fascination with the body can, however, be used for productive as well as repressive ends. In his collection of short stories, *Skinned Alive*, White's world is one in which the imperatives of survival are uppermost for his human figures. His characters have a unique culture all of their own – a culture of desire, memory and resistance – and that culture is what proves most ferocious in reaction to the forces which attempt to snuff it out.

White accords singular distinctions to the human figures who populate his world. Their identities ignite in their sensations. If, as White suggests, dominant societies can only unite through the poor mundanity of power relations, then his characters' aberrance and deviance are salutary and rich in the extreme. Like the world-wide gay community which surrounds White's work and informs it from multiple tangents, his world of human figures amasses around their distinctions, their craziness and their independence. The crucial element in this creative proliferation of human attributes has been the fact that White's life has been one vast incitement to friendship. It is a life which has run headlong into every other kind of human life. However, the wildness of the world in his writings is tempered by its intricate stratification. It is a world immersed in gratuitous hierarchies and obtuse ceremonials, extending from the arcane protocol that governs his first novel, *Forgetting Elena*, to the intricate rhythms of Parisian society in *Sketches from Memory*. The layers of that world are mysterious in the way in which they appear absolutely predetermined, and it is the rôle of White's heroic figures to splinter those ostensibly fated strata with wilful, sexual caprice. The preoccupations of White's characters are those of his own life, and White is a writer whose life has often been confused with the first-person narrators he creates. Part of the aim of this book is to show where that overlap between writer and narrator ends, and where another, more probing voice begins.

Edmund White is a pre-eminent writer of the contemporary city: both the cities of North America which he documented from his travels in *States of Desire*, and those of Europe, especially the city of Paris where he has lived since 1983. More than ever now, the power of the city is crucial: virtually all the sensations of contemporary life flood from it, and the imperatives of the city bring together and drive all creative communities, including the gay community. But White incessantly transforms his cities, with imagination and desire, and the most vivid manifestation of this is the city's metamorphosis into the form of an island. The city and the island are the spaces which White simultaneously inhabits. Throughout his life, he has travelled from city to island, from island to city. His life and work have a double compulsion and a double location in the city and the island. These are the exhilarating arenas within which sex and identity are worked through in White's world, where borders are always broken, and sedentary senses torn apart. His cities possess a precarious insularity which is also that of the human figures in his writings, forever offered or exposed to the jolt of invasion.

From his childhood cities of the American Mid-West, Cincinnati and Chicago, White's urban panorama shifts to the New York of the 1960s and 1970s – decades of physical and cultural uproar. But his preoccupation with the city as the formative zone of ecstasy, liberation and calamity comes into its own with his move to Paris. White's fascination is for the city's self-irony and its intricate contradictions – a love of the city as a place of masks, where social strata can disintegrate into moral free-fall and then shamelessly reform themselves into entirely new configurations. Paris fulfilled to the hilt that desire for brazen self-contradiction and for the pleasures of re-invention. Paris, for White, is socially moribund but incurably enlivening. His capacity to evoke a frantically futile social arrangement, already highly developed in New York, came to full fruition there. Paris is also a city with a phenomenal literary history which has always been read in intimate tension with English-language culture. Centrally, for White, Paris is the city of the legendary gay writer and thief Jean Genet, who seemed set for a lifetime of squalid petty crime and imprison-ment before his sudden literary fame of the 1940s propelled him into the stratospheres of Parisian intellectual and aristo-cratic life. White spent six of his years in that seductively hostile city constructing his extraordinary biographical study *Genet*, following Genet's life through the intersecting social and anti-social spheres he inhabited in Paris. In White's world of Paris, the city simply scintillates as it accommodates the diversity of its enormous sexual components; but it is also hilariously intent on trying to screen away the final non-existence of its legendary glamour and glory.

White's islands take these social screens and masks to their extreme. They are city islands which pulse with trapped and dreaming flesh. White spent much of his time in the 1970s on the infamous Fire Island, New York's gay nirvana of that decade. Fire Island, along the Long Island coast from that other dream island of Manhattan, was transfigured by White into the unnamed island of *Forgetting Elena*. White creates an island existence of amnesiac frenzy whose inhabitants breathe a rarefied atmosphere of sharp urban ritual, containing too a prescient intimation of the devastation to come in New York. The island is the site of a revolution which abruptly evanesces once it has expelled the elements that questioned the power of its rituals. The island is scarred by the blazes of its momentary, headlong physical insurrections. White's islands are inhabited by self-obsessed populations whose contradictory gestures and hierarchical acts are the evidence of deep desires and bursting tensions. In his later novel *Caracole*, begun in New York but completed in Paris, White formulated his first island society after his move to Europe as a heady concoction of Imperial Venice, Occupied 1940s Paris, and the contemporary New York whose elaborate cultural machinations he had just exited from. The island community of *Caracole* is vividly charged, festive and decadent; living under the domination of a stultifying alien power, it is pulled between invisible complicity and outright revolution. (Though *Caracole* has been viewed as White's one 'heterosexual' novel, in some ways it's the antithesis; in terms of its political resonances, it forms a liberatory exclamation of celebration for the history and survival of gay life.) The island is where human life is impelled to liberate itself, whatever the consequences of that act may be.

White has always lived and created his work on islands. His island communities are the manifestation of his own inhabitation of a vast succession of the world's islands – first, in the United States, Manhattan, Fire Island, and Florida's Key West; every summer for decades, the island city of Venice, itself fragmented into a host of smaller islands; for many years, after his arrival in Europe, the hauntingly beautiful Île Saint-Louis in the heart of Paris; the island of Crete and its Venetian port of Xania; the Île de Ré, off the Atlantic coast of France; and, from many visits in the late 1980s and early 1990s, the island of Büyükada, across from Istanbul in the sea of Marmara, a bizarre and silent terrain of opulent villas, intricate promenades and dark passageways.

The city and the island form a pressurized zone where White's human figures collide at random between moments of intense sexual self-interrogation. His world is one of deeply stratified ritual in conflict with exuberant and spontaneous eruptions of lust and mischief. White's characters gaze into the endless subterranea of their identities, and spend their time evolving schemes to explore deeper into that proliferating and always transforming mass of identity; then suddenly, when that absorbed figure hits and seizes another human figure, all hell breaks loose, and the spectator of White's world is propelled on a vertiginous journey, from city to city, from island to island, from body to body. It is a world where inner exploration collides with an urgent longing for sexual contact, caught in a spectacularly disciplined crash of language.

White's move from New York to Paris is the vital point both in his life and in the development of that mastery of language in evoking the desiring human body. It is also a move that spans many of the critical events and preoccupations – such as the onset of AIDS and anxiety about the future of culture – that would become the key obsessions of the end of the twentieth century. New York and Paris were utterly different worlds. In the New York of the late 1970s and early 1980s, White had inhabited a factional literary and artistic scene that often appeared to be as intent on acrimonious infighting as it was on refiguring sexuality and language. The New York cultural scene fluctuated between narcissistic self-absorption and tirades of denunciation. In his creative or sexual contacts (the two forms of human liaison are often closely interlinked in White's world) with some of the figures who have determined the ways in which language and the image are used in contemporary culture – such as Robert Mapplethorpe, Susan Sontag, Robert Wilson, James Merrill, William Burroughs, among many others – White's manoeuvres had to be intricate. White is a prodigious absorber of his surroundings and of the contemporary moment, and in inhabiting that multi-faceted scene, to a great extent he incorporated it. He became a chameleon of the city's culture.

White began gradually to acquire a reputation over the 1970s with the publication of his two novels of that decade, *Forgetting Elena* and *Nocturnes for the King of Naples*. From his bases in New York's Greenwich Village and then in the East Village, he was taking imaginative and actual journeys beyond the city's limits. In the two fiction projects he began working on at the time, *A Boy's Own Story* and *Caracole*, he was exploring the equally exotic and arcane territories of childhood and his island communities. The actual journeys were more gruelling. Documenting an unparalleled moment of change in gay life, he travelled exhaustively – though intermittently – around the entirety of North America gathering material for *States of Desire*. And, towards the end of the 1970s, he was shuttling incessantly from New York to the outlying university towns to teach courses in American and English literature. Despite this travelling, it was the relentless polyphony and experimentation of New York itself which saturated White's world. He experienced everything from the insulated and paranoid environment of Burroughs' subterranean home – the 'Bunker' – to the blaring gay discos and clubs. New York made up a vast creative assault with its rancorous and aggressively contradictory mesh of noise, language and imagery.

The heady culture of New York was compounded by the sexual energy concentrated there. The infinite sexual permutations of 1970s New York gave extraordinary scope for handsome young gay men such as White, and this imposed a different kind of mobility to his incessant travelling. In his writings on Robert Mapplethorpe – whose work embodies the mixture of raw outrage and adept sophistication which animated the cultural life of the city at that time – White emphasized the limitless mobility of the photographer's hunt for sexual partners. Like the Irish painter Francis Bacon moving seamlessly between London's Soho and Belgravia, Mapplethorpe led a life which encompassed extremes of income and social standing, of squalor and luxury. Distinctions of race and money were cancelled in the overriding will to interrogate identity and beauty. White shared that mobility and its dual benefits of ecstasy and of insight about how societies operated. Living and fully experiencing this defining moment of evanescing social structure was to enable him, after his move to Europe, to treat the far more solid social limits of France and Britain with the same invisibility.

New York's gay sex and drugs scene of the 1970s and early 1980s is the stuff of extravagant legend, focusing particularly on the bath-houses, bars and piers of Manhattan. Here, too, all social distinctions evaporated. White's New York was constellated with bath-houses and bars where the immediate compulsion in acts of sexual penetration negated superfluous and bogus social structures. The random anonymity of multiple sexual encounters – in the recesses of the bath-houses, and on the more dangerous piers – was a powerful driving force. There was no sex without drugs, whose open availability lent an atmosphere of hallucinatory and neural excess to the moment. White's travels around North America also enabled him to experience intensively the sexual culture and surroundings of other cities, notably those of San Francisco, where he lived for six months in 1972. The way of life was wildly defiant and chaotic, although even during its pre-eminent decade, the 1970s, that wildness was beginning for some to evolve into habit and nostalgia. The sex scene powering much of the creative experimentation of New York continued in full flood, until the realization in 1981 that the onset of AIDS meant this key moment of gay history had been short-lived.

The initial confusion and anxieties about the AIDS virus began to solidify into one focus with the growing pattern of cases and deaths. White charted the initial nuances of fear and

bewilderment in the short stories about AIDS collected in 1987
– together with those of Adam Mars-Jones – as the volume
entitled *The Darker Proof*. As AIDS delineated itself from the
mixed variety of mundane sexual diseases which 1970s New
York had blithely taken in its stride, a sense of panic started to
set in. White has highlighted a feeling of sharp collective
anticlimax as one of the principal characteristics of that
moment. Despite the attacks of anti-gay campaigners, it had
seemed that the liberation of gay life was irreversible. Though
that new life had become streamlined into routine in some
respects, the potential remained for endless transmutations into
original zones of sexual life and socially oppositional life. One
key factor was that the ignorance or hostility of the American
family towards homosexuality, which had determined many
young gay lives in the 1950s and 1960s – including White's
own – had now partly disappeared, along with that hostility's
enforcement through psychiatric treatment. American family
life, at least in the large cities, had become subject to a new
openness and tolerance in the years following the Stonewall
uprising, and White's participation in that uprising and his
subsequent writings played their part in those developments.
On a wide scale, the culture of protest of the late 1960s and
early 1970s, with its focus in collective and vocal denunciations
of the Vietnam war and of the corruption of governmental
power, had questioned and overhauled all of the structures of
authority in America. In particular, the innumerable declarations of sons and daughters, about both their sexuality and
their political engagement, had changed the nature of the
American family in the years before the onset of AIDS.

All of this was suddenly transformed with the cohering of
scattered medical reports into the profile of a disease possessing
blind horror. In time, the entire cultural configuration of New
York would be altered by AIDS. The anticipated future of art
in the city collapsed with the deaths through AIDS of such

figures as Keith Haring and Mapplethorpe. New York became a desperate landscape of absences. Where European cities such as Berlin in 1945 had the vital architectural components of their landscape obliterated, New York in the 1980s began to have its essential human elements summarily excised from its landscape.

Edmund White left for Paris in 1983, along with his lover John Purcell, and became one of the essential absent components of New York. The decision to leave New York behind was not, however, primarily the result of any desire to put distance between himself and the escalating trauma of disease and death which the city now represented for many of its inhabitants. For one thing, very few of White's friends had actually died by that stage. And AIDS already had its hold too upon the population and imagery of Paris, although there the disease was viewed less hysterically, more clinically than in New York (much of the pioneering research into AIDS had been done in Paris). AIDS did not threaten the identity of a strongly cohesive gay community as it did in New York, since such an entity simply did not exist in the more diffuse and discreet arena of individuals that made up Parisian gay life.

White's arrival in Paris was far more the desire to excavate a new creative site that in many ways was the elegant, arrogant negation of its wild counterpart in New York. Paris, for White, was the discovery of an enthralling and challenging new environment. Where New York was fractious and ephemerally experimental, Paris possessed an immense and entrenched cultural history. It breathed out that history, transmitting it atmospherically and tangibly, especially to an American like White who was well aware of the depth of European culture. Though conscious of the lengthy lineage of American writers who had moved to Paris in both the pre-war and post-war years – figures as diverse as Ernest Hemingway and James Baldwin – White was largely indifferent to the influence of that migration. Those writers had arrived in Paris for every conceivable reason under the sun, not as part of a collective movement, and White's motives were as idiosyncratic as most of the others' reasons for relocating themselves there.

An element of cultural competitiveness has existed between New York and Paris for most of the twentieth century, and was hotly under debate at the moment White arrived there. It was argued by writers such as Serge Guilbaut (in his 1983 book *How New York Stole the Idea of Modern Art*) that Paris had lost its claim to be the originating crucible of all experimental art and writing around the time of the Second World War when – so the argument went – the avant-garde had transplanted itself wholesale to New York. White had seen and experienced the aftermath of that cultural shift during the prolifically experimental 1960s in New York. But he was aware too that a vital culture around producing a new and disruptive imagery and language of the human body and its sexuality had been reactivated in Paris in the 1940s, and had sustained itself to the present day. Work by writers such as Jean Genet, Jean Cocteau and Georges Bataille – preoccupied with the intimate proximity between sex and death – was still richly influential and resonated into the contemporary world. Those two seminal preoccupations formed a volatile concoction which had heightened relevance for the 1980s and 1990s. White's engagement with that work gave him elements for his new language of precarious physical desire.

In some parts of the literary scene back in New York, the feeling developed that White had abandoned the city just as it was being precipitated into a far-reaching crisis – encompassing both the homosexual and the heterosexual communities of the city – which he should have stayed to confront. The same sense of White's having escaped a situation with crucial responsibilities had been felt when he had left New York after the Stonewall riots to live for six months in Rome. At that time, he had been unknown. But by 1983, with the impact of *States of Desire* and the publication in the previous year of the hugely successful *A Boy's Own Story*, White had acquired the status of a senior commentator in his non-fiction, and of an authoritative imaginer of gay life in his fiction. His loss to New York was compounded by the pervasive sense there of a terminal situation. An irreversible leakage had begun of those who remained in New York, into death from AIDS and into the fearful abyss of knowing things would never be the same again. The onset of the Reagan years from 1980 had released decrepitude and corruption into the city's atmosphere – together with a high degree of governmental incompetence and apathy towards AIDS research – and this consolidated the prevailing unease about things going badly wrong. But as it turned out, White had not abandoned New York. He remained a vital part of the city's discourse about AIDS and its strategies of resistance and refusal, with his writings and numerous visits back to the city.

In addition to White's desire for a challenging cultural site outside of the United States, other more pragmatic factors were at work in his move to Paris. The heated intellectual acrimony enacted within closed New York circuits had proved alienating and exhausting. London was discounted as an option for being too like New York. In financial terms, the dollar's strength meant that living in Paris was feasible and attractive. An arrangement with *Vogue* magazine gave White a regular monthly sum in return for reports on the cultural life of Paris and its ascendant fashions. And White's sex life in Paris, while very different in venue and intensity from that in New York, would be just as adventurous and consuming. But crucially, he had been awarded a writing grant from the Guggenheim

Foundation, primarily to work on his novel *Caracole*, and had the opportunity to choose the best European city as a writing environment for what was initially planned to be a year's stay. Paris was to become an immensely enveloping arena, and White's nurturing of a network of friends who were more diverse than their New York counterparts meant that the initially provisional stay rapidly acquired its permanence.

Paris, at the time of White's arrival in the city, was impelled by a mood of political and cultural elation which he receptively absorbed. Two years earlier, François Mitterrand's Socialist government had been elected in uproar. That moment's sensation of impending transformation had only two parallels in recent Parisian life: the Liberation of 1944 and the student street riots of 1968. Much of that impression of a positive upheaval and of a separation from the past would prove to be mistaken, at least as far as the often caustic assessments of Mitterrand's fourteen-year presidency after his death in 1996 were concerned. The illusory sense of victory and accomplishment following the Socialists' coming to power resulted in the premature disbanding of many militant groups, particularly those with feminist and anti-racist preoccupations. But certainly, the first years of the Mitterrand government appeared to break with the oppression that had been endemic to France in its relations with its residents from North Africa and in its political dealings with its former colonies. And Mitterrand's Minister of Culture, Jack Lang, attempted to use his power to crack apart the ossified structures of the country's culture and media, with radical popularizing measures intended to promote experimentation and openness.

Paris, in the early 1980s, had a culture that was firing. It was the vibrant and provocative world centre of philosophy, with the work of writers such as Michel Foucault, whom White knew from his visits to the United States (where Foucault had lectured and assiduously explored the gay sex scenes of San Francisco and New York). Foucault would die of AIDS in the year following White's arrival in Paris. The legacy of Roland Barthes, whom White had also met in New York shortly before Barthes' death in 1980, was still strong. In Paris, White was to encounter the prominent philosophers Julia Kristeva and Philippe Sollers, whose work since the 1960s had been aimed at putting the nature of language itself under intense interrogation, by recasting it as an ecstatically mobile and potentially liberatory substance. And Paris was the home to a vast array of writers (in addition to film-makers, theatre directors, artists, dancers, and fashion designers), many of North African or Eastern European origin, with urgent and captivating preoccupations. These writers – such as Tahar ben Jelloun and Milan Kundera – were often intentional or involuntary exiles from their own countries and languages, but there were also French-born fiction writers with original, explicitly sexual obsessions whom White was to encounter, such as Hervé Guibert and Pierre Guyotat. For White, his arrival in the culture of Paris immersed him in a hugely inspiring creative framework.

In Paris, White's work would respond to that atmosphere prodigiously. He would engender a language that corresponded to his existing concerns from his years in New York, but with extraordinary new vision. He would produce works which extended his earlier books in terms of their evocation of sexuality, and also in their capacity to formulate opposition to the powers influencing a society that was under sustained manipulation as a result of the impact of AIDS. The spread of the disease was habitually utilized over the course of the 1980s and 1990s as an opportunity to entrench conservative governmental power and morality, through the media and through legislation. All White's work from 1985 responded directly and with tactile sensitivity to his own diagnosis as being HIV-Positive in that year.

Edmund White's unique world forms a wholehearted exploration of how creative languages and assailed human bodies can
survive into the future: it is a world in which extremity is
pronounced centrally, and with inflammatory love.

Part 1

Terrains of Memory –
Cincinnati to New York City

The origins of great writers with spectacular lives are invariably marked by a relative mundanity. Edmund Valentine White III was born in Cincinnati, Ohio, in the North American Mid-West, on 13 January 1940. He remembered: 'I grew up in a very conservative world – the suburbs in the Mid-West in the 1940s and 1950s.' His father, a civil engineer by training, was already prosperous as a self-employed broker of chemical equipment, and the war years of White's early childhood provided a source of great profit for his father's business; he already employed a large staff of engineers at five locations across the Mid-West. White's father was a stern man, openly racist and homophobic, but also idiosyncratically kindly (although most of that kindness was directed towards White's one older sister, Margaret). In a deeply conservative and in-bred city such as Cincinnati, White's social rôle was to replicate his father, who even possessed the same Christian names, which he had himself inherited from his own father. The inescapable dynamics of replication and divergence that such a relationship imposed would haunt White throughout his early life. And it was a relationship which White subsequently worked to transform, from the posthumous and ephemeral fragments of memory – such as the intangible smell of the noxious cigars which his father smoked – into a resonant narrative of oppression and desire.

White's mother, Delilah – who, like his father, was originally from rural Texas – had been thirty-six years old when he was born. Since his parents were older than those of most of his friends, White often had the feeling in his first years that he was being brought up by strangely self-absorbed and distant grandparents rather than by parents who could engage intimately with him. Neither of his parents read fiction, and his father was even hostile to the idea of literary culture. White's mother was a short, fat, curly-haired woman whose time was occupied with her husband and children; the large family house itself was run by black maids. In the year that White had been born, his father had started an affair with a secretary at work, and an acrimonious divorce followed when White was seven years old. While White's father soon married his secretary, his mother would never remarry. Deeply embittered and wanting to make a definitive break from her ex-husband, she took White and his sister to live several hundred miles away in Chicago, eventually settling there in the quiet suburban community of Evanston. The suburb was regarded as progressive educationally – its schools were integrated between black and white children, which remained rare in the period before the American civil rights movement. White's grade school in Evanston, Miller, had adopted an experimental educational practice named 'creative dramatics', whereby the structure of competition between pupils was entirely eliminated, and all pupils were encouraged to extend their imaginative capacities, projecting themselves in their written work and drama classes into the lives of other people of all ages, cultures and historical moments; for White, this experiment was inspirational. His next school, Haven Intermediate, was less of an eccentricity within the American educational system: the pupils there were brought up to be patriotic, and when military heroes from the Second World War such as General Douglas MacArthur visited Evanston, White and the other children stood proudly to attention as the motorcades drove past. He commented: 'In Evanston, we never stopped to wonder whether it was a good thing to be pro-American.' The YMCA youth clubs of Evanston were all named after American presidents; White joined the Eisenhower club. The Chicago winters could be glacial, and White complained that 'as a child, I remember, I used to pray God not to let me freeze to death as I walked home from school'.[1] Although she received alimony from her ex-husband, White's mother was determined to demonstrate that she could pursue a successful career herself, and she worked relentlessly as a child psychologist, taking a position as a visiting school inspector and eventually running a clinic for mentally retarded children. White himself could, when it suited him, assume that same disciplined work ethic. As a middle-aged and divorced mother of two children, White's mother found it hard to establish new relationships with men, despite her desperate desire to do so; White also matched her in this sense of isolation and excision from forming part of the sexual life of America. By the age of twelve, he had understood that his own developing sexuality was an aberration in America. From his reactions to the male figures in the books he read and in the films he watched, from his lustful fascination with the bodies of the boys and men he saw around him, and also from a deep instinctual conviction – he knew that he was and would remain gay.

White was a beautiful adolescent, with deep, dark eyes, a wryly pouted mouth always teetering on the brink of a beguiling smile, and fine hair slicked across from a side-parting. But his imagined self, as he approached his teenage years, was on a different planet altogether from his physical appearance. At the age of twelve, he painted a self-portrait in which he mercilessly represented a face of grey skin, studded with wild eyes and spiked with desultory hair. Painting was just one element of the prodigious creativity of White's adolescence – he also played musical instruments, acted and danced, and read widely, assimilating material from virtually every culture. He remembered that: 'The one good thing about being brought up in the Mid-West is it's such a vacuum that you have to compensate, and you feel that all world culture is open to you.' He spent his evenings exploring the contents of the local public library in Evanston. Many of his early attempts at writing were in the area of poetry: 'I was very facile and shallow – I could write in any form, very quickly. I could also translate from Latin verse, from Horace and Virgil, directly into English verse. It was an eerie but talentless facility.' With his mother's encouragement, he collected together a manuscript of his poems under the title *A Crop of Pins and Pearls*. He was also beginning to make his initial attempts at writing fiction, in the form of novels and short stories. In his mid-teens, he wrote a first novel entitled *The Tower Window*, based on the painful consequences of a rare 'heterosexual' date he had with a schoolfriend named Sally Gunn, which had made White – exposed as he was to the oblique but condemnatory American media pronouncements on homosexuality – all too aware of what he believed to be his cripplingly anti-social and diseased desires.

Alongside his confident early creative projects, White's childhood sexual experiences were equally prodigious and precocious. He estimated that by the time he left the all-boys' boarding school, Cranbrook, which he attended in Detroit after transferring from Haven Intermediate, he had accumulated more than a hundred sexual encounters – most of them with boys of his age. The boarding school itself, White noted wryly, was the one place where sex seemed not to take place, even covertly, despite the acknowledged reputation of boarding schools as hotbeds of buggery. It was while travelling through Mexico on holiday with his father and step-mother that White had lost his virginity, in a thrilling, if sordid, encounter with a middle-aged pianist from the bar of the glamorous hotel in Acapulco where they were staying. Among White's other sexual contacts with adults, he especially liked to recall an incident involving his maternal step-grandfather, during a visit he had made at the age of twelve to the rural Texas farm where his grandparents lived. He described the incident: 'My grandmother let me bunk with my grandfather and he and I made passionate, unending love all night. So far, so good but in the morning I heard him in the living room telling the others, "That Eddie is such a sweet boy, we just hugged and kissed all night long." My grandmother cooed with affection, "Well, isn't he the sweetest *thang*," but my mother and sister subsided into ominous silence.'[2]

Although he found these encounters compulsively exhilarating, White would increasingly torment himself in his teenage years about the sickness and marginality of his homosexual desires and acts, while at the same time defiantly affirming his homosexuality to his parents. Looking back from a distance of fifteen years on this torment, he wrote: 'I heard once of a boy who literally had a horn on his forehead that was growing *inwards*, that was driving its point deeper and deeper into his brain, slowly and methodically destroying his faculties one by one. I was that boy, as I watched my obsession with men overtake me.'[3] White's feelings towards sex at this point were an inextricable mixture of revulsion and fascination, and when he announced to his mother that he was gay, at the age of fourteen, it was an outburst that contained both anguish and defiant self-assertion. White's constrained domestic life with his mother and sister in their Evanston apartment periodically boiled over into an over-heated triangle of frustrations and powerplay, and his sudden and spontaneous outburst about his homosexuality came at just such a moment of exasperation, while he and his mother were engaged in doing the washing-up together. After White had told his shocked but finally indulgent mother that he was gay, she arranged a consultation for him with a psychiatrist. White experienced the session as one of mutual hostility. His mother later told him that the psychiatrist had reported a negative diagnosis to her: 'I was borderline psychotic, unsalvagable, and I should be locked up and the key thrown away.'

Although vocally defiant about his homosexuality, White also felt deeply troubled about the limitations he felt it would impose on his future life, largely because he already wanted to pursue a writing career and believed then that being gay would restrict him in his subject matter, denying him access to 'universal' heterosexual experience. He remembered this dilemma – of desperately wanting sex with men but feeling it was insane or, at least, creatively limiting – as the main preoccupation of his teenage years: 'It was as though I were writing two separate books in my mind.' In an attempt to resolve this dilemma and seeing only one possible solution, White then asked his incredulous father to pay for him to receive a prolonged course of psychiatric therapy, with an eccentric doctor named James Clark Maloney whose clinic was in the same Detroit suburb as White's boarding school; the father of a school friend, himself a doctor, had recommended the psychiatrist to White. Psychoanalysis and psychiatry were immensely fashionable institutions in 1950s America. Psychiatric therapy was by this time an ingrained American preoccupation, and it promised to cure any social deviation, given sufficient time and money. The incompetence of the treatment which White received from the drunken, amphetamine-crazed Maloney – with its unequivocal goal that he must give up his perversion – marked his views on the subject of therapy for life. He continued to be fascinated by Freudian models of sexuality, but he was also deeply sceptical, later engaging with the influential 'anti-psychiatry' concepts of R.D. Laing and Thomas S. Szasz (which polemically explored the idea of lunacy as productive or revolutionary), together with Carl Rogers' style of therapy, an attempt to defuse the power relations operating between the therapist and patient. White's treatment continued for many years with other therapists, extending well into adulthood. The result of the therapy White underwent as a teenager was to instil in him a sense of emotional paralysis and of a lack of connection with reality. It convinced an exhausted White that he was emotionally empty – and that he was enlivened neurally and driven physically only by the power of a sexuality that was strictly forbidden and stigmatized as pathological. His emergent creativity was exempt from those prohibitions, but when its sexual charge was extracted, it too was left void.

As his final piece of written work at Cranbrook, White submitted a novel entitled *Mrs Morrigan* to his tutors; he also handed in a long essay on the work of the French writer Marcel Proust, with its preoccupation with the nature of memory. White left Cranbrook in 1958 and began to attend the University of Michigan in the campus town of Ann Arbor, located at an equal distance away from his mother in Chicago and his father in Cincinnati. He joined the same all-male campus 'fraternity' or club to which his father had belonged, 'Sigma Nu', which required him to live in a hall of residence with its own distinct set of arcane rituals, including sessions of naked all-night torture for new members; on arrival in Ann Arbor, White proudly received his Sigma Nu membership certificate. He was expected to take part in a ceremony, modelled in part on racist Ku Klux Klan rituals, in which the hooded Sigma Nu members solemnly swore to protect the chastity of American womanhood – 'I was only too willing to oblige,' White remembered. The Sigma Nu was legendary for the drinking capacities of its members, who would drink themselves into a stupor at every available opportunity. Although White himself was not a great drinker at this point, the atmosphere of constant, chronic inebriation had its particular advantages for him: 'The boys were always so drunk that they could barely notice what was going on and I managed to have sex with quite a few of them, which I liked.'

In contrast to the anachronistic and reactionary system of the Sigma Nu, the University of Michigan itself was beginning to acquire a reputation as a base for extremely progressive, radical politics. White had decided to study Chinese there, inspired by his growing preoccupation with eastern religions such as Buddhism – the idea of a spiritual existence from which raw corporeal compulsions could be effortlessly subtracted was highly attractive to him at this time; but he was an indolent student, and his professors often had to call him by phone at the hall of residence to order him to get out of bed and attend classes. His one focus of engagement was with the sociology of ancient China. He was still making his early experiments with fiction, and while studying in Ann Arbor wrote a picaresque novel entitled *The Amorous History of Our Youth*, about the adventures of two brothers who are separated at birth; he was also avidly reading the poetry of Rimbaud, together with that of Ezra Pound, T.S. Eliot and Wallace Stevens.

Along with Buddhism, White's other main preoccupation of the time was with the conflict between socialism and the capitalism espoused by his father (together with virtually all of America). White was drawn to communism – an explosive subject matter at such a precarious moment in the age of the Cold War – as a stimulating ideal with the potential to cancel out the inhumane emotional nullity and repression which he associated with a capitalist society. As a young man who was both gay and receptive to communism, White felt that he was 'rubbing shoulders with Satan himself', as he put it. He often discussed his political concerns with a close friend he had met while still at Cranbrook, Marilyn Schaefer, who was herself preoccupied with the attractions of communism; eight years older than White, she had been a painting student at Detroit's postgraduate art school, the Cranbrook Art Academy, which was situated alongside White's boarding school. Marilyn Schaefer had been a political organizer for socialist causes in her native state, Iowa, before attending the art school; the period when White had met her was that of the Soviet Union's most violent repression of Eastern European countries such as Hungary, but he would often watch her passionately defending the Soviet communist system to sceptical listeners. 'I was madly in love with her,' he remembered, and he often wondered what married life with her would be like. They would remain lifelong friends. White graduated from the University of Michigan in 1962 and considered going on to do postgraduate work in Chinese at the more prestigious Harvard University. Instead, he decided to move to New York, attracted by the glamour of urban life and the presence there of a lover he was pursuing, a young actor he had met at the university named Stanley Redfern, with whom he would live during his first years in the city. After spending the early summer of 1962 in Chicago, driving a delivery van as a stop-gap job, on 19 July he flew to New York, where he would remain for the next twenty-one years.

The period of White's move to New York proved to be politically tumultuous. Three months after he arrived there, in October 1962, America was transfixed with apocalyptic anxiety by the confrontation between the United States and the Soviet Union that took place over the siting of Soviet nuclear missiles in Cuba. During the period in which White had been a socialist at university, many of his fellow students had travelled to Cuba to help with the sugar harvest and offer their support to Fidel

Castro's communist régime, which had seized power in 1959; White himself had been firmly pro–Castro, and now viewed the Cuban crisis as an absurd spectacle engineered by the Kennedy government to consolidate its power. Then, thirteen months later, John F. Kennedy was assassinated in Dallas. Both events had made most Americans feel that the sky was falling in on their heads. But White had always viewed Kennedy as a bogus and insincere figure, with confused and authoritarian political ideas: 'His death meant nothing to me – I was more moved by Marilyn Monroe's death,' he remembered. He later found a resonance of his own views in those of Jean Genet, who, as White later wrote, 'denounced Kennedy as the man who had launched the Vietnam War, bungled the Bay of Pigs invasion, built up the CIA and chosen Johnson as vice president'.[4]

Sexually, White experienced his arrival in New York as a thrilling revelation. In Cincinnati, Chicago and Ann Arbor, he had been able to find only the slightest visible traces of a furtive and fearful gay life, but walking through New York's Greenwich Village district on those summer nights of 1962, he was aware of a highly evident and vibrant community of gay men existing alongside the dominant but tolerant Italian population of the area. He could see that community of gay men inhabiting the streets – especially a long avenue of small tenements, bars, restaurants and shops named Christopher Street, which ran between Sixth Avenue and the Hudson River – and clearly possessing their own distinct environment of bars and restaurants. As he soon appreciated, that community was highly fragmented, acrimonious and often scathingly self-deprecating. Crucially, it was silent and powerless in the face of political, religious and physical attacks and oppression. But it existed, in the city where White was now living, as a young gay man – and those basic facts were enough to elate him. He found a small apartment in MacDougal Street – a bustling shopping street of red-brick tenements fronted with iron fire-

escapes – at the southern end of Greenwich Village, the area
which formed the axis for much of New York's intellectual
culture and experimental art, as well as for its gay life. While
living at MacDougal Street with Stanley Redfern, White began
to take part in that gay life. His principal way of meeting other
gay men for sex was by cruising the Greenwich Village streets
at night. Cruising constituted an entire culture of exchanged
gazes, gestures and words, and White cruised relentlessly. But
he remained deeply anguished about his sexuality, and continued to pay for seemingly endless, futile sessions of psychotherapy which finally convinced him that he should break off
his relationship with Redfern, on the rationale that he could
never 'achieve' heterosexuality while living with a gay lover.

White hoped to develop a successful writing career in New
York, and he began to turn out novel after novel; they were all
rejected. Retrospectively, he believed that he had been too
conscious while writing of desperately wanting a literary career,
and consequently had tried to write ingratiating novels that
could slide their way into the existing literary market-place,
rather than create their own original space within it. White
pursued his doomed strategy until the end of the decade, by
which time he had accumulated the manuscripts of five unpublished novels. For White, his novels contained distinct elements
of a gay content – sometimes explicit, sometimes subterranean,
subliminal or metaphorical – and he believed that this also put
editors off, since American gay fiction was virtually non-
existent at this time (with a very few exceptions such as the
already world-renowned Christopher Isherwood's 1964 novel,
A Single Man), and its readership was still undiscovered. In
the years leading up to and following his arrival in New York,
White also wrote a considerable number of plays and musicals
– over the years, he would accumulate the manuscripts of
twenty-three plays and musicals – and there he had a little
more success. He managed to find a young producer, named

Ashley Feinstein, for one of his works, a play inspired by his socialist concerns entitled *The Blueboy in Black*, which he had written while still living in Ann Arbor. Although the production of the play – about a black maid who disrupts the life of the white family she works for and then goes mad – coincided with the then-current issues of racial segregation and civil rights equality, its Off-Broadway run in 1963 was extremely short and unnoticed. Among the cast was the black actress Cicely Tyson, who had acted in Jean Genet's play *The Blacks* when it was staged in New York for the first time, two years earlier. Although White would later dismiss his work for the theatre as 'dreadful',[5] he remained enduringly attached to this element of his writing and would return to it in the following decade, never completely abandoning his ambitions in the theatrical form.

On his arrival in New York, White had immediately begun to apply for corporate jobs. After several rejections, he was offered a job as a staff writer and editor with the huge publishing corporation Time-Life. It was a job which his father thoroughly approved of, since he considered that White was joining a monumentally secure company. The Time & Life building – an imposing limestone and aluminium skyscraper which had been built only three years previously – was on Sixth Avenue, in the very heart of Manhattan, and White found the location exhilarating. His office was on the thirty-second floor of the forty-eight-storey building, with a view looking north over Central Park. With his dark suits and ties, short hair and glasses, White looked indistinguishable from the rest of the corporation's vast work-force; he kept his gay life of cruising the night streets of Greenwich Village a strict secret from his colleagues, though the office atmosphere was, at least on the surface, unpressured and leisurely. White's work load at Time-Life was erratic and often virtually non-existent: the company was grossly over-staffed, and he would often be given weeks to compose a short text of several hundred words for one of the ongoing projects. Alongside its weekly magazines, *Time* and *Life*, the company specialized in historical textbooks and current affairs publications with a sociological, educational aim. The prose White wrote and edited for these publications had to be simple and direct. At the time when he began his job, he underwent the company's six-month training programme, in which he successively followed every lowly job in the building, from that of mail boy to research assistant, before becoming a writer and editor; ultimately, the programme was designed to instil in the employees a collaborative spirit and the need to give a stylistic uniformity to the company's publications. The company usually hired an 'authority' – a renowned historian or scientist – on the chosen subject matter to write or dictate a rough draft of the book, which was then repeatedly edited, added to, and rearranged into 'bite-sized pieces of cutely-presented information', as White put it, by a succession of editors, including White himself. His responsibility was often to write captions for the picture essays – sequences of photographs or drawings that formed a narrative or sub-plot of their own – which were then used to accompany the main part of the books. The resulting publications possessed an authoritative aura and sold in their hundreds of thousands. White was always highly conscious of the reader he was writing for at Time–Life (just as in his unpublished novels of those years he was aiming either for a particular imagined 'market', or for a gay readership which was yet to materialize); this keen awareness of his reader would remain an essential element in the composition of most of his own book projects, where the reader could, in turn, be implicated, alienated and intricately seduced. In the case of writing anonymously for the Time–Life reader, White commented: 'It was assumed that the reader was intelligent but uninformed, and that you could broach absolutely any subject as long as it was relevant to your area.'

White worked on wide-ranging series of books about the history of science and, particularly, the history of the United States. He often became exasperated by what he perceived to be the pre-eminence given by Time-Life solely to American culture, and the disdainful lack of regard accorded to other world cultures and their histories: 'It was as if everyone was benighted, until they struggled up out of the slime and finally arrived in America in 1962!' The project which most fascinated him was one that documented the Italian High Renaissance and its leading figures. One of the final projects which he undertook for Time-Life (at the end of his association with the company) was a textbook charting the origins of the human race, entitled *The First Men*, for which he wrote the initial chapters from material supplied by a number of eminent anthropologists. His language was by then precisely nuanced and evocative, meshing together human actions with a vivid sense of visual environment: 'On a late spring day 400,000 years ago, a band of about 25 craggy-visaged men, women and children stopped at a sandy cove on the Mediterranean coast. They were looking for a place to stay, and they chose a spot, perched on a sand dune and protected by a limestone cliff, at the mouth of the Paillon valley. Today, the city of Nice, France, rises around their ancient campsite, but archaeologists have unearthed the place, called Terre Amata, where these 25 primitive visitors once made a brief stopover.'[6] Although White's Time-Life projects were habitually undertaken at a restrained pace, he occasionally had to work to urgent deadlines, and over his seven years there he learned to assemble and edit fluent prose accounts rapidly, a quality he would apply to his subsequent journalism, always undertaken with clarity and at considerable speed. The work at Time-Life also served to develop the sociological preoccupations that White had already formed while at university; he would bring these preoccupations to bear twenty years later in researching his biography of Jean Genet, showing the intricate interaction of Genet's life with the society of France from the 1910s through to the 1980s.

The years of routine work in his office at Time–Life gave White an escalating feeling of lassitude and mundanity as the 1960s went on. He remembered: 'It was a job I should really have left after two or three years. But it was so cushy and well-paid, with very little work. I was like a bird in a golden cage.' Despite White's sense of being in suspended animation in the air-conditioned, unchanging Time & Life building, he was aware by the end of the decade that it had been one of immense upheaval in America's political and cultural scene, as well as in its gay life. As the decade ended, White watched America shatter into fragmented disarray. The country was saturated in governmental corruption and incompetence, embodied by the out-of-control Vietnam war, which was claiming thousands of young lives in the age-group of men a few years younger than White. For the youth of European cities such as Paris, revolution was now literally realizable, as the street battles of May 1968 in that city demonstrated, backed by a film and performance culture with a parallel revolutionary intent. In the United States, the greatest perceived threat to social stability came from the militant Black Panther movement, which regarded the anti-racist civil rights legislation of earlier in the decade as superficial and deceitful. The decade had been one whose very texture had been determined by the assassinations which pierced it: the killing of John F. Kennedy had been followed five years later by that of his presidential candidate brother Robert, and the two inspirational black leaders of the decade, Malcolm X and Martin Luther King (with their deeply divergent views on the rôle of violence in black liberation) had also been gunned down. 'Martin Luther King's assassination deeply moved me – the whole time was such an accumulation of deaths,' White remembered. During the mid-1960s, the response of protest to the prevailing political chaos had been distinctly pacifistic. But the element of violence used in the revolutionary struggles of South American and newly de-colonized African countries – with their resonant icons such as Che Guevara – grew in influence and attraction over the final years of the decade. The degree to which political power was seen as intrinsically violent – and only to be effectively com-bated through violence – became evident with the vast protest riots around the Chicago Democratic Convention in August 1968, which were ferociously repressed by the police.

It was the decade in which culture and the actions of the individual became essentially political – the ability of a person to sidestep adopting a position either against or in favour of the dominant social arrangement was curtailed. Every act, however individual or intimate, became meaningful in the social sphere. One of the great slogans of the decade which was to prove of lasting inspiration to White declared that 'the personal is political'. The impact of drug culture – notably that of LSD, with its attendant philosophy – was especially strong. Much of the decade's urban culture saw itself as political in style as well as intention, from the wall of noise of rock bands such as the seminal Velvet Underground, to the more oblique and subversive strategies of art. The cultural scene of New York was particularly under the ambivalent influence of the artist Andy Warhol (who had masterminded the Velvet Underground); Warhol's work oscillated between images of race riots and appropriations of the ultimately bland – but strangely compelling – icons of American consumer culture. Even after Warhol was shot and almost killed by the lesbian revolutionary Valerie Solanas in June 1968, the counterculture – powered, in any case, by imageries of violence – just became wilder.

The gay cultural life which White experienced in the New York of the 1960s remained tentative and marginal, largely existing on the peripheries of the counterculture until the end of the decade, even though it suffered a parallel degree of oppression and censorship to those factions whose protests were vocally public or violent. A vibrant gay culture was mainly apparent in the areas of cinema and performance. New York film-makers such as Kenneth Anger and Jack Smith produced works with explicitly gay subject matters – such as Anger's 1964 film *Scorpio Rising* – which articulated their sexual preoccupations through experiments in narrative and visual style. Though highly inspirational to film-makers associated with the counterculture at large in both America and Europe, such films as Anger's were often neglected by gay men, whose interests usually lay in the field of more mainstream cinema, such as Hollywood musicals and melodramas. In the area of theatre performance, one tiny theatre space in Greenwich Village, the raucous Caffè Cino – which White visited many times with Stanley Redfern, who also acted there – was the principal arena for the development of performance works which demonstrated the emerging gay sensibility, with extravagant spectacles of camp dialogue edged rawly with social protest. As with the gay cinema of the 1960s, performances at the Caffè Cino were innovative in their form as well as in their gay concerns, adopting the revolutionary experiments in staging and acting styles from the European theatre of the 1920s and 1930s.

Throughout the 1960s, the gay population of New York – and of the entire United States – was the mostly passive target of religious fundamentalist condemnations, of repressive legislation that prohibited gay sexual acts in most states, and of a relentless barrage of media jokes, sniping and attacks. The mid-1960s, in particular, saw a flood of mainstream media attention directed negatively at gay life, most notably in the form of a special magazine feature, 'The Homosexual in America', published in *Time* in January 1966. The American media had always been predominantly anti-gay, but the precarious social climate of the time, together with the gradually increasing prominence of gays in the public arena, exacerbated these attacks against what was largely depicted as a destabilizing or pathological element within American society. The historian Juan A. Suárez has commented: 'The greater visibility of gay communities in the early 1960s, facilitated in part by the relaxation of the gay-hunts of the 1950s, led nationally circulated newspapers and magazines such as *Time, Life, Newsweek, Harper's,* and the *New York Times* to publish stories on "the gay lifestyle", with the desire to capture the subculture for the public eye. Shifting in tone from patronizing tolerance to rabid homophobia, these writings tended to combine the points of view of sociology and clinical psychology.'[7] White was well aware of the painful irony that he himself held a position of responsibility within a corporation, Time-Life, whose public position towards gay life was to denounce it as insane and dangerous to society. Since gays had become accustomed by the dominant social climate to regard their sexuality as criminal, diseased and sinful, self-directed hatred was widespread in the gay community. At the end of the decade, most gays – including White himself – still conceived of the idea of a gay culture as ridiculous and as a contradiction in terms. The idea remained strong that invisible assimilation by gay men into heterosexual society was the only tenable solution to their dilemma. But the first clear signs of an insurgent gay culture started to emerge in the final year of the decade. Although White would retrospectively consider much of the late 1960s counterculture to have been naïve in its intentions, its influence on gay liberation was utterly determining. Many young gays were using LSD to take them – at least mentally and momentarily – outside society, and gay community groups were beginning to form in New York and to adopt the political vocabulary of other criminalized and marginalized groups.

White's exposure to that radical culture of late 1960s New York now began to convince him that gay life was far from the lamentable disease he had become accustomed to agonize about. For the first time, he could now conceive of gay identity as potentially vital, creative and fulfilling, despite the tangible sense of oppression that permeated his environment. He was spending most of his evenings in Greenwich Village, cruising the streets at night and meeting friends in the smattering of Mafia-operated gay bars where customers – though exuberantly wild and noisy – were always fearful of police raids. White's physical appearance in 1969 was still largely determined by his respectable daytime office employment at Time-Life, although he had grown longer sideburns and his hair was fashionably thick and luxuriant on top. He began work on a new novel at this time, entitled *Forgetting Elena*, set in an imaginary island domain based in part on the gay resort of Fire Island, close to New York, where he was increasingly spending his time in the summer months. For the first time, with *Forgetting Elena*, White attempted to develop a distinctive, intricate language and an independent voice in his fiction, rather than producing something that would simply attempt to conform with the literary market. He recalled that with *Forgetting Elena*, 'I tried to write something that would please me alone.'[8] The writing of the novel took off in a captivating and exhilarating way that White hadn't experienced before: 'I felt as though possessed. There was a certain hum that would be generated by the book when I was writing well . . . I wasn't fully aware of all the implications of my book but that didn't matter so long as I mastered the tone or rather obeyed it.'[9]

On the night of 27 June 1969, White was one of two hundred
or so people crowded into the steaming-hot Stonewall Inn, a
small gay bar located at 53 Christopher Street, a few doors
down from the junction with Seventh Avenue, in Greenwich
Village. Judy Garland, an important gay icon, had been buried
that same day in New York after her death in London from a
drugs overdose; the gap between her brittle but glamorous film
appearances and her calamitous private life of excess and
melodrama had given endless imaginative scope for gays. The
mood in the bar – usually a cacophony of laughter, exclamations and Motown – was edged with melancholy. The
Stonewall was a relatively long-established fixture in the rapidly
changing New York gay bar scene; it had been open for over
two years, and along with its clientèle of gay men in their late
twenties and early thirties, it was particularly the haunt of drag
queens (other gay bars around Greenwich Village had loose
affiliations with other elements of the gay community, providing a base for the emergent leather and S&M scenes). The
Stonewall was basic and sleazy, with no running water behind
the bar and a constant illicit hand-to-hand exchange of drugs
and stolen items. It was owned by the Mafia, and the financial
rewards for its operators were huge; regular payments had to
be made to the local police, who habitually undertook only
token raids in the early evenings (at times pre-arranged with
the owners), to check the customers' proofs of identity. The
raid that night, at twenty past one, was unexpected and
brusque. For White, raids were nothing new, and he took the
intrusion in his stride as everyone was bundled out onto the
street. The plain-clothed police officers attempted to make a
few arrests out of lugubrious habit, but the mood suddenly
turned from passivity to anger and refusal: that transforming
instant of resistance, its exact source unknown but long-
debated, was retrospectively viewed as the crucial formative
act of contemporary gay identity in the United States. White

alternately watched and participated with exhilaration as the confrontation exploded into outraged taunting directed at the police, and into bursts of intermittent violence between the police and the protesters; the police officers, overwhelmed and out-numbered, retreated back into the bar and radioed for assistance as the crowd outside began to set it on fire. A squad of riot police arrived and advanced in formation towards the protesters, driving them towards Sixth Avenue; some of the protesters darted into a side-street on the right, Gay Street, doubled back along the adjacent Waverley Place, and then triumphantly emerged back in Christopher Street *behind* the line of riot officers. The spectacle of drag queens dancing high-kicks and jeering in a haphazard line at the rigid line of riot officers served to shatter the power of the police utterly. For White, those few hours out on the street in the hot Greenwich Village night passed in a blur of sudden movements of human bodies, of oscillating sensations of fear and elation, but it was that sense of a blow – simultaneously gratuitous and fatal – dealt to the previously unassailable power of conformity that remained vividly with him.

On the following evening, a Saturday, the crowds were still larger. The demonstrators formed groups in the street to exchange ideas and to deliver short declarations about their future course of action; White spoke about the need for all gays to join together and act decisively as a radical group, and to see themselves as part of the larger community of revolutionaries. He had spoken in public before, while at university, in defence of communism. A number of black activists mingled with the protesters and gave them encouragement from the perspective of the blacks' own struggle against oppression. The gay poet Allen Ginsberg arrived to offer his support. The skirmishes between the celebrating gay protesters and the increasingly provocative police officers continued for the next few nights around the burnt-out bar, but with little actual violence. Although the managers of the bar (who had feared in the first chaotic moments that the crowd was protesting against the Stonewall's Mafia ownership) re-opened it almost immediately, the bar soon closed down again, the victim more of the whims of the fluctuating bar scene than of any clear intention on the part of the police or protesters. But the Stonewall riot itself passed into legend, and its anniversary began to be marked each year with a march – staged in New York and in other American cities, and eventually world-wide – organized by the emergent Gay Liberation Front. In the months following the riot, left-wing gay activists attempted to forge links with the assailed Black Panther movement, many of whose members were being arrested and killed during this period. In the spring of 1970, the Black Panther leader Huey Newton called for an alliance between blacks and gays; but while the Black Panther movement began to disintegrate rapidly, the gay movement would consolidate itself spectacularly over the next decade.

Shortly after the Stonewall riots, White wrote his first essay about gay liberation, 'The Gay Philosopher', in which he captured the exhilaration and potential of the moment. For White, gays now led philosophical lives because of their urgent need at each moment to reinvent their identities, as gay culture gathered in strength and freedom. He denounced the stultifying influence of psychoanalysis on the development of gay culture, arguing that as a consequence of its stigmatization of homosexuality as a disease only curable by therapy, 'all theoretical thinking about homosexuality has come to a standstill'.[10] He also polemically placed the new sexual freedom of gay culture at the very forefront of the fundamental social and familial transformations which at that moment seemed imminent: 'For gay men who have no family pressure to stay together, no social responsibility to raise a family, why should they struggle to create a lasting affair? Perhaps the promiscuity of many gay men is a vanguard experiment, a sort of trial run for the rest of the society.'[11]

Although New York was an arena of sexual and political elation for many gay men following Stonewall, White himself was absent from the city for much of the next year. At the end of 1969 he decided to leave his job at Time–Life, to take on the more precarious but potentially fulfilling occupation of being a full-time writer and journalist. He was aware that, if he chose, he could have remained for his entire working life at Time–Life, doing the same anonymous work there; suddenly, after seven and a half years, and approaching his thirtieth birthday, he could no longer face that prospect. With his years of corporate service, he was entitled to a then-substantial payment of 7,000 dollars from the company's profit-sharing scheme to launch him into his new life. He decided to use the money to finance an extended period living in Rome, where he hoped to work on his writing undisturbed; he had also considered Paris as a possible destination. His mother had once taken him to Rome for a childhood holiday. And from childhood, White's idea of the unified cultural entity of Europe (unburdened by the continent's incessant internal hostilities and its real divisions of culture and nationalism) had loomed large in his mind as an attractive presence with unlimited creative potential, as it did for many Americans of his age. To some extent, Rome was an arbitrary and gratuitous choice as White's destination for an extended stay abroad, just as Paris would be thirteen years later: the abstract cultural resonances of the city (the contrary to the over-specific, exhausting demands of New York at that moment) took him there.

In Rome, where he arrived in January 1970, White found virtually no gay culture at all in the chaotic streets of family apartments and raucous domestic transactions. Italy had experienced many of the countercultural and political upheavals of the late 1960s which White had witnessed in the United States, and he saw a heavy police presence in every street; but these upheavals had, at that point, left the subterranean gay life of Rome untouched. For the first few weeks, White felt as though he was in a film by Michelangelo Antonioni, with what he saw of the city – as he walked endlessly through the streets – being filtered through a strange sense of separation, which only made everything more attractive and beguiling. The intense street life went on until well into the night under the windows of the apartment White rented in the riverside Trastevere district of ancient alleyways, churches and palaces. The city seemed visually raw and shocking, even after the brusqueness of New York – on his first day there, White watched a rotting horse carcass floating down the River Tiber. He found the city's inhabitants intimidating, their behaviour determined by an intricate code of etiquette he could hardly decipher. One thing he did understand was that, as a young single man living alone, he was regarded as 'highly suspect, morally', as he put it; as well as his gay sexuality, his domestic routine also had to be concealed – whenever he went shopping for food, he took a suitcase with him to transport his purchases, since only women and servants were supposed to carry shopping bags. He began to take Italian lessons from a private teacher, and had soon mastered the rudiments of the language. His only sexual contacts with Italians were with decadent aristocrats past caring about their place in the lugubrious upper echelons of Roman society, and furtive encounters with scared businessmen in darkened cinemas. However, White did meet and became lovers with other young expatriate American men. The city's visible sexual culture was so suggestively heterosexual that White, to his amazement, sometimes caught himself involuntarily cruising women in the streets. He even had a brief sexual relationship initiated by a young Roman poetess (although this encounter, like all of White's meagre sexual contacts with women in his twenties and early thirties, was characterized by bemused lassitude and impotence on his part). He would remember his time in Rome as one completely dominated by the idea of sex: 'I think I used to be like a dog in the sense that if I came to a new city, I would want to stake out my territory – I wanted to race around and meet everybody, sniff at everybody, pee on everything. I wanted to say: Does Rome belong to me? And Rome wouldn't have belonged to me unless I'd slept with half the people. Or tried to.'[12] While living in the city, White worked intermittently on the manuscript of a film screenplay, entitled *Cipriana*, which he hoped would succeed in relaunching the career of a popular Hollywood actor of the 1950s named Farley Granger whom White had met briefly in Rome, where Granger was then living after his American career had collapsed. Although the only film pro-ducer who read the manuscript, Carlo Ponti, rejected it dismis-sively, White otherwise found that whenever he told an Italian that he was a writer, he received a respectful, undisputed acceptance of this identity which he had never had in the United States. He found the city intoxicating – he was drinking heavily at the time – but his sense of being an alien presence there remained strong. He began to grow thinner and listless from self-neglect and alcohol, and, despite his attachment to the city, was finding it hard to write there. He experienced his stay of six months in Rome (until his money had run out) as a kind of sensory hallucination – a quality he would later transmit to the language of his novel *Nocturnes for the King of Naples*. Naples was a city which White travelled to from Rome and found to be a vast, compelling concoction of noise, dirt and sex. He would return to both Rome and Naples for visits during the 1990s.

White made a short stop-over in Paris, where he stayed at a

hotel on the Île Saint-Louis, on his way back from Rome to the United States in July 1970. On arriving back in New York, he was immediately seized by the overt signs of gay culture which had appeared during his absence. Greenwich Village now seemed to be constellated with thriving gay bars, each catering to a particular sexual specialism, and the streets were packed with cruising gay men. The vast nineteenth-century bath-houses around Manhattan were now being redesigned as sites of sexual encounters for a specifically gay clientele. The gay culture of Greenwich Village had become explicitly political, with groups of radical activists making angry demands for the repeal of anti-gay legislation across the United States. With the suppression of the Black Panthers now virtually complete, the new prominence of gay liberation made it a strong and increasingly independent voice in the American counterculture. White adapted his visual style and his physical appearance to the new decade: he wore unkempt clothes, grew a moustache and let his dark brown hair become much longer, tousled and unruly. Back in New York, he began making a living by doing pieces of journalism, and by undertaking editing and writing work wherever he could find it (including freelance work for Time-Life), and often contributing to technical textbooks. He had already started writing book reviews for magazines such as *Newsweek* in the late 1960s – 'reviews of a very vigorous, aggressive and hateful sort', as he remembered them – and continued to do this. But he now also managed finally to find a publisher for his fiction for the first time, with the positive response by Anne Freedgood at Random House to the manuscript of his novel *Forgetting Elena*, which had already been largely completed by the time he had gone to Rome. The novel had since been rejected by many other publishers, but the translator Richard Howard, whom White had encountered at this time and shown the manuscript, was enthusiastic about the novel and smoothed the way for its positive reception at

Random House. White began to work on preparing his novel for publication.

White spent six months during 1972 in San Francisco, where he rented a house in the salubrious but bohemian district of Russian Hill, high up above the city. A relationship he was having there with a lover who had also moved from New York was working out badly, and White spent many of his days and nights languishing around the house, drinking vodka and watching the wall of fog move in and out of the San Francisco Bay. Many gay New Yorkers would spend a period of time in San Francisco over the 1970s, investigating its reputation as more sexually experimental (particularly in the area of S&M sex) than New York, if lacking the intense urban excitement that usually returned those visitors to the East Coast. Despite his depressive mood at the time, White managed to observe much of the rapidly developing bar and bath-house scene that was establishing itself in San Francisco – a scene just as specialized as its New York counterpart, but notably more relaxed, since the gay population of San Francisco congregated in strength in particular areas of the city, such as Folsom Street and the newly gentrified Castro Street, where they were able to exert their political will and lead a life relatively free from harassment. But White's deep sense of melancholy in San Francisco made him feel isolated from the city's thriving sexual culture. From Russian Hill, he moved to a house out in the Berkeley Hills, across the Bay, and spent his last months on the West Coast there.

In San Francisco, White had again been working as an editor, this time as the well-paid senior arts editor of a new literary magazine, the *Saturday Review of the Arts*. He had been able to secure the job through his long track-record as an efficient editor at Time-Life and through his rapidly expanding network of contacts in the publishing world of New York. The entire magazine operation had then been moved from its initial base in New York to San Francisco, taking White with it. He managed to arrange jobs on the magazine for several of his friends from New York – including a young man named Patrick Merla, who, almost twenty-five years later, would edit a volume of coming-out stories, *Boys Like Us*, to which White contributed an account of his adolescent encounter with the Mexican pianist. Part of White's job on the magazine was to commission wide-ranging articles on art and literature; among the freelance photographers whom he employed to illustrate the articles was Claude Picasso, the then-impoverished son of the artist. One of the first issues of the *Saturday Review*, due to be published at the beginning of 1973, was to be a special issue around the work of Vladimir Nabokov, whose novels – especially *Pale Fire* and *Lolita* – White found endlessly fascinating. In October 1972, he wrote to Nabokov, who by this time was in his early seventies; he was living in a luxurious hotel in the Swiss lakeside town of Montreux on the vast royalties from *Lolita*. White explained the project and enumerated the writers he had asked to contribute essays on Nabokov; he also asked Nabokov whether he himself would be willing to write an essay for the issue. Nabokov rarely wrote to order, but he was impressed by the project and sent White a short essay entitled *On Inspiration*. White was sufficiently encouraged to send Nabokov his own novel *Forgetting Elena* when copies of the book became available at the beginning of 1973; to White's astonishment, Nabokov responded positively, telling White that he thought his novel was itself 'an example of inspiration'.[13] Although Nabokov had died by the time White published his second novel in 1978, he accorded White an extremely rare distinction when, in the summer of 1975, he told the interviewer Gerald Clarke from *Esquire* magazine that White was one of the American novelists he most admired, along with J.D. Salinger and John Updike. Nabokov never endorsed the work of American writers, and this sudden and unusual burst of enthusiasm would make editors in the United States view White's work with particular respect. White himself, twenty years later, suspected that Nabokov – whose sense of irony was advanced – had been playing a characteristically paradoxical game on the American interviewer (and on White himself) by blurting out his admiration for a largely unknown young novelist, after a lifetime's sustained reticence. Although White remained deeply touched by Nabokov's praise, he believed that it might well have been the mischievous evidence of an ironical last-minute conversion to effusiveness on the part of Nabokov – in the same way that the film director Luis Buñuel, whose life-long atheism was legendary, had amused himself at the end of his life by telling friends that he was going to send for a Catholic priest and receive absolution at the moment before he expired.

White had been unsettled in San Francisco, and he moved back to New York at the end of 1972, shortly before *Forgetting Elena* was published. Although he had now been writing fiction for almost twenty years, since the age of fifteen, this was the first occasion on which he had seen his fiction published in book form. He had already had an immense amount of his non-fictional writing published, but it was almost always work that had been arbitrarily requested by Time-Life or by other publications, and assembled according to an externally imposed formula – often scrambled with other contributions and published anonymously. With *Forgetting Elena*, White could mark a distinction between that previous work (which continued, in its evolving form, as White began to gain a greater degree of control over his journalism and editing assignments) and a work that was clearly and tangibly his own, in its conception and execution. For the first time, he could assume the identity of a writer.

Forgetting Elena is set in an insular world of intricate human and social interaction. The narrator must simultaneously immerse himself in the arcane hierarchies of that world and also challenge them, in order to gain the power to determine his own status and identity. A primary inspiration for the tone of ritualistic obsession in the novel was White's reading of the tenth-century Japanese classic of court life in the Kyoto imperial palace, *The Pillow Book of Sei Shonagon*, and of Ivan Morris's book about that closed society, with its promiscuous, constantly shifting but rigidly hierarchical nature, *The World of the Shining Prince*. White's island in *Forgetting Elena* is one of slippages, of abandoned movements, of sudden bursts of cacophony from silence, and of sheer instants of individual ecstasy created within an overwhelming banality. One of the characters on the island declares: 'We all know that human emotions are banal, that only a handful of motives exist (lust and greed and particularly vanity); and even fewer sentiments – notably love, fear and hate – which form, at that, an extremely unstable triad in which any element may transmute in an instant into any other. But the islanders are not reconciled to this parsimony of human nature. They crave a whole host of new sensations and reflexes.'[14] White's amnesiac narrator is a figure who reflects both of those worlds – that of the dominant but numbed and limited society, and that of a new, revolutionary arena of desire – and is able to traverse the border between them without difficulty, because of his lack of memory about his own social rôle. Like two of White's subsequent novels, *A Boy's Own Story* and *Caracole*, the novel charts an initiatory experience. And it is in itself an investigation into the language of initiation, as the essential medium that both originates human experience, and defines that experience out of the linguistic materials of time, space, youth and desire.

One morning, in a house full of men on an island, the nameless narrator awakens into his new world: 'I am the first person in the house to awaken, but I am unsure of the implications.'[15] He is deeply alert in a sensory way and able to make adroit mental calculations, but his memory has been obliterated. As a result, every movement he makes has to be provisional, a small step towards the establishment of his identity. He may possess no power at all or absolute power over that identity: everything is unknown and has to be established or created in that world. The narrator works out that he is a young man, and that the group of men sleeping in the house are his companions; he has a first memory of their adventures from the previous night, when they visited a hotel, danced there and watched with studied insouciance a house blazing in flames on the inland hills, detachedly appraising 'the lamentable lack of blue in the flames'.[16] From his initial contacts with the men in the house – particularly Herbert, who seems to hold a position of special power within the group – it becomes apparent to the narrator that every action he takes will be assessed on a scale extending from originality to futility. On his first day of exploring his rôle on the island, wearing just a pair of swimming-trunks, he finds himself given exhausting, pointless work to do by Herbert, raking pine-needles on a hillside: a slave's task that can never be completed. He rebels against the act's futility and gazes in fascination at the flesh of his own penis growing in erection, then joins and finally leads an elated, spontaneous procession of men – punctuated by one woman – as it ceremonially progresses, constantly increasing in size, along the island's sandy beach.

Some of the participants of the procession clearly know the narrator's identity, but his oblique attempts to make them fully reveal it are always frustrated. He walks with one of his arms around the woman, Elena, and the other arm around one of the men from his house. The woman seems attached in some way to the narrator and invites him to her own house, along with some of her companions, who appear to form a kind of dissident or overthrown element within the island's power structure. The woman prepares to read from a manuscript she has written on the 'history of the Valentines', but the distracted narrator is seized by the inadequacy of language itself, and by its separation from the immediate speed of life: 'I await the woman's reading with the hope that it will deliver me from the landscape. These books and poems have a way of fighting off the world. Terrible new things are happening all around us, but people write only about a few old things. Even their "suffering" has a familiar ring. Books overexplain and at a rate slower than the understanding requires – in fact, too slowly to be understood.'[17] The narrator leaves; but once all the other people have gone away, he returns to the house, where he and the woman – whose submissive attachment to the narrator is desperate and intense, in contrast to his own lethargy and bewilderment – make love. The narrator notes that an 'offensive smell rises off our bodies – offensive but interesting'.[18] Later, the narrator returns to the hotel with his men to dance deliriously all night; the island's power factions induce him to snub the woman, who commits suicide. The narrator is revealed to be the 'Prince' of the island, with Herbert as his 'Regent': Herbert is attempting to instigate a new régime of social behaviour, ostensibly less hierarchical and repressive than its predecessor, but in actuality just as loaded and ritualistic. The narrator's memory coheres for a moment during the ceremony of 'arrival' that celebrates his special identity, but then it fragments and collapses all over again in the novel's final sentences.

The language and vocabulary of the novel are pitched between a sensual evocation of the body and a self-directed concern with their own expressive idiosyncrasies. The book's first chapter circles back chronologically beyond its own time-scale to gather up essential elements of its characters' vocabulary of the previous evening, and the entire structure of the novel is determined by its language's push towards an explication of itself which only reinforces its own ever-expanding multiplicity of meaning and resonance. The vocabulary of White's characters is always subject to whimsical revision as they evolve new terms, expressions and prohibitions. And the upheavals of memory experienced by the narrator work to inflect every event differently at each moment. A particular preoccupation of the novel is with the process of finding a name and representation for the male body and its sensations, especially in the course of the hallucinatory sequences in which the narrator finds his body metamorphosing in front of him: 'If I were blind and beginning consciousness this instant, would I be able to start from these few points of sensation and sketch in a fully accurate picture of my body? Since I feel nothing below my shoulders and above the slight cinching of my drawstring, would I imagine that I came in two separate sections, one floating above the other on a cushion of air?'[19] The name of the author, and the author's body, are also implicated in this process of transformation – one of the factions in the island's power struggle bears the family name of Valentine, White's middle name (and that of his father), and the word 'white' itself is an object of exploration: 'Is white an indication of age or position or bachelorhood, or what?'[20] The novel is finally about the urgent creation and simultaneous cancellation or deferral of a language for gay identity. White commented: '*Forgetting Elena* was essentially a series of structures constructed over the void: a spider's web stretched across nothingness.'

The publication of *Forgetting Elena* passed with little attention, noted simply as the first appearance of work by an original young novelist. No reviewer of the time emphasized (or even apparently noticed) its gay content. In the context of the period when the novel was conceived and largely written – immediately before the Stonewall events of 1969 – the amnesia of the narrator is both a wilful oblivion towards the demands of a life in heterosexual society, and a socially induced (and therefore at least partially innocent) amnesia about his true identity as a gay man. In retrospect, White – whose own memory is excellent, apart from an occasional tendency to forget people's names – was interested particularly in this contradiction between the wilfulness and the innocence of amnesia. In connection with the evading of tiresome social responsibilities, the former kind of 'guilty' amnesia clearly came in useful. But, for White, that 'guilt' attached to memory also connected to his self-reproach at not himself possessing a coherent sequence of emotional memories – an absence which he felt sabotaged his ability to progressively sustain his life and his work. He noted: 'Like the narrator in *Forgetting Elena*, I'm an amnesiac – a guilty, not an innocent amnesiac.'[21]

It would be another five years before White published his next novel, *Nocturnes for the King of Naples*. During those years, he was often still working as an editor, including a stint at the bi-monthly arts magazine *Horizon*, where he initially worked full-time, and then part-time, feeling as underemployed as he had during the 1960s while working at Time-Life. He often filled in his time sitting idly at his desk by leafing through books on architecture and gardening from the magazine's library. He also wrote a number of articles of his own for *Horizon*, including one on the painter Jasper Johns. White would work on several abandoned fiction projects during those years, notably a never-published novel whose manuscript he alternately titled *Woman Reading Pascal* and *Like People in History*. But one particularly determining factor in the long gap between his first two published novels was that the intervening period would coincide with the crucial years of sexual experimentation in New York's gay culture, and White was to play a full part in those experiments.

Fire Island, the inspiration for the hierarchical island of *Forgetting Elena* – and the place where much of the novel had been written – was central to that sexual culture, despite its distance from the city itself. It was one of the key sites for New York gay life, with its sexual transactions and celebrations, during the second half of the 1960s and throughout the 1970s and early 1980s. White had first visited the island in 1965 with a Swedish friend named Kaj Areskoug, and spent large parts of every summer there over the next seventeen years. The beach procession which figured as a central moment of the narrative of *Forgetting Elena* had been inspired by a similarly exuberant and spontaneous procession that had taken place on Fire Island in the summer of 1968 (the one woman in the actual procession alongside White had been his friend Marilyn Schaefer). The island – a long spit of land, only one or two hundred metres wide, that ran parallel to Long Island – was reached from Manhattan by a journey along Long Island by suburban train to the port of Sayville, followed by a ferry ride across the Great South Bay to two of the island's main settlements, Fire Island Pines and Cherry Grove. The settlements faced the bay and the mainland of Long Island, but a short walk across the narrow width of the island brought visitors to the beach and the endless Atlantic waves. The richer inhabitants could take a seaplane direct to the Fire Island Pines harbour from the Manhattan quayside, and all through the summer, luxury speedboats and huge white yachts packed the harbour. When the island reached the peak of its celebrity, special buses ran directly from Manhattan to the ferryport, and visitors such as White could make an immediate transition from their Manhattan lives to their Fire Island lives: 'You'd get on the bus and there'd be cute boys in shorts serving you Martinis. You could instantly let your hair down and you'd see very funny and bizarre things – leather guys in full chains doing knitting!'

With its gorgeous landscape of grey timber houses on stilts, white sand beaches and pine woods, Fire Island had served as the location for Andy Warhol's 1965 film about its metropolitan inhabitants' obsessions with lust and money, *My Hustler*. Wild deer wandered around the dunes and raised wooden walkways, unconcerned by the island's human population. The islanders would sit out on their terraces each evening to watch the spectacular sunsets over the ocean. It was a world away from the chaos and noise of Manhattan – the only sounds on Fire Island were the cries of sex and seagulls and the breaking of waves, since all motor vehicles were banned after the poet Frank O'Hara was knocked over and fatally injured on the beach by a taxi. The island had been one of the retreats of the New York gay cultural scene as far back as the 1920s. Cherry Grove had had strong elements of a gay community throughout that time, while Fire Island Pines shifted suddenly from being a heterosexual resort in the mid 1960s. The entire island had been completely swamped by a tidal wave in 1938 and many of its houses swept away; even in the 1960s and 1970s, it retained an air of precarious fragility, heightened by storm warnings and occasional emergency evacuations. The most severe storm during the years White spent on the island happened in the summer of 1976; White was one of the very few who refused to be evacuated, happily ignoring the last-minute dashes of the island's panicking inhabitants for the final ferry to safety, and preferring to see the storm through. 'I was one of the die-hards who just wouldn't go back,' he remembered.

The island's wooden houses were occupied every weekend over the summer months by a community of lawyers and businessmen (with their 'houseboys'), writers, artists and beautiful idlers who together established an alternative island society there, more relaxed than its Manhattan counterpart, but equally ritualistic and fickle. The various small communities dotted around the island – White usually stayed either in Fire Island Pines or, occasionally, in Water Island, a small settlement with a strangely primitive atmosphere of isolation – were rigorously segregated according to the wealth and age of their inhabitants. White noted: 'Everyone on the island pretended to be equal – in their sawed-off blue-jean shorts, with their tans and their bodies fresh from the gym – but there were tremendous disparities of income between the over-achieving executives and the out-of-work hustlers.' Since renting houses on the island was always extremely expensive, young gay men would often arrange to rent a house together for the summer in groups of five or six, and then distribute the small rooms of the houses between them. Around the bigger houses, young houseboys would make frantic preparations throughout the weekdays for the owners' brief weekend visits. Above all, the reason for being on Fire Island was sex, pursued both indoors and out in the open air, especially in an area of pine trees, bushes and winding pathways between Fire Island Pines and Cherry Grove that was known as 'the Meat-Rack'. Parties went on all night in the settlements, and a principal activity of the island's inhabitants was the ingestion of complex sequences of drugs, timed according to a schedule encompassing day and night, in order to enable full participation in every precious moment of the island's life. Much of that life revolved around the island's three discos – held in Fire Island Pines at the Sandpiper restaurant and at the Botel hotel (which also hosted a legendary Sunday afternoon 'tea dance'), and, in Cherry Grove, at the Ice Palace nightclub. The pressing nightly dilemma for inhabitants of Fire Island Pines lay in judging exactly the right moment to leave the Botel and head for the Sandpiper. White remembered: 'This was the great question. It was all very Versailles-like. If you went too soon, hoping to set the trend, you could easily be left out in the cold if nobody followed you – but if you lingered too long, you'd be unfashionably late!' Away from the settlements, many casual visitors slept rough on the beaches, where an incessant interchange of looks and gossip went on during the day's sunbathing. The compulsion for seduction was tempered by the opportunities for voyeurism which the island afforded. The English film-maker Derek Jarman, who lived rough on the island and filmed it at around the same time that *Forgetting Elena* was published, evoked its idyllic separation from the pressures of New York: 'The shrubs in the woods that lie along the shore were heavily scented, full of fireflies, silent floating will-o'-the wisps . . . This world had a purity that one never encounters in "civilized" surroundings.'[22] Fire Island was a compound of an original Eden and an ultimately decadent arena of sexual pleasure and caprice. It continued to exert its imaginative pull after the onset of the years of AIDS – which would abruptly depopulate much of the island – and retained its dreaming population of gay New Yorkers into the 1990s.

The gay sex scene of the 1970s in New York itself was harder, wilder. Sexual contacts were made on the Manhattan piers, in bars and clubs, and in the grandiose, labyrinthine bath-houses which dated from the end of the last century, when many of the immigrant inhabitants of the Manhattan tenements had no access to hot water or bathing facilities in their own homes. Other, more salubrious gay bath-houses had been converted by entrepreneurs in the early 1970s from the swimming pools attached to the once-elegant turn-of-the-century Manhattan hotels which were now less fashionable and falling into decay. One of White's favourite bath-houses was the Continental Baths, located in the basement of the formerly luxurious Astoria Hotel, which attracted vast crowds of gay men throughout the 1970s. Another bath-house which White often visited was the St Mark's Baths in the East Village, which was used particularly for specialist S&M sex – 'a serious, no-frills venue', as White remembered it. By contrast, the Continental Baths became a New York legend for the raucous pool-side concerts given there on Friday evenings by the singer Bette Midler with her pianist, Barry Manilow. These concerts always exasperated White, who found that they distracted the customers of the Baths away from the rhythm of urgent sex which was their usual preoccupation: 'I was so sex-obsessed that I found it irritating when she was there, because everybody stopped their sexual activities to listen to her. I was the person fuming away in the background, hoping everybody would hurry up and get back to work! I was usually stoned on grass or quaaludes or acid, and so not really too focused on show-business.' One of Andy Warhol's transvestite 'superstars', Jackie Curtis, also performed regularly by the pool-side. The huge bath-house was equipped with its own bars and restaurants, and even with its own hairdressing salon. Beautiful young Puerto Rican drug-dealers waited for clients in specially assigned cubicles. Sexual partners discarded one another wordlessly after rapid encounters in the bath-house's many darkened areas, and then passed on to the next body – and the next – until the point of satiation or exhaustion was reached. Derek Jarman also visited the Continental Baths at this time, and left a vivid outsider's account: 'The Baths were on the West side above Columbus Circle, in an old building: eleven dollars entry. The dance floor was alongside a very large swimming pool with fountains, surrounded by beach chairs. Off to the side was a labyrinthine white-tiled Turkish bath whose corridors ended in pitch black. The scalding steam took your breath away; in the darkest recesses a continuous orgy was under way, but the heat was so searing that only the most intrepid could get it up . . . I met one young man who had lived there for three months; he had only left the building a couple of times.'[23] For White, the Continental Baths represented a startling cultural revelation as well as a compelling orgiastic spectacle which welcomed his participation. He began to encounter young heterosexual couples who were visiting the Baths in evening clothes, believing that the vitality of gay sexual culture evident there was something they could learn from, and relate to their own lives. For the first time, White became aware that gay culture could be perceived as equal or superior to mainstream heterosexual culture, in terms of its experimentation with the idea of physical beauty, and with its emphatic refusal of the monogamous, familial structures upon which a corrupt and war-torn American society was moored. He remembered: 'It was a very special moment in the acceptance of gay life. It struck me for the first time at the Continental Baths that gays were being seen as chic and exemplary.' But the location of those experiments in the bath-house scene was to be short-lived. The Continental Baths went into ruinous decline with the AIDS panic of the early 1980s, and by the mid-1990s, the building had been converted into a welfare hostel for alcoholics.

It was in the gay bars, clubs and discos of Manhattan that the essential contribution of drugs to the wild delirium of the sex scene was most apparent. Where LSD had been pre-eminent in the 1960s, the preferred drugs now became amphet-amines and cocaine, usually absorbed with large quantities of alcohol. The gay culture no longer subsisted as an insecure annexe to the sprawling counterculture of the 1960s, which had been self-defined by its attachment to the mental explora-tions provoked by LSD; New York's gay culture now defined itself on its own terms, and its drugs were used to promote physical endurance in order to sustain the orgasmic elation that formed a crucial axis of that culture of the body. Cocaine was also an icon of the increasing affluence of elements of the gay community as the 1970s wore on. White had an exhaustive knowledge of the entire scale of gradations presented by the bar and club culture of Greenwich Village, which had expanded hugely since the late 1960s days of basic venues such as the Stonewall; only San Francisco now rivalled New York in the complexity of services offered by its bars and clubs. At one extreme, there were relaxed settings for romantic encoun-ters, and at the other extreme, intricately furnished venues for out-and-out orgies of fist-fucking and beatings. In the latter category, one of White's personal favourites was the 'Mine Shaft' in the West Village, which he would document in his book *States of Desire*: 'Something of a dress code prevails at the Mine Shaft. A man outfitted in dress slacks and sandals or an alligator shirt might be turned away, while somebody in muddy boots, torn jeans and a t-shirt stiff with come would be readily admitted . . . Through an archway is a large very dim room. Along one wall in doorless cubicles couples stand and carry on. Elsewhere slings are hung from the ceiling; men are suspended in these, feet up as in obstetrical stirrups, and submit to being fist-fucked. One flimsy wall in the centre of the room is perforated with glory holes. Two staircases lead downstairs to still darker rooms, cold cement vaults. In one is a bathtub where naked men sit and wait to be pissed on. Roosting on a toilet, often enough, is another human pissoir.'[24]

The Manhattan piers, located at the western end of Greenwich Village's Christopher Street, would form the setting for the opening passage of the novel White was working on during the mid-1970s, *Nocturnes for the King of Naples*, in which he evoked the incessant movement of men hurrying in the dead of night among the dilapidated warehouses and the covered walkways that extended out into the Hudson River, and whose gazes rapidly evaluated potential sexual partners through the darkness. The piers had an entirely different atmosphere to the more communal bath-houses and bars, where it was tacitly agreed that the element of violence in a sexual act could be immediately terminated by one of the participants at any time. The piers, by contrast, existed outside the intricate commercial system that controlled the bars and bath-houses, and they were also beyond all supervision. For White, the piers were both potentially vicious and thrillingly atmospheric. Many older gay men avoided them, since the possibility of assault, robbery or murder was always present. Pickpockets were constantly lurking in the darkness beside the fucking men, waiting for their moment, and the wooden floors were covered with broken glass. But the piers provided a special pleasure. In the bath-houses and bars, sexual encounters were dependable and fore-seeable; but on the isolated piers, that predictability was replaced by the sensation of being vulnerable to abrupt, unknown sexual collisions in the darkness. Like White, Derek Jarman was attracted by the way in which the piers formed intense islands of sex and danger in the heart of the city: 'This night-life was charged with an excitement far greater than drugs; as you stepped into the dark you entered the world of strangers, on the derelict piers you left the imprisoned daylight world behind . . . The piers had their own beauty; surrounded by water, they were a secret island.'[25] The arena for gay sex in New York was uniquely multi-faceted and exhilarating for committed participants such as White. But even during its heyday in the mid-1970s, a receptive visitor such as Jarman could be pessimistic about the future of the city's sex scene, with its vast commercial structure, and its relentless oscillation between venues and between bodies: 'This life could become as wearying as a treadmill in a rodent's cage.'[26]

Throughout the 1970s, White was consuming increasing amounts of alcohol, along with the intake of drugs which participation in the sexual culture of the bars and bath-houses demanded. He often wrote in an alcoholic haze, as the gap of five years opened up between his first and second novels. The imperatives of that decade were primarily towards experiencing its sensations, and White's projects of documenting and imagi-natively transposing those sensations took time to finally bring to fruition, with his two books of the end of the decade. For White, it was a moment which, even then, appeared irreplica-ble; though he saw no reason why the burgeoning sex scene should not continue and develop, he was experiencing the exhilaration of forming part of the very *first* moment when such an open, outright sex scene for gay men had existed in New York. It was also deeply pleasurable for White that it was taking place while he was in his thirties – still handsome and tireless – so that he was conscious enough to enjoy it, but not so brash that he blithely took it in his stride (or so mature that he regarded its innovations with weary irony). But White's drinking took its toll as the decade came to a close. His sustained participation in that unique sexual furore required a degree of almost mandatory intoxication that sometimes stopped his creative life in its tracks.

The creative life of New York itself in the late 1970s was similarly marked by its excesses as well as its unique experiments. Despite his alcohol consumption and the expanses of time he spent in the Manhattan bath-houses, White still managed to play an important rôle in that scene. The atmosphere of the New York districts which White frequented – Greenwich Village and the East Village – had a restless, bohemian quality, pitched between angry social protest and acrimonious factional in-fighting. Over the last years of the 1970s, the more languorous hippie scene which had prevailed since the mid-1960s in those areas faded away, and was uproariously replaced by a younger punk culture which picked up on many of the preoccupations of Andy Warhol. Especially productive borrowings from Warhol included his idea that anybody could make art or music, his fascination with blatant consumer culture, and his advocacy of a metropolitan clique of stylish creative figures powered by arrogance, rancour and self-obsession. That cold edge to New York's culture was tempered somewhat by the preoccupation of many of its ascendant artists and musicians, such as Patti Smith and Tom Verlaine (the two seminal figures in New York punk culture), with French writing and art; rather than espousing the work of the East Village Beat poets who had been fashionable for the last two decades, such as Allen Ginsberg, this new generation engaged more with revolutionary figures such as the French writers Genet and Artaud, and with Rimbaud, who had advocated and embodied a wild but ecstatic self-destruction. These preoccupations of the late 1970s New York cultural scene helped to alert White's attention also to the potential seductions of more contemporary Parisian culture, which he would soon encounter through his meetings in New York with Michel Foucault and Roland Barthes.

White's physical appearance had changed since the early 1970s; he now once again looked clean-cut and studious, certainly more so than in the years following his release from his office job at Time–Life, when he had grown his hair longer and adopted a more haphazard sartorial style in keeping with the times. Now, despite his moustache and the beginnings of deep vertical lines at either side of his mouth, he still looked like an overgrown college student (not least through an intentional desire to appear as young as possible in cruising situations and bar encounters). Although he often dressed in leather to visit the Greenwich Village bars, White's habitual appearance was markedly different from the dominant 'clone' culture of the time, where many gay men adopted a uniform of muscular flesh, denim and leather. The clone culture was notoriously codified for immediate recognition of sexual preferences. Although some gays viewed the clone culture as being too rigid for a gay community attempting to free itself of restrictive behaviour, White appreciated its large element of irony. Gays now dressed as – and even followed the careers of – the kind of blue-collar workers, such as truck-drivers and telephone repair men, that they had lusted after in the time before Stonewall. Clone culture also had positive resonances of the concerns with replication and plagiarism which were becoming intensely fashionable in the cultural thinking of the time.

White had been living on the Upper West Side, but now moved south-east across Manhattan, taking a cheap, rent-controlled studio apartment in Lafayette Street, in the East Village. It was a distinctive location. The building which housed his high-ceilinged apartment – part of a terrace known as Colonnade Row – had, when it was constructed in the 1830s, been one of the most prestigious addresses in the entire city, but it had long since fallen into splendid decrepitude. In the first half of the twentieth century it had served as a brothel. The elaborate Corinthian marble columns at the front of the building were crumbling and pitted with age. Lafayette Street itself was a major avenue of traffic, with street noise throughout the day and night, but White's apartment was at the quieter rear of the building, with folding wooden shutters that could be closed over the huge windows. His writing days in the Lafayette Street apartment tended to be arranged in short bursts around his sexual pursuits (the St Mark's Baths, in particular, was situated very close to the apartment) and were always intercut with his journalism assignments and editing work. The East Village was a down-at-heel but creatively thriving area where many young writers lived, and White's lover at this time, Christopher Cox, was himself a writer who also worked as an assistant to the composer Virgil Thomson. Cox would later become an editor at the Ballantine publishing house, where he specialized in the work of gay writers. Cox was a possessive lover, always jealous and resentful of White's other lovers and his nights spent in the bars and bath-houses.

It was through Virgil Thomson that White met one of his heroes, Christopher Isherwood. Thomson was a long-standing friend of Isherwood and invited him to dinner, along with Cox and White, during a visit Isherwood made to New York from his home in Los Angeles. For over a decade, White had been fond of Isherwood's novel *A Single Man*, one of the rare gay novels he had been able to find during his first years in New York. For White, the meeting was a revelation, since he found that Isherwood, who was in his mid-seventies, responded openly and with warm enthusiasm to the far younger writer. White had become habituated to the rivalry and rancour that he encountered among New York writers, even those who formed part of his immediate circle and age group. He was deeply impressed that Isherwood was still avidly following the ongoing transformations in gay life, together with the religious fundamentalist opposition to its development. Isherwood was absorbed in trying to balance the pre-eminently physical axis of gay life with his own long-term spiritual preoccupation with disembodied eastern religions (a dilemma which had also been White's during his university years). He and White would keep in touch for the seven remaining years of Isherwood's life, and White later wrote: 'Isherwood was as inspiring as a man as he was as a writer . . . He had the same graceful sense of humour linked to the same unvarnished truth-telling that I'd always admired in his writing. His response to flattery, for instance, was a great roar of laughter; there was not a pretentious bone in his body.'[27] Isherwood had attended the dinner with his lover, the artist Don Bachardy, who would, in the closing months of Isherwood's life, chart the final facial gestures of the writer's decrepitude and decline with loving cruelty, in a series of line drawings which White found compelling as a document of the extremities of the human figure.

One of White's closest friendships of this time was with a professor of literature named David Kalstone. White had first met Kalstone in 1969, shortly before his departure for Rome; after his return, they met up again and began to spend much of their time together. Initially, their shared interest lay in visits to the New York City Ballet, but they soon began to make frequent journeys together to Venice. Kalstone had published essays about many contemporary American poets, and dedicated one of his collections, *Five Temperaments*, to White. From his friendship with Kalstone, White himself developed a critical engagement in writing about the work of poets such as James Merrill and James Schuyler – work of great density and intricate word-play, whose influence would surface in the multi-layered language of White's novel *Nocturnes for the King of Naples*, and eventually too in his 1985 novel, *Caracole*, which he was beginning to formulate at this time. He had come across the work of many of the Beat poets too; but at this time, the work of poets such as Merrill was viewed as utterly antithetical in its intellectual style and introspective concerns to the wild and blatant forms of Beat poetry, and White's allegiance to Merrill and Kalstone meant that his essays focused primarily on their chosen forms. White had also become a close friend of the eminent professor and translator of French poetry Richard Howard, who had helped him to find a publisher for *Forgetting Elena* as well as introducing him to the poets Elizabeth Bishop, John Ashbery and Brad Gooch, and the painter Joe Brainard. Howard also alerted White to the experiments which were being pursued by contemporary Parisian philosophers, such as Roland Barthes and Julia Kristeva, in investing written language with an excessive, orgasmic texture which they termed 'jouissance'. White began to inhabit a tightly-knit circle of New York gay poets and scholars which formed one of the numerous and diverse satellites of his creative life at the end of the 1970s, alongside his friendships with activists, with young novelists, and with figures involved in innovative performance and visual art.

The most astonishing of those figures experimenting with the borders of performance was Robert Wilson, with whom White had an affair in the late 1970s. Wilson had trained as an architect and possessed a deeply spatial, sculptural sense of the human bodies whose actions and gestures comprised his spectacles; he detested theatrical décor and rarely used it to frame his performers, preferring instead to design intricate arrangements of light around their figures. His work shattered the limits between theatrical performance and other prominent art forms of the late 1970s, such as art installations and rock music staging (he would later collaborate with the musician Tom Waits on a project entitled *The Black Rider*). Wilson had a strong sense of the tangible presence of duration in the performance space: many of his spectacles lasted for more than ten hours, and he closely collaborated with people he saw as existing both at the peripheries of society and of 'normal' perceptions of time and space, such as the deaf and the autistic. Although Wilson choreographed his performers to move with exactitude through disciplined physical trajectories which were hypnotic and compelling for their audiences, he was also prepared for his spectacles to occasionally explode into what he called a 'visual bombardment'.[28] For White, these works, with their magisterial control over the body, were awe-inspiring. But in many ways, they were the antithesis of the multiply resonant mischief he wanted to accomplish with his own work, and he could be caustic about the way in which he saw Wilson's maniacally structured works as embodying a 'fascist aesthetic' (not the same as a political fascism, although the two modes could be permeable, as in the work of the film-maker associated with Nazism, Leni Riefenstahl): 'These works exalt the spirit and preclude humour or irony. To the degree they summon erotic energies, they disguise or transcend them; this is the art of sublimation. They transport us to another world and lead us there seamlessly.'[29] In the flesh, Wilson looked like an elongated version of White, as though White's more solid figure had been sculpted by Alberto Giacometti. Wilson wasn't openly gay, and in their sexual relationship White experienced him as a strangely self-obsessed human being, preoccupied with hierarchical gestures, and capable of oscillating from instant to instant between deep, garrulous emotion and a glacial, asexual austerity. White worked on a play which he intended to be directed by Wilson, but the project never came to fruition.

The other seminal figure of late 1970s New York visual culture with whom White formed a close relationship was the photographer Robert Mapplethorpe. At this time, Mapplethorpe was just beginning the propulsive ascent into notoriety which would make him one of the world's most celebrated and financially successful artists at the time of his death, a decade later. In the late 1960s he had lived with Patti Smith, but then took gay lovers and became a prominent feature of the Fire Island scene. He and White occasionally did journalistic assignments together, but White was far more captivated by the extravagant sexual content of Mapplethorpe's work of the time. He had been working for the last few years on a sequence of explicit images of gay S&M sex. This work raised the question – hotly under debate, particularly through the writings of Susan Sontag, at the time of Mapplethorpe's friendship with White – of the degree to which the iconography of S&M sexual culture was linked to the iconography of violent political fascism. White's view on the question, articulated in an essay published in 1979 entitled *Sado Machismo*, was that S&M represented a sexually intense liberation from violence, and an individual dispersal of totalitarian power. Similarly, the visual icons of S&M represented an oppositional defusing of totalitarian icons. For White, the liberating beauty of Mapplethorpe's work was the opposite of the coercive 'fascist aesthetic' he saw operating in Robert Wilson's spectacles. Mapplethorpe's work often used naked black men as models, and (though he later noted that he had photographed their penises in exactly the same way as he photographed lilies and orchids in his later work, as objects of phenomenal beauty) he was attacked for a racist exploitation of black bodies. White wrote a text at this time for a gallery exhibition of Mapplethorpe's work in Holland, emphasizing that the deviant but salutary irresponsibility of Mapplethorpe's art – and its overriding exploration of human beauty – excluded it from such a narrow social prohibition.

Although White was six years older than Mapplethorpe, he found that Mapplethorpe treated him as a fraternal mirror for his own avid sexual investigations: 'He'd sit forward in his chair and look me in the eye, his gaze unflinching and curious, his smile complicitous.'[30] Mapplethorpe also used White as an occasional baby-sitter for his unruly boyfriends. He took a number of photographs of White, including a portrait of White's screaming head, which – though it would form part of his daily life in Paris a decade later – shocked White so much at first viewing that he immediately hid it away. What most impressed him about Mapplethorpe's infinite charm was the way it enabled him to traverse divisions of society, income and race in New York with an utter fluidity: 'If his sexual tastes sometimes led Robert into the poorest sections of the city, his success carried him to the richest. I never knew whether I'd see him skulking off at two in the morning with his leather or catch him in black tie in Paris or Gstaad or London. His manner never changed, because it worked equally well wherever he found himself. With his rich friends his simplicity came off as a form of sophistication; with his poor friends it seemed like simplicity, which is what it was.'[31] Mapplethorpe would die of AIDS in March 1989, shortly after photographing his own emaciated head alongside a walking cane tipped with a glaring skull. In the aftermath of his death, a touring exhibition of his work, *The Perfect Moment*, caused an immense furore – with both accusations of obscenity and protests at the governmental funding of the exhibition – as it travelled to art institutions around the United States; it created a particular uproar when it reached the Contemporary Arts Center in White's stultified place of birth, Cincinnati.

White's second published novel, *Nocturnes for the King of Naples*, appeared in 1978. It would also be the first of White's novels to be published in Britain, in the following year. For the title of the new novel, he had recycled the title of an unproduced play he had written in 1963. Unlike *Forgetting Elena*, which had contained accounts of heterosexual sex and used an elusive style in which the essential substance of the narrative had slipped away from the amnesiac narrator, White's new work was fundamentally and tangibly a gay novel, both in its subject matter and in its delirious, ecstatic style. The editor who had accepted the novel for St Martin's Press, Michael Denneny, would become one of the central figures in the American gay publishing scene of the 1980s and 1990s. In the previous year, White had co-authored a sex manual entitled *The Joy of Gay Sex*, modelled in part on its hugely successful heterosexual counterpart, *The Joy of Sex*, which had been published six years earlier by a British novelist and therapist, Alex Comfort. In the context of the mid-1970s, placing a volume on gay sex directly alongside a volume on heterosexual sex, in the same publishing series and with the same visual design, had a striking impact: 'It was as though every home should own both,' White commented. Apart from their different sexual focus, the crucial dissimilarity in content between the two volumes was that White and his co-author, a psychiatrist named Charles Silverstein (who was White's own therapist at the time), devoted large sections of their book to spelling out cogent answers to questions of gay legal rights, and also to dealing with practical matters, such as the drawing

up of documents by which gays could bequeath their property
to their lovers rather than to family members. White had been
paid a large fee for the commissioned project, which had drawn
on the ability he had developed as a staff writer and editor at
Time–Life to produce lucid documentary text at a very rapid
rate. He and Silverstein had produced the book in only three
months, over the spring of 1977 (Alex Comfort asserted that
he had himself written the original volume in a mere three
weeks). White's main preoccupation during the time when he
had been working on the project was that he was frustratedly
spending every single waking hour writing about sex acts rather
than practising them. He had approached the project in much
the same sociological way as he had with *The First Men*; but
The Joy of Gay Sex gave him a very particular reputation as a
writer and editor. By attaching his real name to the manual,
which was widely advertised and sold well, White had very
openly signalled his gay identity as a writer and his commitment to a strongly sexual, explicitly orgasmic gay culture.

The style of *Nocturnes for the King of Naples* itself has an
orgasmic, delirious quality. The book is a unique document of
the imagination in its compulsive interaction with the human
body. Less than ninety pages in length and more of a novella
than a novel, it forms the most concentrated articulation of
White's concerns with the shattering power of memory and the
beauty of the male body. Where *Forgetting Elena* is an initiation
into an unknown and unexplored territory, *Nocturnes for the
King of Naples* is an attempt to convey the experience of having
been initiated, of finding the body now enveloped within an all-
pervasive medium that is both sensationally new and terrifying
to the adapting consciousness – which itself spins wildly into
hallucination as it tries to document that experience. Like all
of White's books up until *Caracole*, the novel forms a first-
person narrative, with the direct implications for the reader
which that insistently seductive intimacy entails. The book is

addressed from an undisclosed place of exile to an absent 'you' – a figure that is never explicitly identified and oscillates in address according to the nameless narrator's whims. That 'you' could be a particular older lover, or the reader (in the way that Jean Genet's novels often break off their narrative to address the reader as a mischievously taunted 'you'), or even a deity who – although omniscient and disembodied – can still be approached on familiar, sexual terms. White described the book as 'a long love letter to an absent beloved' and 'an overtly gay love story in a mystical tradition that blends the carnal with the spiritual'.[32]

A man is standing at night on a derelict pier, watching other men covertly approach one another for sex among the ruined buildings. The atmosphere is one of industrial decay, the surrounding presence of water and whispered voices: 'The men I was searching for now became palpable. They leaned out of the low shelf of night. They whispered, if they were in twos, or shifted their weight from foot to tentative foot if alone. At the far end of the vaulted room in a second-storey window, one gnat-sized man knelt before another.'[33] All of the cruising men find sexual partners, apart from the narrator, who has to go home with a man so physically or emotionally disfigured that he fears the narrator will abandon him when he sees him revealed in the light. That disfigured man has known a former lover of the narrator's, and the connection ignites a sequence of memories and hallucinations in the narrator that take up the remainder of the book. In particular, the narrator is obsessed with his childhood. He remembers his father as a decadent but rigorous figure, incestuously attracted by the youth of his own son, but only as one small element in an undifferentiated lust directed towards the world at large. The narrator's father and mother are divorced – 'When my father left us, I sat in my bed, holding my knees, listening to my mother's screams'[34] – and he recalls discovering his mother's body after she commits suicide by inhaling the exhaust fumes of the family car. The narrator remembers travelling as a youth to visit his errant father, who is leading an orgiastic, narcotically sustained life in a Spanish villa crowded with hangers-on. When the narrator tells his father during an outing to Granada that he is gay, the father disregards the confession entirely, simply pleased to have the prospect of less heterosexual competition (even though his heterosexual affairs are supplemented by regular sex with a visiting English boy). The father arrives wretchedly at his son's bedside one night, complaining that he has injected too much heroin, and the narrator notes how the strong imaginative attraction of incest between them has now been transformed on his side into physical disgust for the ailing figure of his father (who, the narrator relates in an aside, is now dead): 'All along, I suppose, I had wanted this passionate, ridiculous pasha in my bed, had wanted him to hold me in his legendary arms. But now that he was here, so reduced, I loathed him.'[35]

The narrator breaks off his memories at intervals to address as 'you' a figure who sometimes jars into focus as a suave older lover (also now dead), and at other times becomes a far less distinct presence, melting into imagery that is purely open to the reader's interpretation. The location of the book's action similarly oscillates openly, shifting between New York, suburban America and Rome. But the narrator is an adrift exile wherever he is, always vulnerable and uncomprehending of social conduct. He describes his arrival in Rome: 'My indifference to this city was real enough, at least at first. Not knowing the language, I walked everywhere. I was afraid to take a bus; I didn't know which end to get on, or the routes, or how to pay.'[36] Finally, the narrator's memories take on substance only through the medium of sex – the narrator has been vigilantly searching for his absent lover 'in the bodies of hundreds of men I've ransacked, tearing them open as though surely this one must be concealing the contraband goods'.[37] And the narrator attempts to transmit his memories by giving them a vital physical form for the reader or absent lover, assembled succinctly in 'a tale that lies coiled, messy but alive, in the hot hollows of memory. Take your stick and poke the steaming entrails. Read them; read me.'[38]

The book's language is pitched between ecstasy and melancholy. The narrator notes at one point that he has lost control over the design of his book, and it's certainly the case that the book's language would be equally powerful even if all the elements of the narrative were re-arranged at random. Language transforms itself incessantly and suddenly, from a blur to precision and back again, unnerving the reader. White commented: 'I wanted a haziness of mood to be played off against moments with a great exactitude of detail.' The evocative texture of language is paramount, in its overriding desire to make sexuality and beauty materialize. That texture is a dense material of metaphor, myth and description. Although White was drawing on a wide tradition of allegorical love poetry and mystical religious poetry, a particular inspiration for the poetic density of the book – with its strategy of inserting ellipses of time and space between the novel's episodes and images – was his contact with contemporary American poets such as James Merrill. Unsurprisingly, the novel possessed a language that appealed to poets (the British poet Jeremy Reed, for example, regarded it as White's outstanding work). A further inspiration for White was his engagement with trying to find a parallel in language for the imaginative power of cinema, with its highlighting and juxtaposition of a particular sequence of vivid images, and its capacity to oscillate suddenly between different moments in time and space through strategies of montage and flashback structures. White remembered: 'Before I would start writing a scene of *Nocturnes for the King of Naples*, I would try to visualize a strong image that you could come away with. I was seeing it cinematically and trying to create a verbal equivalent to a powerful cinematic image.' He also intended to give to the language of the novel what he saw as a cinematic quality of being intense and streamlined in its emotional impact, without the need for superfluous scene-setting description and explanation.

The book again received only a limited amount of attention on its publication, but White's writings were now beginning to attract their own readership. His intentions with the book were, to a considerable degree, insular and self-absorbed. Although the reader's presence is occasionally invoked and implicated in the book, White made no attempt at establishing a specific relationship between himself as the author and his audience (as the constant variance in the book's tone of address and style indicates). As a result, he was shocked at the responsiveness of that audience: 'I thought I had been almost perverse in how few clues I gave to the reader, and I was amazed at how much was made of so little. That is, if you go back to the text, there are only the strangest little traces of slime to indicate where the snails once crawled, just a few phosphorescent, glimmering paths, and I was astonished by just how much intelligent readers were able to get out of this, and to reconstruct more or less the same picture I'd intended.'[39] It was the very openness of the book – with its lack of a voice giving any definitive or sealed form to its compelling events and sensations – that attracted its audience and allowed them to engage imaginatively with it. In the context of the moment when the novel was published – an identifiable American gay literature was only just beginning to gain a status within the publishing world and to establish its audience – White's readers additionally had to work hard to pick up the sparsely scattered clues about the book's very existence. But for readers who were eager for such innovative and contemporary gay books, that relative obscurity didn't present special difficulties. (On its British publication in

1979 the theatre director Neil Bartlett – later a close friend of White's, but at the time a young student – searched out the book with both trepidation and excitement.) A few gay novels of the time, all very dissimilar in style – in particular, Andrew Holleran's *Dancer from the Dance* and Felice Picano's *The Lure*, alongside White's work – now began to adhere together as the first foundations of a new gay literature.

White was later to remark that 'in *Nocturnes* there was some homosexual content, partially autobiographical but largely wish-fulfilment'.[40] That element of autobiography in the novel was mainly formed from White's fragmentary evocation of his experiences on the Manhattan piers, and of his time spent living in Italy at the beginning of the 1970s. But this concern with writing *through* the experiences of the author prefigured a much more sustained autobiographical preoccupation in White's next novel, *A Boy's Own Story*. For White, *Nocturnes for the King of Naples* had presented 'an exaggerated, condensed and abstracted version of my childhood' – a version in which, for example, he had transformed his father 'into an amoral playboy, more attractive than the boring, self-made business-man he actually was'.[41] The resulting portrait of the narrator's parents is largely imaginary, apart from details such as the divorced mother's anguish. The autobiographical element of *Nocturnes for the King of Naples* is largely subliminal, swamped by White's captivated elevation of his power as a writer over language itself. In *A Boy's Own Story*, the autobiographical element would be far more explicit, although equally placed at the service of a transformation of identity through language. White's stated key concern in *Nocturnes for the King of Naples* – to use his fiction as a means for the fulfilment of his wishes – would be reactivated in the other novel he was starting to work on at this time, *Caracole*, a fairy story of social initiation and revolution. But before White had fully developed either of those projects concerned with identity and fantasy, he would produce a non-fiction book, *States of Desire*, with a very different language charged with immediate, political pre-occupations.

Following the publication of *Nocturnes for the King of Naples*, White was able to find regular work teaching courses in creative writing and literature at universities in the area surrounding New York. He had already taught occasionally at Yale University in New Haven, to the north of New York. Teaching courses in creative writing – a subject rapidly escalating in popularity – was one of the principal ways in which emerging American writers of White's age often supported themselves. The work was more sustained than White's freelance journalism, and was usually better paid, by a small margin, than his editing work. He also found the work initially stimulating, since it dealt in an unmediated way with investigating the intricate processes of creating fiction, and White enjoyed being challenged and intimidated by his brash young students. He worked for a lengthy period at Johns Hopkins University in Baltimore, and had to spend much of his time engaged in gruelling commuting between the two cities; later, however, he found work teaching courses – including one on Proust's work – at Columbia University in New York itself. But after a few years of teaching, White began to find the work repetitive and increasingly arduous, since he discovered that he was only ever presented with a narrowly limited range of challenges from his inexperienced students, and that there appeared to be a finite amount of productive input he could contribute to his discussions with the students. Although he would return to teaching briefly at the beginning of the 1990s, he was already reluctant to immerse himself permanently in a professor's sedentary life.

While spending much of his time teaching and commuting, White also continued to undertake journalistic assignments for a range of New York magazines; these were now more often on subjects of his own choosing, and frequently took the form

of profiles of writers whom White admired. He was sometimes
able to ask the magazine he was writing for to hire Robert
Mapplethorpe to take the photographs which illustrated the
profiles (despite Mapplethorpe's imminent world-celebrity, his
name attached to the photographs accompanying White's articles appeared in insignificant, small print). On one occasion,
White and Mapplethorpe visited the novelist Truman Capote
for a feature for *After Dark* magazine – a 'soft-core gay porn
magazine that had literary pretensions', as White remembered
the publication. It was a sweltering summer's day, and White
recorded with acuity the spectacle of Capote languishing in
terminal decline, repeatedly interrupting the interview to disappear for narcotic sustenance. Mapplethorpe was stunningly
beautiful at this time, but Capote was too far gone to appreciate
his attentions. White described Mapplethorpe posing Capote
and White together for a joint portrait: 'Mapplethorpe told us
to look at each other, at the window, at him and we did so
rather stiffly as though we were puppets gloving arthritic
hands. The sweat flowed freely over our bodies. Although
Capote, as he told all the world, was homosexual, he seemed
not even faintly interested in the handsome Mapplethorpe.'[42]
As they parted, Capote gave White some world-weary and
fatalistic words of bleak encouragement about his future as a
writer.

The most extraordinary of the assignments which White and
Mapplethorpe collaborated on was a profile of the novelist
William Burroughs, commissioned by the *Soho News*. Over the
next few years, White would become one of the two most
celebrated gay American novelists alongside Burroughs, who
was already in his late sixties when White met him. But in
many ways, Burroughs was the antithesis of White: his work
revolved around lust (along with paranoia and the creative
potential of sustained drug consumption), but he was absolutely
indifferent to the rapidly developing gay culture instigated by

the Stonewall riots. He belonged to an earlier generation for whom gay identity was intractably tortured and solitary, rather than liberatory and communal; White had fully experienced the two disparate kinds of gay life on either side of Stonewall. Nevertheless, Burroughs' work deeply fascinated White (just as he would later engage with the work of Jean Genet, another gay writer for whom the idea of a salutary gay culture was scandalous). Burroughs had just published his novel *Cities of the Red Night*, and White vividly captured the obsession in Burroughs' work 'with teenage boys, with beautiful, heartless redheads covered with erotic sores, who hang one another to the point of ejaculation and whose eyes light up as they come or die – a complex network of boys who fade and cross-fade through time and inhabit other boys in other centuries'.[43]

White and Mapplethorpe followed Burroughs on a tour around his home, a derelict basement locker room known as the 'Bunker', located in the down-market Bowery district of New York: 'He led me into his spare room, rooted around in a filing cabinet through pornography magazines with titles like *Teen Punk* and *Jock Scene* . . . He tours me through the toilet – here are the old urinals, no longer functioning, and here the stalls with their marble walls and 1920s graffiti.'[44] Occasionally, Burroughs would interrupt the tour to demonstrate to White and Mapplethorpe the efficacy of items from his immense armoury of lethal weapons, including a blowpipe and a machete-like metal rod which he used to slice cardboard boxes in half. Because of his deep admiration for Burroughs, White was concerned about offending his feelings with the profile's tone of bemused awe and gentle mockery. He had given his article the title 'This is Not a Mammal' (the writer Susan Sontag had told White that this was the thought that went through her head while shaking Burroughs' hand for the first time). But White discovered that Burroughs was utterly oblivious to any negative commentary on his life or work. White remembered: 'Burroughs was a master of publicity. Even if you wrote nasty things about him, you later came to realize they were exactly the nasty things he wanted you to write about him. He set you up.' He and White remained friends of a distant kind; in later years, Burroughs would shift his activities from writing to painting, and moved to the Kansas countryside, where he kept cats and gave his paintings their finishing touch by blasting them from long-range with his beloved shotguns.

For much of 1978 and 1979, White spent all the time he could spare from his university teaching and journalism travelling around the United States, from city to city, compiling his book *States of Desire*. The idea for the book – a kind of expansive travelogue that would chart White's encounters with gay men of all ages and incomes, together with their environments, their houses, bars and clubs, in every major American city – had been proposed to White by the publisher of the gay magazine *Christopher Street*, Charles Ortleb. The magazine was innovative, since its high literary content contrasted with the predominantly pornographic gay publications of the time. The first four of White's accounts of his journeys appeared initially in *Christopher Street*, before being collected together in 1980 alongside chapters based around a series of new journeys undertaken specifically for the book, which was to be published by Dutton. Extracts from the book also appeared, as White's work on it progressed, in American gay magazines such as *The Advocate*. The moment of White's travels was an exceptional one. It was the maximal point of gay liberation – although when White travelled to the Mid-West and Florida, he often met gays who were nostalgic for the more covert thrills of the 1950s when 'Sex was furtive and dirty and exciting',[45] or who simply disapproved of gay liberation on social or religious grounds. And it was the last moment before the impact of AIDS would transform the gay culture of America irreparably.

White's travels also coincided with the time when the virulently anti-gay campaigner Anita Bryant was at her most influential; but, despite her prominence in the South of the United States, White met many gays – particularly in San Francisco and New York – who were clearly oblivious to Bryant's taunts, believing that the gay culture they inhabited had, over its ten-year existence, become so consolidated that it was now well out of the reach of any serious threat.

White's travels took him to every large American city. He was visiting many parts of the country for the first time, and – in addition to their intention of documenting American gay culture – his travels also constituted a sustained exposure to the pervasive consumer culture of America at large (for example, he encountered a shopping mall for the first time in his life). Since he was researching his book on an extremely tight budget, he relied completely on the hospitality of the gays he encountered, and found himself making new friends wherever he went – a contact in one city would pass him on to a contact in another city, and on and on, in a long chain of men. White was particularly suited for following that kind of random trajectory between men from deeply different backgrounds, since he was able to engage on a human level with absolutely anybody, however much their views on gay issues happened to contradict his own. His gay characters in the book were adeptly drawn, ranging from portraits of forthright young men struggling to make a living while exploring their gay identity, to wealthy old businessmen anxious for their sexuality to be invisible outside the narrow confines of their insular gay circle. As a kind of an itinerant ethnographer, White recorded an array of coming-out stories, all endlessly rehearsed and using the same evolving vocabulary, but each one also unique in its narrative and testifying to the vastly nuanced expanse of gay experience.

Only rarely did White encounter a contact who refused to

speak to him – a gay horse breeder in Kansas City, in the Mid-West, 'wasn't buying any', as White put it, and told him flatly that he hated gays and was indifferent to gay liberation. And except in the Anita Bryant strongholds, he met with only occasional evidence of homophobia in the cities he visited; where there were discernible traces of it, it often appeared to White to be edged with envy at a newly developing culture of freedom and evident sexual pleasure. White reported on a bus journey in San Francisco with a new friend: 'On the bus we sit next to a pack of loud-mouthed nine-year-old boys, one of whom shouts, "Bet you guys give each other nice blow-jobs." '[46] San Francisco had the reputation of offering the most intense sexual experiences of all American cities, particularly in the area of S&M sex, and another of White's friends gave him a graphic account of how things had changed in the seven years since White had lived there, and what was now available: ' "The guys down in the Folsom area," Denton says, "are into heavy-duty sex – bondage, fist-fucking, you know. There's an S&M baths, The Slot, where you can rent rooms with slings in them for fist-fucking. The shower is outfitted with a long tube for douching. The place is dingy, raunchy, the floors are on a slant. Then there's another baths, The Handball Express, also for fist-fucking, though not quite so extreme." ' White, always a conscientious researcher, noted: 'I visited the area many times.'[47] But he was deeply critical about the way in which the city's gay population had a markedly polarized division of income, leaving many young gays destitute. And homophobia still ran deep, even in such an ostensibly enlight-ened city – in the year before White's visit, a gay city councillor, Harvey Milk, had been murdered, together with the mayor of San Francisco, by a former councillor who had been enraged by the ascendant political power of the city's gay community.

White enjoyed the degree of notoriety which his name was

beginning to attract with the publication of *The Joy of Gay Sex* and his pieces for *Christopher Street* (the audience for his two novels was still very limited at this time). In the North-Western city of Seattle, he attended a surreal gay benefit evening at an old vaudeville hall, where he realized for the first time that being known as the co-author of *The Joy of Gay Sex* accorded him the status of a gay celebrity: 'The master of ceremonies, an old hand at conventions, reels off the names of the sponsoring gay groups without consulting a list or placing inverted commas into his tone and then throws the spotlight on the reigning drag Empress of Seattle – and on me, the "famous sexual authority".'[48] In other cities he remained anonymous, content simply to stand back and objectively observe details about the customers in the gay bars, before interviewing a small cross-section of each city's gay community. He noted the idiosyncrasies of the men he met, often wryly – on the West Coast, he was bemused by the preoccupation of gay business-men with arcane but intensely fashionable consciousness-rais-ing therapies, and in the gay cowboy bars of Texas, the rigid etiquette of the enormous men dancing together fascinated him. Occasionally, he inserted short accounts of the sex he had with some of his contacts.

White also intercut the objectivity of his accounts with some of his own individual memories as a gay man who – although not yet forty years old – had lived through immense changes in gay culture. The tightly-knit and nervous groups he observed in Florida and Tennessee evoked for him the secretive gay life he had caught glimpses of during his adolescent years in the mid-1950s, while his experiences in San Francisco were utterly new and at the cutting-edge of contemporary gay life. His travels also took him back through his childhood as he passed through the Mid-Western cities he had not returned to for many years. He visited the Chicago suburb of Evanston, where he had grown up. And while in Cincinnati, on the same journey, he met up with his terminally ill father for the first time in ten years. After a single evening spent together, they parted for the last time on a note of tentative acknowledgement of one another's now vastly disparate lives.

Towards the end of *States of Desire*, White wrote about the city for which he had abandoned the Mid-West in order to make his new home, New York. As with his account of San Francisco, White was concerned to chart the complexity of the city's bar scene and its overwhelming emphasis on anonymous sex, powered by the consumption of intricate combinations of drugs; he also evoked the rôle of Fire Island as New York's summer annexe, with sex taking place outdoors at night on the beaches and in the bushes, rather than within the cramped heat of the backrooms in the city's clubs. White also noted that, whereas San Francisco appeared to be a cultural void in terms of art and literature, New York was riddled with its competing artistic factions (White noted that he himself belonged to several of these factions simultaneously). The counterculture of the late 1960s had unleashed such a mass of contradictory and confused demands and innovations – in all areas of culture, and in the tense rapport between the individual and society – that the entirety of the 1970s in New York had, to a large extent, been devoted to sorting out the debris from that time, and attempting to develop the period's creative impetus and retain its adrenalin. Gay life in New York was one of the very few areas in which that sustaining of the furore of the late 1960s had been accomplished with success – in the form of an increasingly flourishing gay radical culture – and also with pleasure, in its sexual culture. This contrasted sharply with the 'hangover' of anguish which beset many of the other late-1960s radicals in New York – and elsewhere, both in America and Europe – often leading them to become reclusive and desperate, and in extreme cases turning them to the violence of terrorism or to suicide.

It was the gay sexual culture that he observed across America that most preoccupied White. He saw it as absolutely essential to the consolidation and self-definition of gay life in the face of objections and persecution from governmental or religious institutions. On his travels, White had met many gays who felt that sex needed to be more discreet and linked to specific relationships. But for White, the quantity of sex had to be a matter of freedom for the individual gay man to determine: 'I am, I must confess, suspicious of those who denounce others for having "too much" sex. At what point does a "healthy" amount become "too much"?'[49] He felt that gay sex had much to offer as a model in the wake of the shattering of social structures which the 1960s counterculture had seemed to accomplish – it was now widely believed that the family structure (with its oppressive paternal power, and with marriages often based on economic priorities) was moribund, together with the patriotic attachment to the idea of the nation which the protests against the Vietnam war had eroded. In this vacuum, the importance of sex as an embodiment of liberty was crucial for White: 'I would say that with the collapse of other social values (those of religion, patriotism, the family and so on), sex has been forced to take up the slack, to become our sole mode of transcendence and our only touchstone of authenticity.'[50] White felt that the course of the 1970s had seen a vast increase in creative and enduring gay friendships that originated in sex, and also an attempt by the gay community to instil a degree of flexibility and equality into human relationships that formed an urgent example for heterosexual society. Those experiments were still in progress and far from accomplished: 'The radiant community has not yet been born. In the meanwhile we make do.'[51] However, the period immediately following the publication of *States of Desire* was to be one in which sex would acquire an aura of lethal menace rather than of liberation, and in which values such as those of family life and patriotism would rise from the dead with the election of the reactionary Reagan government, with its explicit hostility to all surviving traces of the 1960s counterculture.

For White personally, the outcome of his travels was to give him a clear insight for the first time into the degree of social division between elements of the gay community, especially in terms of wealth. This was what most disturbed him in his thoughts on the future of gay culture, since he grew conscious that parts of the gay community would happily become invisibly complicit with any reactionary power which prioritized wealth. In that sense, he concluded: 'Writing the book radicalized me.'[52] A lesser but related source of unease for White was his experience of witnessing the more negative aspects of the thriving gay consumer culture that had appeared in the decade since Stonewall – in particular, the vast profits being made from the bar and bath-house venues of big cities (still mainly owned by heterosexual businessmen, just as the Stonewall Inn had been owned by the Mafia), and the escalating property prices in gay resorts such as Fire Island and Key West. Here, the dilemma was hard to resolve – White was troubled by the reactionary effects of wealth on gay men and their sense of community, but it was only with extensive financial resources that the venues for gay culture could become owned and directed by gays.

The rapid, lucid language of *States of Desire* was entirely different from that of *Nocturnes for the King of Naples*. The need for White to communicate his pressing political concerns – with matters such as wealth and oppression – made him keep his vocabulary as pared and direct as he could. No element of the delirious language of his two published novels survived in *States of Desire*. But the tone of his language remained personal, and it retained its keynote of initiation, with White intimately accompanying his readers as their guide: 'Let's move on to a tour of the bars. Though it's only ten, don't worry, we won't be too early.'[53] In *States of Desire*, White worked to find a language that would both articulate and solder together his individual and his political concerns. For this to succeed, he had to make explicit for the first time his own relationship as a writer with his audience, in the form of an 'us'. In vividly spelling out that relationship, White stressed how every book he wrote needed to innovate a new style, in order to reactivate the always ephemeral force of language: 'For language to stay honest it must start from the beginning each time. Nothing can ever be fixed in words – when it is, the fixative kills the butterfly and stills its most distinctive characteristic, motion. As a writer I've cultivated an acute distrust of all words, not just catch phrases. I see them as slender lianas that must be thrown across the chasm between us again and again; they can bear the weight of meaning but not for long.'[54]

States of Desire appeared early in 1980; the initial critical response to the book was largely negative, since White was accused of having been élitist in only travelling to meet gays in large cities and so neglecting the American hinterland of small towns and rural communities (White's travels had in fact been limited by factors of money and time, rather than by a preference only to visit cities). And some reviewers simply found its content outrageous. But the book rapidly became an essential volume for gay travellers. As a contemporary testimony to a country in sexual upheaval, it served to demonstrate to the gay communities of New York and San Francisco that gay liberation had scarcely made an inroad in other parts of the country, and to gays in out-and-out weird cities such as Salt Lake City (the centre of the gay-hating Mormon religion) that other environments existed in which their lives could be led with far less of a sense of celestial oppression. The book also formed a documentation of the highly structured bar scene of New York, and also that of San Francisco, where gay culture was most entrenched and commercialized. White was particularly happy to have his book praised by Christopher Isherwood (who preferred it to White's novels) and by the habitually taciturn William Burroughs; Truman Capote told White that he had especially liked the episode in which White, while touring the cities of Texas, recalled his very satisfying sexual encounter as a child with his Texan step-grandfather.

Then, the year after its publication, the book's identity and relevance suddenly shifted. The gay culture in many of the cities White had visited became decimated by the onset of AIDS. In 1986, White – by then living in Paris and watching the situation in America from a distance – would write an 'Afterword' to a new edition of the book, emphasizing how much of gay life had now, once again, 'gone underground'. He saw AIDS as revealing America to itself in a fundamental way, and he viewed the scope of the calamity as paralleling that of Vietnam in its potential to transform the very identity of America: 'The AIDS epidemic has rolled back a big rotting log and revealed all the squirming life underneath it, since it involves, all at once, the main themes of our existence: sex, death, power, money, love, hate, disease and panic. No American phenomenon has been so compelling since the Vietnam War, which itself involved most of the same themes.'[55] *States of Desire* now came to be widely viewed as an invaluable eye-witness account of a unique but irretrievably lost moment in American sexual history. However, other retrospective critics were more harsh: James Miller, a biographer of Michel Foucault, while appreciating White's evocation of the New York and San Francisco bar and bath-house scenes, dispassionately summarized the book as a 'saucy travelogue'.[56]

After completing *States of Desire*, with its exhausting schedule of travelling, White spent the autumn and winter months of 1979 recovering on the gay island resort of Key West, the final link of a long curving chain of islands stretching down from the coast of Florida towards Cuba. Key West – a former smuggling outpost which still retained its illicit, sleazy aura of mischief – had also been one of White's recent destinations for *States of Desire*. At this time, the island's town remained idyllically decrepit, its lethargic community largely tolerant of its gay visitors (although a minority population of drunken rednecks occasionally became whipped into homophobic frenzy by religious anti-gay campaigners such as Anita Bryant); the island would, however, shortly metamorphose into a more salubrious up-market resort, and its property prices had already begun to soar. White rented a house on the island with Christopher Cox, and Virgil Thomson came to stay with them. White's mother also visited him there – she was now writing her autobiography, entitled *Delilah: A Life in Progress*, which she would pay to have published by a vanity press in 1981, with an 'Afterword' by her son. On Key West, White began writing the first chapter of a new novel, for which he chose the title *A Boy's Own Story*; he would work on the novel off and on over the next two years. He was preoccupied at the time with his response to the recent death of his father. White had known that his father was terminally ill with heart disease, and so his death had come as no surprise; what most struck White was how, on hearing the news that his father had died, the monumental presence and power – with its sexual resonances – which his father had held and inflicted upon White, especially during the years of his adolescence, completely evanesced. White's haunting sense of a rigid cycle of replication existing between father and son, particularly strong since he shared even his father's name, was abruptly broken. He could now feel his memory transforming his father from a figure of oppressive power to one of nostalgia. The liberating death of his father triggered a creative burst and also a productive subject matter for White. While his father had already figured as a tangential presence in both of White's previous novels (as the omnipotent source of the futile raking of pine-needles in *Forgetting Elena* – an act White had frequently had to perform himself as a child – and as a glamorously debauched variant of his own dour self in *Nocturnes for the King of Naples*), White now decided that he wanted to write a novel which dealt more directly with their relationship and with his own adolescence. All through the winter on Key West, he drank heavily; while he made rapid and fluent progress on his novel, he was aware that his permanent drunkenness meant that the novel's tone fluctuated wildly between meticulous evocation and bursts of intense emotional excess. On Key West, White also completed the first chapter of his novel *Caracole*, which he had already been working on intermittently for three years. But he now decided that he would suspend work on that project (James Merrill had told him that the completed chapter was a disaster), and concentrate instead on *A Boy's Own Story*.

From 1980 until the time he left New York for Paris, three years later, White held the administrative post of 'Executive Director' at the New York Institute for the Humanities, attached to Columbia University, where he had been teaching. The social historian Richard Sennett had given him the job. The Institute, funded in part by the Hungarian financier George Soros, existed to debate topics which its participants perceived to be important to contemporary culture. Despite the grandness of his job title, White's duties mainly consisted of organizing a regular weekly seminar at the Institute, to which he invited guests to present their research in progress; the sessions always took place at lunch-time, around a horse-shoe-shaped table, and the participants took along their sand-wiches in brown paper bags and ate them as the speakers delivered their talks. Soros' aim was to bring as many Eastern European intellectuals as possible to New York, and White found himself spending much of his time finding apartments for Polish and Hungarian expatriates. White himself invited the British novelist and historian Marina Warner to come to the Institute to present the research in progress she was undertaking for her book *Monuments and Maidens*. She remembered her appearance at the Institute for the Humanities and her first encounter with White there: 'I was finding it a very daunting atmosphere. I talked about the public bodies of women in France and how breasts signified one thing, naked torsos another: fecundity, liberty, the Republic, and so on. Then a voice came from the back, from the far end of the table: "I've just been looking at a whole collection of gay pornographic magazines of the 1950s and it strikes me that attitudes to male bodies can be analysed in a similar fashion. Have you ever considered the semiotics of penis size?"' [57] As it happened, she had, and she and White were soon friends.

White was given an office at the Institute, and often used the space in the evenings to work undisturbed on *A Boy's Own Story*; he believed that working on the novel within the atmosphere of the Institute served to inflect his fiction with its intellectual concerns with the nature of memory and sexuality. The regulars at the Institute's seminar included White's friend David Kalstone, Richard Sennett (who was researching the visual depiction of the human body within the city), and Susan Sontag, whose presence dominated the seminar. Sontag had been a vastly influential figure – and a crucial arbiter of New York cultural taste – since the publication of her collection of essays, *Against Interpretation*, in 1966. Although she and White were close friends at this time, White always felt that Sontag was casting him as a kind of enthusiastic underling to her pre-established genius. Although he was now forty – and only seven years younger than Sontag – White saw himself being manoeuvred into the position of the lovable young acolyte, slightly idiotic but always earnestly well-meaning. Certainly,

Sontag was a legendary cultural figure in New York, but White increasingly found his assigned subsidiary rôle within the intellectual crucible of the Institute for the Humanities to be an undignified one. He began to contemplate leaving New York for another cultural centre of influence, where he wouldn't need to start off at such a hierarchical disadvantage. White's friendship with Sontag would continue for several more years, until the 1985 publication of his novel *Caracole*, in which White depicted a female character that, in part, satirized Sontag's exercise of power within the New York literary world, and led to the abrupt end of their friendship. But even during White's time at the Institute for the Humanities, the tensions emerging from their differing views on aspects of gay culture were evident. White had often been suspicious of the way in which Sontag had staked her claim on defining a gay camp sensibility; he doubted that anything so precise as a 'sensibility' of camp could be assembled from the provocative and intentionally elusive vocabularies of gay life. In *Caracole* (which he had started work on by this period), White would also mischievously satirize the Institute's seminar as a glorified 'chatbox'. The cultural priorities of the seminar were often rarefied, and concealed labyrinthine dynamics of power and personal ambition. But the seminar also served to instigate investigations into areas of culture which were then virtually unknown in the United States (and Britain), such as the idea of a dissident sexuality, and the relationship between gender and consumerism – subjects which would soon become vital mainstream concerns for cultural debate.

Among the most prominent guests of the Institute was the gay French philosopher Roland Barthes, who was one of the principal inspirations for Sontag's work. Barthes had remorselessly incised the imageries and icons of French consumer culture in his 1957 book *Mythologies*, which – together with the continuing influence of Pop Art – had a huge impact in the way advertising culture became an object of fascination in New York in the 1970s, as a cultural form that was viewed as simultaneously both powerfully insidious and pleasurably banal. At the time White met him at the Institute (for the one and only time), Barthes was working in a more lush and individually inflected style than that of his seminal work of twenty years earlier; he was now absorbed in investigating the evocative force of the visual image – particularly, in his final work, *Camera Lucida*, of the photographic image – and in mapping the endlessly shifting languages of love, sexuality and the human body. White found Barthes, who was in his early sixties, to be subdued and melancholy, and preoccupied with death. His mother had recently died, and he would himself die in 1980 from injuries sustained when he was hit by a van while crossing a street in Paris (the injuries had been slight, and it was widely assumed that Barthes had lost the will to live as a result of his mother's death). Although Barthes' work – with its attachment to the form of tangential, insular fragments – was seen as negating the literary author and making the intricacies of theory supplant the formulas of fiction, he told White of his growing desire now to write a novel, with an elaborate narrative like those of nineteenth-century classical French fiction. At the same time, he wanted to create a fictional narrative that tangibly connected with the fragmentary sexuality which he had been exploring in his recent theoretical work. For White, Barthes represented the fascinating allure of French intellectual culture – both innovative and deeply traditional – which helped turn his attention towards Paris in these years.

At this time, White also met the gay French philosopher Michel Foucault, who – in common with Barthes, though their strategies were different – was attempting to evolve a language which would encapsulate sexual desire. Where Barthes had used sensual fragments, Foucault employed rigorous historical analysis. Foucault presented his work in progress to the Institute for the Humanities, and also attended a bookshop reading which White gave in New York from his own work in progress, *A Boy's Own Story*. Foucault was no stranger to American gay life: he had often spent extended periods of time in the United States since 1975, initially while teaching at the University of California at Berkeley, which had given him the opportunity to immerse himself in the sex scene of nearby San Francisco. At the time White met Foucault, he was working on his multi-volume project *The History of Sexuality*, which would occupy him until his death in 1984. Foucault spoke to White about his friendship with Jean Genet, whom he had known in the early 1970s when they had both been involved in political activism in support of prisoners and persecuted North Africans living in Paris. White asked Foucault questions about the raw details of his masochistic sexual experiences in the United States (questions of a kind that White felt must never have been posed to Foucault in France, where he was revered as a living intellectual legend, alongside such figures as Barthes and Jacques Lacan). White was impressed by the sensational contradictions that drove Foucault's life and work. He saw Foucault as a human being irresistibly attracted to totalitarian power at a primary, sensory level, and to the intoxicating revelation of sexual power which the iconography of fascism could release. But what most startled White was the intellectual tenacity which Foucault applied to combating that attraction, and the way in which Foucault's creative work sprang directly from an endless tearing of the body's identity, resulting from the violent collision between the lust for power and the absolute refusal of the structures of power.

White's activities at the beginning of the 1980s also focused on the pleasures of collaborating in the development of a new gay writing, alongside the more rigorous demands of the Institute for the Humanities. In March 1980, together with a small number of his fellow New York gay writers, White formed a literary club which they named, with gentle self-mockery, the 'Violet Quill'. The intention was to create an environment for discussing work in progress that was distinctly separate from the faction-ridden responses to gay writing in the New York press and magazines, and distinct too from the kind of rarefied intellectual atmosphere that the Institute for the Humanities exuded. White described the less exacting priorities of the Violet Quill: 'We'd meet once a month in one another's apartments. Four of us each time would read our latest pages, then settle down to high tea. We were more competitive about the richness of our desserts than the quality of our prose. The mood was certainly friendly and collaborative; we thought of calling our organization The All-Praise Club.'[58] The sessions gave White an enduring passion for giving public readings, or readings to his friends, from his work in progress (rather than from his published books). The other writers who formed part of the informal club were White's lover, Christopher Cox, the novelists Felice Picano, Robert Ferro, George Whitmore, Michael Grumley and Andrew Holleran – who, at this point, was the best known member of the group, having in 1978 published his acclaimed novel *Dancer from the Dance*, which had captured much of the period's exaltation of physical beauty and sexual ecstasy. An occasional visitor to the club was the eminent film historian Vito Russo, who owned a vast collection of gay films; Russo read to the Violet Quill from his seminal study *The Celluloid Closet: Homosexuality in the Movies*, which was to be published in the following year. All of the participants of the club were around White's age or slightly younger, and all were poor. White remembered there having been around ten or twelve sessions of the Violet Quill in all; Felice Picano's diaries of the time, consulted by the gay historian David Bergman, indicated that the number of meetings was as low as eight, with the encounters dissolving in March 1981. The principles of the club were all-embracing, and any gay writer could join; the limited number of participants indicated the extent to which a contemporary gay American literature was still in its most tentative, formative stages. To some degree, the sessions served to allocate territorial areas among the participants: White, who read extracts from *A Boy's Own Story* to the group, was seen as the writer preoccupied with gay adolescence, Holleran with the bar scene and Fire Island, Picano with the genre of the gay thriller. With so few participants, these 'monopolies' still left large gaps of subject matter about gay life unclaimed. But for the first time, the writers of the Violet Quill were now confident that they were writing specifically and openly for a gay readership which existed and would be receptive to their work – a readership that was beginning to expand rapidly and to consolidate itself visibly, with the establishment of exclusively gay bookshops across the country and the increasing prominence of magazines such as *Christopher Street*. White believed that, despite its adamantly non-combative nature, the Violet Quill incited all of its participants to produce their best work to date, with the supportive atmosphere forming an invaluable springboard of solidarity.

By the mid-1990s, together with White, only Picano and Holleran would still be alive from the members of the Violet Quill. Picano published his monumental novel *Like People in History*, spanning forty years of gay history, in 1995. Picano's ebullient narrator evokes both the uniqueness of his and White's generation of gay men, and the merciless divine injustice that wiped it out: 'Why create such an extraordinary generation of beautiful, talented, quirkily intelligent men, and then why let them all die so rapidly, one after the other? . . . We'd been the first generation of gays to force ourselves or to be forced out of the closet. We had to experience the traumas of coming out, and of making the gay movement happen . . . But despite that, we were almost godlike in our creative power.

Face it, we pretty much created the seventies! Its music, its way of socializing, its sexual behaviour, its clubs, clothing, its entire sense of style and design, its resorts, its celebrities, its language! We were always creating, always doing something!'[59] In his 1997 volume of memoirs, *A House on the Ocean, A House on the Bay*, Picano observed that he had himself probably escaped that decimation only by a freak chance – he had suffered from an anal fistula for six years over the late 1970s and early 1980s, which meant that he found it too painful to be sexually penetrated. In the year following the publication of *Like People in History*, Andrew Holleran's novel *The Beauty of Men* (only his second since *Dancer from the Dance*, eighteen years earlier) concentrated on a more poignant and subdued evocation of contemporary gay existence away from New York, laced with the loneliness of the survivor. Holleran and Picano, along with White, were compelled to respond to that experience of being rare survivors. Every other participant in the Violet Quill had succumbed to AIDS.

The first intimations of the lethal power of AIDS – as an illness crushingly different from the innumerable but ultimately innocuous sexual diseases that had constellated the previous decade – appeared at precisely the time that the Violet Quill was in full flood. The initial confused reports of a 'gay cancer' – of unknown origin but leading to certain death in some of its sufferers – began to cause panic over the course of 1981. The reports were initially received with incredulity, although this was often edged with a sense of prescience – the British novelist Oscar Moore, who died of AIDS in 1996, wrote at the end of his life about this premonition: 'Even before it had started, we knew. Even before anyone had whispered words such as fatal in the same breath as pleasure, we had guessed.'[60] For many gay intellectuals, such as Foucault, the prospect of a new disease which apparently set its target exclusively on homosexuals, and avoided heterosexuals, was almost too ironical a twist of nature – although, as it transpired, the disease would also affect heterosexuals, particularly through infected blood transfusions and drug addicts' shared needles. Semen and blood were identified as the two most likely media for the disease's transmission. As a result, almost the entire basis of New York's gay male sexual culture (excepting some S&M and fetishistic sex), with the exchange of semen as its most valuable currency, was abruptly reversed into a fear of physically absorbing semen, at least anally. From this point onwards, all of White's work would be underlined and accented by the disease; his life, too, would be irreparably transformed, since he was well aware of the likelihood that he had himself been exposed to the virus. Although White would not lose any close friends to AIDS for a further five years (with the deaths of David Kalstone in 1986 and his editor Bill Whitehead in 1987), he felt immediately involved in the growing outcry about the disease. At first, White believed that it was essential not to respond with sexual abstinence or austerity to the disease and thereby capitulate to it, since that would simultaneously entail a catastrophic social surrender: 'When I first found out about AIDS, I wanted to deny it because I felt it would be used by straight people or the religious right or by regressive elements in the gay community as a way of reducing our freedoms, which I perceived then to be mainly sexual freedoms. The idea of closing the baths or enforcing safe sex seemed to me hideously repressive and against everything we'd struggled for in the sixties and seventies.'[61] But, as the death toll began to mount, White soon realized that the possibility of the gay community simply being obliterated by AIDS overrode his reluctance to sacrifice the hard-won sexual liberation of gay life. The fact that he had recently published *States of Desire*, and had co-authored *The Joy of Gay Sex*, gave him the public persona of someone able to provide authoritative information about the disease and the kinds of sex that would avoid it (although, for the disease's first years, reliable sources of information to pass on were few and far between). White helped to found the first of many AIDS research and support groups in New York, the Gay Men's Health Crisis group, in 1981, and became its first president.

Despite the threat of AIDS, there was no way that White's – or anyone else's – sex life suddenly ended. At the end of 1981, White met a lean, elegant man in his mid-twenties named John Purcell. White's relationship with Purcell was arranged by a 'match-maker', as he put it. White's friend Rudy Kikel – a wealthy, eccentric poet in his early forties whom White had met through Richard Howard – had befriended Purcell while they were both living in the fashionable Beacon Hill district of Boston. Purcell had grown up in the town of Concord, close to Boston, and was from a family which, though not rich, had a high social standing there – White called Purcell a 'little Boston aristocrat'. Purcell had recently moved to New York and was living in Gramercy Park, an exclusive square of houses around a private garden, working as a houseboy for an older gay man. Kikel had called White to tell him that he was going to be visiting New York, and they arranged to go together to see the stage version of Harvey Fierstein's *Torch Song Trilogy*. On the way, they called by at the Gramercy Park apartment to see Purcell, who at that moment was in the kitchen, absorbed in preparing dinner. White remembered: 'I was dazzled by his beauty.' When he indicated to Kikel his interest in Purcell, Kikel told him: 'You know you can have him, but he'll cost you around $10,000 a year.' White replied: 'That sounds fine to me.' He invited Purcell to dinner a few days later, and they spent the night together. Purcell had no objections at all to this idea of a semi-luxurious dependence, and moved in with White at his Lafayette Street apartment. He had attended a number of colleges, but was accustomed to regard the prospect of salaried employment with horror. He had a magisterial assurance that the financial needs of his life should be supplied for him, with little or no effort on his part. He was polite and attentive, and White loved having him by his side. It was Purcell's beauty and friendship that had entranced White, rather than any deep sexual attraction between them: 'It was never a great sexual affair,' he remembered. After the first few months of their relationship, they would virtually stop having sex, though they usually slept together in each other's arms after evenings spent in the Manhattan bars and bath-houses, having intense bouts of anonymous sex. By temperament, Purcell was intermittently excitable but more usually languid. He liked to watch television incessantly, and the noise made it impossible for White to write in their one-room apartment. Finally, White had to rent another small apartment nearby, in the SoHo district, to serve as Purcell's television room. Purcell objected to being 'banished', as White put it, from Lafayette Street, but the arrangement worked out well.

A Boy's Own Story appeared in the United States in 1982. The novel was edited at the Dutton publishing house by Bill Whitehead, who had already worked with White on editing *States of Desire* (although much of the press response to *States of Desire* had been negative, the furore created by that book helped White subsequently to secure a contract for his novel). White found Whitehead to be a productive and friendly collaborator, and it was this personal association which led him to offer the novel to Dutton rather than to the publishers of his previous novel, St Martin's Press. As White remembered, Whitehead took a very relaxed editing approach towards the novel's wandering narrative and fluctuating style of language, believing the novel to possess an attractive complexity all of its own in its exploration of the power of sex and the nature of memory, and he made only very minor grammatical changes to the work in preparing it for publication. Susan Sontag wrote an approving comment for the cover of the novel, and White believed that this was determining in the book's overwhelmingly positive response from both gay and heterosexual reviewers. The publication of the novel had already been anticipated for over a year among New York's increasingly large visible gay readership, since White had given many public readings from the manuscript of the novel as it had progressed, as well as publishing an extract in the prominent gay magazine *Christopher Street* (where extracts from both *States of Desire* and *Nocturnes for the King of Naples* had also appeared). Even so, White was shocked by the way in which interest in his novel suddenly accelerated immediately in advance of its publication – he would walk into a bookshop event expecting to find a sparse scattering of friends and familiar faces awaiting his reading from the novel, and would find the space electric with expectation, and so crammed with young men that he could barely make his way to the front.

Susan Sontag had told White to change the title he had been using for his novel from the outset, telling him it sounded too trite, but White stuck to *A Boy's Own Story*. With the novel's title, White was aiming to evoke the garish adventure books he had absorbed as a child; his intention was to intimate with his novel that childhood was more overwhelming, both sexually and emotionally, than the sterilized and limited representations those books offered to adolescents. The title also had resonances for White of the practice of documenting oral history (particularly widespread in America during White's youth), whereby an ethnographer took down the testimony of a witness to a particular period of history before it could be lost. The onset of deaths from AIDS during the period of the book's composition gave it precisely such a quality of endangered testimony. And for White, childhood itself was always ephemeral in substance and vulnerable to being lost through the fragility of memory. He saw the narrative of his book as deeply individual, but also as an act of witness to the universal terrain of childhood.

The novel's preoccupation is with the origins of gay sexuality and how they impact on the consciousness of a male child, whose view of what forms the healthy, acceptable and dominant nature of the social world is – to his horror – clearly mismatched with his own sensations and experiences. White's intention was for the book to establish 'a relationship of healing', as he put it, from himself as an adult gay man to his anguished childhood self. The figure of the father is crucial in *A Boy's Own Story*: the father is the source of the child's degradation, exerting crushing power over his identity and reinforcing his social fears. But, contradictorily, the novel also conveys a tangible sense of the father being himself deeply wounded by his existence, and of the child's alertness to that wound: 'At such moments, tears would come to my eyes in impotent compassion for Daddy: this invalid despot, this man who bullied everyone but suffered the consequences with such a tender, uneducated heart! Tears would also well up when I had to correct my father on a matter of fact.'[62] This evocation of the father's wound is edged with nostalgia, induced in White by his own father's recent death. The novel is also fundamentally about sex and its visceral power to change human perception and precipitate extreme acts, such as betrayal; also linked to sex, however, is the overriding quality of beauty: 'It seemed to me then that beauty is the highest good, the one thing we all want to be or have or, failing that, destroy, and that all the world's virtues are nothing but the world's spleen and deceit.'[63] In the boy's desire to secure beauty for himself, an immense will to power comes into play. He fantasizes that he is a hidden deity or prince, like the narrator of *Forgetting Elena*. Since the boy does not consider himself to be beautiful, he needs the power to seduce and so inhabit or accompany boys or men who *are* beautiful – or else to rearrange and manipulate the social world around him according to his own conception of beauty, and thereby anchor his place within it: 'I was desolate. I toyed again with the idea of becoming a general. I wanted power so badly that I had convinced myself I already had too much of it, that I was an evil schemer who might destroy everyone around me through the poison seeping out of my pores. I was appalled by my own majesty. I wanted someone to betray.'[64] But, when the boy does finally achieve a sense of power and self-importance in the world – precisely through such an act of betrayal – this sense is simultaneously eroded away by a feeling of deeply pleasurable alienation from that world: the alienation of feeling and acting 'like someone in history'[65]. Finally, the book – like White's two previous novels – is an investigation of memory and its fragmentary, arbitrary nature: 'Like a blind man's hands exploring a face, the memory lingers over an identifying or beloved feature but dismisses the rest as just a curve, a bump, an expanse.'[66]

A father is taking his dog and three adolescent boys out for a ride in a motorboat on a lake at night. One of the boys is the childhood self of the novel's narrator, and he immediately transmits a sense of urgency and presence to the situation: 'We're going for a midnight boatride. It's a cold, clear summer night and four of us – the two boys, my dad and I – are descending the stairs that zigzag down the hill from the house to the dock.'[67] The atmosphere is of deep black water enclosed by darkness, adolescent excitement pitched against paternal remoteness, and the crazy but tentative lust of the narrator's youthful self for Kevin, one of the other two boys (both sons of a business associate of the father's). The narrator is looking back on his childhood as an older man, but avoids giving information about his current self, other than intimating his fascinated sexual attraction for his own younger (and unnamed) self. He depicts his relationship as a boy with his father, the texture of his life at school, and his individual awareness of his gay identity, which becomes articulated in public through effusive behaviour: 'I was a sissy. My hands were always in the air. In eighth grade I had appeared in the class pageant.'[68] The narrative resumes: the boy, aged fifteen, is sharing a bedroom with the other two boys and wants to fuck Kevin, who is twelve and eager to experiment. While Kevin had been belligerent on the boatride, he now appears maladroit, and is easily impressed with the heterosexual experiences haphazardly invented by the older boy. The sexual encounter between the two boys initially misfires: ' "I'll go first," I said. Although I put lots of spit on him and me, he still said it hurt. I'd get about half an inch in and he'd say, "Take it out! Quick!" He was lying on his side with his back to me, but I could still look over and see him wince in profile. "Jesus," he said. "It's like a knife all through me." '[69] Eventually the two boys successfully fuck each other in turn. The nameless boy subsides into languid devotion for Kevin, but this rapidly disintegrates into disillusioned disgust at Kevin's uncouth manner and his family's fragile social status, and into deep unease at his own sexuality and its social implications.

The narrative then back-tracks a year. Longing for escape from his family, the boy meets a city hustler who promises to take him to New York; after the hustler shamelessly cheats the infatuated boy out of his bus fare, he arranges for him to pay to have sex with another hustler. Moving further back in time, the narrator evokes the imaginary childhood friends he devised around the age of seven, at the time when his parents broke up; from this point, the timescale begins to ascend again, passing through the boy's squabbles with his sister in their divorced mother's apartment, and his first gay contacts at the age of eleven with the peripheral but squalidly glamorous owners of a bookshop. The following year, his mother sends him to a rural summer camp, where he has sex with a retarded 'special camper', Ralph: 'To overcome my scruples, Ralph hypnotised me. He didn't have to intone the words long to send me into a deep trance. Once I was under his spell he told me I'd obey him, and I did. He also said that when I awakened I'd remember nothing, but he was wrong there. I have remembered everything.'[70] At his suburban school, the boy befriends a beautiful youth named Tommy, who sends him on a heterosexual date with a girl, Helen; the calamitous encounter gives the boy the hallucinatory impression that his life has become entirely filmic, constituted only of vividly composed moments from which the endless banality of his family life must be edited out: 'When the dresser drawer stuck I winced – this sequence would have to be reshot.'[71] The boy is so desperate for social acceptance that he writes to Helen, declaring his love for her; on being predictably refused, he becomes preoccupied with Buddhism as offering an enticing cancelling-out of turbulent emotional states such as his own. Simultaneously craving and fearing an all-male environment, he asks to be sent to a boys' boarding school. He decides that the only solution to his dilemma about his gay identity lies in submitting to psychotherapy, but his first sessions with the inept Dr O'Reilly only intensify and add to his dilemma. After its circuitous course, the narrative of the novel ends with an incident situated one year after its opening: the boy – ingratiating himself with the society which is repelling him – betrays a marijuana-smoking teacher, with whom he has sex immediately after denouncing him to the boarding school's headmaster. Although the outcome of the incident is messy, the narrative reverses slightly in time to conclude in the very instant of exaltation which the boy experiences at his act of betrayal.

While working on *A Boy's Own Story*, White had felt the need to develop a language to convey his preoccupations with memory and childhood both evocatively and explicitly. In the end, he decided to aim the language of the book at a point more towards the lucid candour of *States of Desire* than the idiosyncratic style of *Forgetting Elena* (he was torn because Isherwood had praised the former and Nabokov the latter). The result was a language which was fluent and beguiling. Even the effects of White's heavy consumption of alcohol and drugs during the composition of the book (which he said made it difficult for him to hold the overall design of the novel in his head) served only to give a texture of attractive, whimsical aberrance to the novel's meanderings through time. The book's language periodically goes completely wayward – as, for example, when White describes past incidents as being 'like a whole rootless plantation of algae' and, immediately afterwards, as pulsing 'like quasars from long–dead stars to reach the vivid planet of the present, they drift like fog over the ship until the spread sails are merely panels of gray in grayer air'.[72] At other times, the language is so precisely focused and exact that it resembles a description from a film–script. Only occasionally does White openly establish his rapport with the reader; then, the tone becomes humbly seductive, and complicitious to an irresistible degree: 'I say all this by way of hoping that the lies I've made up to get from one poor truth to another may mean something most particular to you, my eccentric, patient, scrupulous reader, willing to make so much of so little, more patient and more respectful of life, of a life, than the author you're allowing for a moment to exist yet again.' [73]

The autobiographical content of the novel is far more at issue than in either of White's two previous novels. White said: 'All the while I was writing *A Boy's Own Story*, I kept saying to myself, I wonder if I'll have the courage to put in some truth there.'[74] The book took its source in a number of autobiographical anecdotes and sensations: White, for example, remembered the chance smell of a taxi–driver's cigar as powerfully evoking his own recently–dead father's cigars and thereby forming one of the moments of inspiration for the project. And many of the characters in the book, such as the beautiful boy

Tommy and the 'date', Helen, are based on friends White knew in his childhood. White's strategy of incorporating auto-biographical elements into his novels would change fundamentally over the course of what would become a trilogy of novels initiated by *A Boy's Own Story*. In that first novel of the trilogy, the autobiographical material is absorbed fragmentarily, and used to construct a series of revealing masks for White's youthful self. The novel exerts a transformation of identity on that childhood, working in two related ways. In one way, White constructs what he called a 'normalized' version of his precociously creative and prodigiously sexual childhood self. The boy White depicts is diffident, anguished, and nervous about his sexual encounters, while White himself as an adolescent was garrulous, sociable (though inwardly troubled), and supremely confident both in his first attempts at making art and in his many sexual encounters. In inventing his character, White was motivated by the desire to present a boy shorn of what might be perceived as a bizarre or extravagant approach to sex and art. It was only through the relative anonymity or interchangeability accorded by White to his character that he was able to make that character exude the quality of childhood universality which he was seeking to capture and document. In this context, White noted that 'readers assume *A Boy's Own Story* is autobiographical and of course it is – kind of – but in another very important way it is not, because I made the boy much more ordinary than I was, since I was compulsively sexual from age twelve on. By the time I was sixteen, I'd probably been to bed with several hundred people.'[75] To some extent, White's real self becomes turned inside-out in the novel, so that his actual subterranean fears about his sexuality are placed on the surface of his character's behaviour, highlighted and foregrounded.

The other way in which White transforms his childhood identity in *A Boy's Own Story* is by making his own youth the starting point for a presentation of the great resonant myth of childhood. This is largely accomplished through the novel's narrative journey, which winds, back-tracks and advances through individual trials and challenges. Then, that journey finally transcends the personal, to achieve a fundamentally human form of youth, initiation and betrayal. It was here that White sought to avoid elements that would emphasize either his own 'specialness' as a child (such as his sexual appetite) or his own linguistic style. Whereas in *Nocturnes for the King of Naples*, the narrator's delirious infatuation had been with the material of language itself, White kept his language in *A Boy's Own Story* principally at the service of his narrative (White ascribed the occasional eruptions of an intrusive style into that narrative to the effects of alcohol rather than to any intentional stylistic excess). Childhood itself – with its sexuality – is White's infatuation in *A Boy's Own Story*, rather than language. As a result, childhood is transformed into an informally created myth in *A Boy's Own Story*, one all the more powerful for its direct, slightly out-of-control loquacity. It was also a myth whose beauty and resonance would attract a large heterosexual readership, at least in Britain. In its intentions, this approach is a long way from the sense of total transparency which White would work to construct fourteen years later with *The Farewell Symphony*, the final part of the trilogy – offering, to the maximum extent, the whole truth of the writer's presence, of the reader's presence, and of the presence of the narrative process itself. For White, the essential and daring act of truth in *A Boy's Own Story* was his inclusion of the particular element based on a real incident – the betrayal of the boarding school teacher – which he feared his readers would not accept, and would find bizarre or repulsive (although, in fact, readers seemed happy to accept the incident as the novel's suspenseful climax and as a familiar act). This human act, betrayal, would later join together with a concern for the betrayal of language itself (a betrayal both exacted on and generated *by* language), to become one of White's principal preoccupations in his work on Jean Genet.

In 1980, during the period when he was working on *A Boy's Own Story*, White wrote: 'To find the psychic energy to pursue a long career, it seems to me, a writer must juggle between a vigorous, recording curiosity about the world and the ongoing process of self-creation.'[76] That endless re-creation of the self, within and against the world, is the force that transforms the evocations of a personal history in White's work into a penetrating substance, accumulating in power from book to book. The intersection in White's work between a preoccupation with the forms of memory and an incessantly interrogating exploration of the world – its sexuality, its society: the revolutions of the body and the upheavals of human hierarchies – constitutes the origin for White's probing voice.

Encouraged by the reception in the United States to *A Boy's Own Story*, White began to contemplate writing a sequel. Although he had touched on the subject of psychotherapy in *A Boy's Own Story*, he wanted now to investigate more deeply his negative feelings towards the therapy he had received (with its power to induce or reinforce chronic self-loathing), together with the oppressive social climate of the 1950s and 1960s towards gay identity in general. This project would be realized five years later as *The Beautiful Room is Empty*. But White was also concerned to finish his novel *Caracole*, which had already been in progress for six years at this stage. In the wake of the success of *A Boy's Own Story*, he applied for a writing grant to give him the time away from his teaching and journalism to complete *Caracole*, and he was awarded a Guggenheim Fellowship for the year from the summer of 1983 to the summer of

1984, 'to Assist Research and Artistic Creation', as the Guggenheim Foundation defined their award's aim. Susan Sontag wrote a recommendation for White's application which he considered to be crucial in its success (he had applied unsuccessfully several times before, without her recommendation). The award – one of the most prestigious American cultural grants from a private foundation – gave him the freedom to write wherever he chose for one year. He saw the opportunity not only to escape his teaching, but to leave the overheated atmosphere of New York entirely and to spend the year in Paris. The choice of Paris was, to some extent, a gratuitous one, a pleasurable submission to the fabulous aura of European culture which had already taken White to Rome in 1970. But he had also grown increasingly captivated with contemporary Parisian culture through his encounters with figures such as Barthes and Foucault, and Paris was the city on whose wartime history the imaginary city setting of *Caracole* was partially based. White had also been fascinated by the new political culture of Paris during a short holiday he had spent in the city in 1981, at the beginning of François Mitterrand's presidency. Purcell, who had attended a college in Florence and liked the idea of living in Europe again, was happy to accompany White to Paris. The amounts paid by the Guggenheim Foundation were calculated individually, according to how much the recipient usually earned, and White was allocated $18,000 for the year.

White was planning to return to New York after his time in Paris, and so he arranged to sub-let the Lafayette Street apartment for the year; since the apartment was a rent-controlled property, he could rent it out for considerably more than he himself paid, and this would give him another source of income in Paris to supplement the Guggenheim award. In leaving New York, White saw a reprieve from the lacerated atmosphere of the city, in which the forthright, confident gay community of only a few years previously had been overturned into a huddle of anxious figures, preoccupied with the still largely unknown but unquestionably expanding powers of the AIDS virus to exact debilitation and death. White said of the atmosphere of that moment in New York: 'We were anticipating the deluge to come.' Although White was aware that he, too, might be carrying the virus which had nonchalantly begun to decimate New York's gay community, the distance between Europe and the United States seemed a sufficient separation from his own experience to signal a tangible, if provisional, release. But it was in creative terms that White was primarily viewing his departure, and in that sense too, it was to be a vital new beginning.

White's years before his departure from the United States are terrains of memory, which would creatively sustain his life in Paris: the materials of childhood and sexual exploration, in Cincinnati and Chicago; followed by the revelation of the gay community in New York, with its friendships, its culture, its revolutionary battles, and its experiments with the beauty and sexuality of the human body; and finally, the impending calamity of AIDS which darkly edged White's final New York years. They are tumultuous years, moving almost without interval from the exhilarating to the horrifying, and back again. Memory possesses a force of transformation, which – in White's life and work – binds those extremes together and makes an astonishing physical form of them.

Part 2

Edmund White in Paris

Edmund White's arrival in Paris in July 1983 gave him a sensational new lease of life. The city of Paris, at that time, was still experiencing the cultural excitement that had surrounded the beginning of François Mitterrand's presidency two years earlier; the initial determination of Mitterrand's government to provide the conditions for a thriving and adventurous contemporary culture – with new museums, monuments and media systems – was making itself felt in every area of the arts. This cultural impetus, together with an avowed political responsibility to obliterate the everyday racism that had been pervasive in French society over the previous decades, gave the city's inhabitants an infectious and pleasurable sense of momentum – which would, however, have largely collapsed by the middle of the decade. The material results of Mitterrand's intentions failed to transpire (except in the realm of architecture), as the socialist government grew ineffectual over the following years, and the innate conservatism of French society increasingly re-asserted itself; but the moment of White's arrival in Paris was one of uniquely high expectations and idealistic upheavals. Alongside the laudable but intangible

cultural ambitions of Paris, White found the city to be hauntingly beautiful in its visual and tactile forms, with its expansive
nineteenth-century boulevards and streets encompassing districts of intricate alleyways and courtyards from earlier centuries; the city's aura of being scrupulously preserved, its
buildings maintained with pride by its loving inhabitants, was
something that had been almost totally absent in New York.

Along with the transformation in his creative life which the
move to Paris represented, White had also been instigating a
number of fundamental physical changes. Before leaving New
York, he had given up drinking completely. Paris was by no
means the ideal city for this self-imposed austerity, since many
of White's new Parisian friends would take for granted that it
was the most natural thing in the world to enjoy drinking wine
and champagne – indeed, an integral part of life – and would
be baffled by his adamant reluctance to join them in this.
White would never resume drinking alcohol, except when a
particularly elaborate recipe he was working on would sometimes call for the addition of a small amount of wine. The end
of alcohol was a huge step for White, giving him a new cogency
and lucidity in his writing; he had also given up his heavy use
of cigarettes. He did, however, continue to smoke marijuana
whenever the opportunity presented itself. A further break
with White's New York past had taken the form of him shaving
off his moustache, so that he instantly metamorphosed from
having the appearance of a college professor heading into
studious middle-age, to that of a much younger man of
indeterminate occupation. In later years in Paris, White would
favour dark designer jackets and overcoats; but at this point
he dressed casually, often in jeans and T-shirts (a T-shirt
with the logo of the mid-1980s American rap group, the
Beastie Boys, was a particular favourite), while he began to
absorb Parisian fashions with a new, shorter haircut and light-
coloured, well-designed overcoats; his new appearance com-

bined residual elements of American college-boy style with that of a tentatively elegant expatriate.

Part of the influence for this change of style came from John Purcell, who looked much younger than his actual age. Although Purcell spoke no French, he quickly assimilated the visual appearance of a young Parisian gay man, with a cropped haircut – left long on top – and clothes pitched between the athletic and the dishevelled, with torn jeans and big, battered boots. Purcell also rapidly adapted to the leisurely pace of his new life in Paris with White – he was no longer under any social pressure to undertake work of any kind, or even to give the nominal appearance of being interested in working. His unfocused life in Paris occasionally made him listless, and he could be defensive about his idleness with visitors (although this was the last thing White would reproach him for, since he himself prized his idleness as one of his own cardinal virtues – a feeling of an effortless control over time, that could fracture occasionally into bouts of a driving work ethic when writing deadlines appeared, or when the mood suited him, but then unfailingly reappeared). Purcell would undertake a course in art and design at an American college in Paris, and graduated there, but the main part of his time was spent exploring the city streets and investigating Paris's sexual possibilities.

On arriving in Paris, White rented an apartment which a professor who sometimes attended the seminars at the Institute for the Humanities had tipped him off about shortly before he had left the United States. It was on the Île Saint-Louis, a small oval-shaped island in the middle of the Seine which White knew from his time spent staying in a hotel there in 1970, on his way back from Rome to New York. White said: 'If you're a foreigner, you always feel safer on an island. You feel you can understand it better and master it better.' In order to locate himself there fully, he bought a number of books about the Île Saint-Louis from the open-air book stalls that lined the Seine and immersed himself in the island's history. The Île Saint-Louis was connected by a pedestrian bridge to the Île de la Cité – where the Notre Dame cathedral loomed far above the entire surrounding area – and by a further five road bridges (two on the south side, three on the north side) linking it to 'mainland' Paris. The island's main street, the Rue Saint-Louis-en-l'Île, housed a line of small specialist food shops and expensive hotels; the island's main landmark was an ornate church, the Église Saint-Louis-en-l'Île, directly opposite the windows of White's third-floor apartment in the Rue Poulletier, a narrow street which ran from the main street to the island's southern riverbank. Most of the buildings on the island were slowly disintegrating seventeenth-century mansions, containing three or four storeys of apartments, although several of the buildings on the riverbanks were vast palatial structures owned by aristocratic families. The interior of the island had always been one of the poorer quarters of Paris, especially in the decade following the Second World War, and the immaculate cream stone façades often concealed intense poverty. The island had been the scene of arrests of Jewish families and resistance fighters during the German Occupation, and plaques marked the houses from which children had been seized for extermination in the concentration camps. White did all of his shopping along the main street of the island, and came to know the shopkeepers well. He found the island's community strangely self-absorbed and suspicious – he was always amused when the insular shopkeepers warily referred to the inhabitants of mainland Paris as though they belonged to another country – and the island could be eerily quiet and empty in the winter months of river mists, when many of the wealthy absentee owners of the more salubrious buildings were away in warmer parts of the country. During White's seven years on the island, until January 1990, he saw the island become still emptier, as property was bought up for investment and left vacant; the streets became deserted of people and the shopkeepers began to go out of business. The island only came to raucous life during the summer, when tourists on their way to Notre Dame would rampage down the island's main street and form queues outside the legendary Berthillon ice-cream shop.

White's two-room apartment in the Rue Poulletier had a slightly dilapidated air but was spacious, and brilliantly lit with late sunshine in the afternoons. White felt it looked beautifully bohemian in its ramshackle way, like a room in a Tennessee Williams play. He had brought over many of his books and records from New York, but – since he was initially planning to stay for just the year of his writing grant – he kept on display most of his landlady's well-worn furniture and decorations, which formed a bizarre assortment of surrealist tapestries woven by the landlady herself, supplemented by her collection of African handicraft objects. The apartment already contained entire shelves of books on Roman culture. The landlady had left a number of bulky portable heaters arranged around the floor, but White and Purcell simply draped covers over them and forgot about them. As the years went by, the living-room filled up more and more with White's photographs and books, and adapted itself to his and Purcell's presence; but it still retained its haphazard feeling of a space acquired and inhabited by chance. Purcell liked the eccentric collection of neighbours – of many nationalities – who inhabited the rest of the building; he would often visit an aged but vivacious Englishwoman who had been a friend of the black American writer Richard Wright during his time spent living in Paris. White was always intrigued by the Hôtel Lambert, a sumptuous, well-protected mansion on one corner of the island that was owned by the wealthy Rothschild family; he was overjoyed when an old gay aristocrat who lived with the Rothschilds, and had read White's novels, casually invited him for lunch one day so that he was able to see the spectacular interior of the mansion.

On the Île Saint-Louis, White's writing days were usually short; he would work for an hour or so on his fiction after waking up, either lying on his front in bed – naked in summer, or in the cold winter months wearing a huge night-shirt that went down to his knees – with his notebook laid flat on the sheet in front of him. He described this approach to the process of writing: 'My idea of writing fiction is – you lie in bed and you sort of daydream, and you have your notebook next to you, and then you scribble a few lines and then if you do that – just a few pages a day – pretty soon you have a big fat book!' He would frequently read what he had just written out loud to John Purcell. Sometimes, he wrote sitting up on an ancient sofa-bed in one corner of the apartment's living-room, which also served as an informal setting for afternoon tea-parties, with a rickety table and three or four wooden chairs. And he also installed a writing desk alongside the apartment's windows, so that he could work while looking out over the roof of the church. In Paris, White acquired the habit of always writing by hand in ink, in large, luxuriously bound blue notebooks with thick paper, which he bought at a specialist stationery store; he wrote on every second page, keeping the adjoining page empty for any subsequent additions, which he linked to the main part of the text with extravagant arrows. After the Guggenheim award had run out, White would undertake regular articles and book reviews for magazines and newspapers in addition to his work on his fiction, and these assignments took up much of the rest of his day. Even during the Guggenheim period, he wrote pieces for *Vogue* magazine, which had commissioned him to deliver six articles a year on Parisian cultural life. White saw so much that interested him in Paris that he often found that he was far ahead of that schedule for his articles. The *Vogue* articles often concerned newly prominent French novelists and artists, or else areas of the city – such as the Bastille district – that were flourishing as sites for contemporary art and fashion. But White was always able to maintain long stretches of time away from his writing, giving him the freedom to walk leisurely around the island's riverbanks and through the ancient Marais district to the north of the island, and to prepare immense, multi-coursed dinners for the evening's guests; the majority of his time was invariably given over to developing a new group of friends. He delightedly gave the enigmatic indication 'I live on the Island' when his visitors asked how to find his street.

After his arrival in Paris, White soon became close friends with the French translator of his novels, Gilles Barbedette. He had first met Barbedette in New York two years previously – Barbedette had read the extract from *A Boy's Own Story* that had appeared in *Christopher Street* magazine, and had eagerly told White that he wanted to translate the novel into French; he had also found a French publisher for *Nocturnes for the King of Naples*. On that first meeting, White had rapidly seduced Barbedette, but it was the only time that they slept together. White had stayed with Barbedette, who lived in the Barbès district of North African immigrant workers, during his holiday in Paris in 1981. Barbedette was a suave gay man in his late twenties; in English, his manner was warm and intimate, but in French, he was coldly abrupt and incisive, and thereby very much at home in the Parisian literary world. He had translated Nabokov's work as well as White's, and was himself a novelist; he also wrote journalism for the Parisian newspapers. One of his books was an oral history of gay men speaking about their lives in the Paris of the 1920s. Barbedette insisted that, now White was installed in Paris, he should set about meeting the prominent French writers and other expatriate writers with whom Barbedette was on friendly terms. White was hesitant, since his French was still very sketchy (he was attending language classes and trying to immerse himself in the language by only reading French novels, including, for the third or fourth time, the work of Proust). But Barbedette's English was fluent, and he was more than ready to serve as White's interpreter whenever necessary. He also arranged for interviews with White and extracts from his work to appear in the Parisian press, so that White began to acquire a reputation as a successful writer newly arrived in Paris whom other writers were keen to meet. With Barbedette, White soon discovered that Parisian gay writers inhabited far less confined social surroundings than their New York counterparts, and – in sharp contrast to New York gay writers – perceived absolutely no limitations on the subject matter of their work. White had soon absorbed this approach himself, and a decade later, he would declare: 'Because I moved to France in 1983, I seek in my own writing to find the universal aspects of gay experience – and I have the freedom to write about even heterosexuality.'[1]

Barbedette introduced White to the novelist Pierre Guyotat, and the three of them spent a memorable evening together. Guyotat was one of the most famous French writers of his time, reviled and adored in equal measure for his novels set in brothels surrounded by the carnage of colonial warfare, such as *Eden, Eden, Eden*; in France, he was often ranked alongside such legendary figures as the Marquis de Sade. Although largely unknown in Britain at the time White met him, Guyotat would make two appearances at the Institute of Contemporary Arts in London in the mid-1990s, and was notably described by one British newspaper as 'bad, bald, and a big name in the French literary avant-garde'.[2] White was intrigued by Guyotat, who had an enormous shaved head and an austere, monastic manner that belied his work's monstrous reputation as extreme pornography (his early work had been censored and banned even in France, where literary censorship was almost unknown).

White later described how shocked and amused he was by Guyotat's blatant greed at their dinner in Barbedette's apartment; having eaten his own food, Guyotat then snatched morsels from White and Barbedette's plates, before burying his head in the remaining contents of Barbedette's refrigerator. However, in Guyotat's view, it was White who was the more avid eater by a wide margin; he insisted that he was just innocently putting weight back on after a period when he had been so immersed in his writing, he had completely forgotten to eat for several months and had to be resuscitated in hospital from a starvation-induced coma.[3] White wrote an article for *Vogue* praising Guyotat's work, thereby earning himself Guyotat's fanatical – if ephemeral – devotion.

Through White's renewed contact with Michel Foucault – who periodically invited him to dinner parties at his apartment in the months following his arrival in Paris – he also encountered the gay novelist and photographer Hervé Guibert, who was then in his late twenties and had been Foucault's lover. In discussing Guibert's work with Gilles Barbedette, White realized that the element of corrosive literary jealousy that had animated the intellectual circles of New York also existed in Paris, albeit in a different form. It was primarily Guibert's arrogant beauty, White believed, that was the cause of Barbedette's jealousy and his dismissal of Guibert's work as shallow and inept. White himself was deeply impressed on their first meeting by Guibert's beautifully sullen face, with its air of raddled innocence. At first, he was put off reading Guibert's fiction by Barbedette's condescending scorn for it, just as he became hesitant about befriending Guibert and so incurring Barbedette's wrath. But later, he came to read Guibert's novels with horrified fascination; they were relentless evocations of acts of sexual torture and violent humiliation, in which Guibert himself often featured as a prominent character. Guibert's inspirations included the writers Jean Genet and Antonin

Artaud, together with the painter Francis Bacon: work which spectacularly incised the human body, and created new and exhilarating imageries and languages for its sensations and obsessions. Despite his increasing fascination with Guibert's novels, White grew to like him less and less personally on their subsequent meetings, under the influence of Barbedette's loathing for him. Guibert developed AIDS and would die in 1991, within a year of Barbedette's own death from the disease. In retrospect, White regretted not having become closer friends with Guibert: 'Gilles died, and then Hervé died, and so I was left with nothing but Hervé's books, and then I realized what a fool I had been.' Michel Foucault too would die of AIDS in the year following White's arrival in Paris. Guibert had described Foucault's physical decline in merciless detail in his book *To The Friend Who Did Not Save My Life*. Foucault never admitted publicly that he had the disease (it was by no means certain that he admitted the fact to himself or was even conscious of it), and on his death, an article on the front page of the newspaper *Libération* furiously denied the rumours that were starting to emerge about the actual cause of his sudden demise, as though it were an insult to his reputation to suggest such a thing. By contrast, Guibert made absolutely no secret of the fact that he had AIDS. At the end of the decade, when he became terminally ill, he gave vividly candid television interviews on the popular book programme *Apostrophes*, which alerted a largely sympathetic French audience to the often hidden evidence of AIDS, and ensured that Guibert's subsequent death would be a highly public event. Of the exceptional French writers born in the 1940s and 1950s and concerned in their individual ways with developing a new language of sexuality – Guibert, Guyotat, Barbedette, and the novelist and film-maker Cyril Collard – all would die from AIDS by the mid-1990s, with the sole exception of Guyotat.

As White noted wryly of Guyotat, 'his sexuality did not involve other living creatures'.[4]

Soon after his arrival in Paris, White met an ebullient young American woman in her mid-twenties named Rachel Stella, who was the daughter of the artist Frank Stella; she had arrived in Paris to undertake art history research, and had decided to stay. She and White became close friends, and she helped him with many of the arduous details of his writing life. White detested typing his own manuscripts, and preferred to simply dictate his hand-written drafts to Stella, as they sat in one or other of the succession of apartments which her mother had bought in Paris as investments. White became eager to publicize his match-making skills after Stella told him she was getting married to a film-maker White had introduced her to, Pierre Aubry. She later opened a gallery in one of the salubrious districts of western Paris, where she exhibited work by young Parisian artists. Rachel Stella's independent and idiosyncratic temperament was mirrored in another of White's older women friends, Marie-Claude de Brunhoff. White had already met Marie-Claude de Brunhoff in New York, ten years earlier, through her work as the representative in Paris of the American publishing house, Knopf. At that time, she had still been married to the celebrated writer of children's books, Laurent de Brunhoff ('Mr Babar', as White called him). She was French but spoke English fluently, in a deep and hypnotic whisper, and always insisted that she and White converse in his native language. She was a few years older than White, and effortlessly combined elements of the flamboyant and the intimately maternal in her friendship with him; she designed and made her own jewellery, and provided White with advice and an explanatory running commentary on the arcane feuds of the Parisian literary world, of which she had an exhaustive knowledge. She also introduced White to the eminent philosophers

Julia Kristeva and Philippe Sollers, former radical Maoists of the early 1970s who were by now the epitome of Parisian respectability. At first, White found these encounters intimidating, since the complexity of the French being spoken – and the expectation that White would have something equally complex to say in response – threw him into a mute panic: 'I was suddenly reduced to this child-like status.'[5] But soon, he was able to face even the verbose Sollers, with his pudding-basin hairstyle and wagging cigarette-holder, without blanching. Marie-Claude de Brunhoff and White spoke at length at least once a day on the telephone, and he believed it was she who was most influential in inducing him to stay in Paris permanently, since her incessant litany of the attractions of Parisian culture and life was captivating. In turn, White supported her through an acrimonious divorce that left her devastated. When White's English-speaking friends met Marie-Claude de Brunhoff, they often found her aloof and bizarre. But White viewed her as his closest friend in Paris, and she was the person who would always be there to help him in moments of desperation.

White's sex life in Paris was markedly different from that in New York. Alongside his relationship with Purcell (which involved very little sex by this time), he began to explore Parisian gay life, which – while acutely conscious of the dangers of AIDS – had none of the hysteria which White had left behind in New York. The bar and bath-house scene of New York, although beginning to disintegrate by the time White had left the United States, had still been the mainstay of sexual contacts there; by contrast, a communal gay scene was virtually non-existent in Paris. A small number of gay bars and night-clubs were frequented by young men in their twenties with hair shaved short at the sides and back, wearing high-laced military boots and the heavy woollen lorry-drivers' jerseys known as 'camionneurs'; but older gay men often shunned the bars, since gay life (though respected and subject to relatively little harassment) was far more covert in Paris than in New York. Many other gay men dismissed the Parisian bar scene in disgust as a 'ghetto' – although a decade later it would be thriving, and the word 'ghetto' would have acquired more positive, if ironical, connotations. In his first years in Paris, White returned to cruising. The main cruising areas in Paris were in the Buttes-Chaumont park and beside the banks of the Seine on the Quai des Tuileries, but White's preference was for the area of public gardens at the very eastern tip of the Île Saint-Louis, much closer to his apartment, where he had numerous sexual adventures in the first year after his arrival in Paris. But Parisian cruising was far more rigorously tied to age than in New York, and for the first time, White – now in his early forties – began to feel the pain of frequent rejection, which was delivered with a more off-hand, wordless dismissal than in New York. Increasingly, in his search for sexual partners, White began to use the 'Minitel' service provided by the French telephone company. The Minitel – 'commercially organized lechery by telephone',[6] as Susan Sontag once crushingly described it – allowed two subscribers to discuss their sexual preferences on a small computer screen, have telephone sex or arrange to meet face-to-face. To his delight, White found himself acquiring lovers of every age, race and occupation, in every district of Paris, and he spent his days travelling from one end of the city to the other between assignations. White was happy to go along with whatever sexual demands his partners had in mind. In contrast with New York, many of his new lovers were ostensibly heterosexual men, often married, who wanted to keep their gay sexual contacts hidden, and White enjoyed participating in the subterfuge. His knowledge of the city, of its inhabitants and of the French language were all rapidly enhanced, along with the variety of his sex life.

By the time that his year's grant from the Guggenheim

Foundation ran out, White had decided to stay in Paris for as long as he could possibly afford it. He found the city endlessly exhilarating, and he had forged a new circle of friends and lovers who actively wanted to keep him there as a permanent part of their lives. *A Boy's Own Story* had been a great success commercially, and was now beginning to appear in numerous translations across the world. With the income from his regular contributions to magazines and newspapers added to his increasing book royalties, he could now imagine supporting himself entirely by his writing for the first time. Although White decided to make a long-term home in Paris, John Purcell would eventually return to New York, in 1987, since he missed the United States and found it hard to find lovers in Paris who met his particular sexual needs (he had a predilection for educated American black men); the separation was amicable, and he remained close friends with White. Back in New York, Purcell began to work in an architect's office. Once White had been able to give notice to the tenant who had sub-let his apartment in Lafayette Street, Purcell moved back in, remaining there until his death from AIDS in 1995.

In the same summer that White arrived in Paris, his novel *A Boy's Own Story* was published in Britain, where it received a mostly laudatory critical response and sold extremely well. At first, the novel had been turned down everywhere it was sent, and seemed destined to be unpublished in Britain, before Sonny Mehta, head of the publishing house Picador, decided to issue the book as a paperback original (this was the first time that White's work had appeared in paperback in Britain). The vastly successful publication of the novel marked a decisive turning point in British literary publishing, pointedly indicating that contemporary fiction with an intelligent and vivid exploration of intricate subject matters – in White's case, those of sex, childhood and memory – could reach and captivate a wide readership and achieve an eminently fashionable status. To White's surprise, the novel was avidly read by a heterosexual readership as well as by the gay community. He assumed that – despite his protagonist's gay sexuality and his obsessions with power and betrayal – his British readers were primarily approaching the novel as a narrative about universal childhood dilemmas, in which his character's gay sexuality and his obsessions were irrelevant; another possibility was that White's readers were simply sympathetic and receptive to gay culture in a way that he had never experienced in the United States. White's readings from the novel around London, in venues such as the Riverside Studios, were delivered to capacity audiences who gave the book a riotous, ecstatic response – 'It was like a landmine had gone off,' White remembered. In the wake of the success of *A Boy's Own Story*, White's two earlier novels were published in Britain together as one volume; although *Nocturnes for the King of Naples* had appeared in Britain before, this was the first British publication of *Forgetting Elena*.

White already knew London from several visits in the 1960s, but he now began to travel to the city frequently, attending parties and cultural events with the new friends he made there. Britain was entering its second term of Margaret Thatcher's government, and – unlike France, with its strong socialist government – the political left in Britain was largely moribund; the Miners' Strike was still in the future, together with the wholesale dismantling of the structure of the British press. The tabloid newspapers were already explicitly anti-gay (the death of the Hollywood actor Rock Hudson from AIDS in October 1985 would be the catalyst for a series of particularly malevolent headlines denouncing gay culture). But, at least in part in reaction to the oppressive political climate of London, innovative creative work was being pursued in the city in the form of performance culture, especially with the work of young directors and musicians; in cinema, particularly with the startling work of the gay film-maker Derek Jarman and his collaborator John Maybury; and in literature, with novels such as those of Salman Rushdie and Angela Carter. White experienced London as a hugely welcoming arena, not least because of the fortunate coincidence that *A Boy's Own Story* was quickly acquiring a vast readership in Britain just at that moment. He felt that he was being acclaimed in Britain not by an insular group of intellectuals – as in New York – or by elements of the factionalized American gay community, but by almost everyone he encountered. His sense of having compulsorily belonged to a ghetto culture in New York, which he had ultimately perceived as an exasperating limitation, was completely absent during his stays in London. And in New York, White had needed to be incessantly combative in the defence of his work, with both friends as well as enemies; in London, the positive response he met brought out his instinct for friendship expansively, and over the years he would acquire a huge network of friends in the city.

One of the most crucial friendships which White developed in London was with the young writer and theatre director Neil Bartlett, who was twenty-five at the time. In many ways, Bartlett embodied the atmosphere of elation and experimentation in London's thriving gay culture at the moment when *A Boy's Own Story* was published in Britain. In London, AIDS was yet to fully coalesce into the urgent and terrifying issue which it had already become in New York, and the city was the site of an expanding network of gay bars and nightclubs (especially Heaven, a vast subterranean space under the railway arches in Charing Cross), and the base for many successful gay musicians and theatre groups. In London, if not elsewhere in Britain, gay culture was receiving a degree of financial support.

Bartlett remembered: 'There was a terrific sense of exhilaration in London in the early 1980s – an explosion of culture – because AIDS hadn't hit, we had the Lesbian and Gay Arts Festival and the support of the pro-gay Greater London Council, with its euphoric, city-wide funding policy. People in the gay movement were actively involved in left-wing politics. Things were moving and happening in London – and Edmund White's writings for me were the kind of soundtrack to that time.'[7] Bartlett himself was intent on instigating gay performance work that was innovative, contemporary and deeply sexual. He wrote at the time: 'In the flesh, I like my theatre *hot* – sexy, colourful, hard-hitting.'[8] But he was also keenly aware of the creative antecedents of his own projects in London, in the work of nineteenth-century figures such as Oscar Wilde and the poet Simeon Solomon. In contemporary London, Bartlett was particularly fascinated by the (already disappearing) clone culture as a historical phenomenon, which he saw as demonstrating that physical appearance no longer had to be viewed as unique in order to be beautiful; for Bartlett, the very multiplication of clones, together with their wilful and adept sense of plagiarism, simply reinforced their beauty.

It would still be several years before Bartlett began to achieve prominent notoriety with his solo performance piece based on Simeon Solomon's life, *A Vision of Love Revealed in Sleep*, staged in 1987 at the then-derelict Butler's Wharf warehouse by Tower Bridge in London. But in 1983, he wrote and directed a spectacle entitled *Dressing Up*, for that year's Lesbian and Gay Arts Festival in London, which drew much of its inspiration from White's recently published books. It was the first time that White's writings had been transformed into another medium. Bartlett constructed a spectacle around the imagery and history of gay identity, manifested through the visual appearance of the male body and through fashion. For the first part of the production, he had done extensive research at the Public Record Office in London, compiling accounts of the eighteenth-century persecution and trials of gay men in London (usually ending with their executions by hanging at Tyburn gallows). These accounts of the lives, dress and language of the London 'Mollies' – a 'particular Gang of Sodomitical Witches', as the influential religious extremists of the time vilified them, and who had their special meeting-places in the back rooms of taverns, especially around Charing Cross – were interspersed with extracts Bartlett had chosen from plays of the period which had tangentially alluded to covert gay life. The material Bartlett had unearthed was performed by his actors in drag or naked, in a great cacophony of gay voices. White's writings formed the basis for the second half of the spectacle, which extended the historical exploration of the production by interrogating contemporary gay life and its imageries. Bartlett used extracts from *Nocturnes for the King of Naples* and *A Boy's Own Story*, along with the accounts from *States of Desire* of White's encounters in the nightclubs and bars of America, in which he had documented a community both tentatively and provocatively assembling its visual identity. On 20 September, White attended the opening night of *Dressing Up*, at the Cockpit Theatre, and met Bartlett for the first time there.

White's friendship with Bartlett was initially intensely sexual. He would often stay with Bartlett in London at his dilapidated council flat in Limehouse's Grenade Street. White remembered: 'It was wild – the windows were knocked out and dogs were always howling. There was almost no furniture – we'd sleep on a mattress on the floor and eat out of a tin can.' White was always delighted when Bartlett would come to visit him in Paris and outrage his staider Parisian friends with his flesh-revealing torn jeans, make-up and leather jackets. Bartlett found the way in which he was instantly whipped up into White's hectic life in Paris to be a captivating experience: 'I'd arrive covered in make-up and chains and suddenly we'd take off for a lunatic catalogue of incredibly glamorous parties – it was all exhausting and ludicrous, wandering among the fabulous ruins of a vanished era of power. He knew everything about Paris – except what the latest hot gay bar was. I think he was now relieved to be having wonderful, ridiculous conversations about cookery in Paris rather than the huge quantities of sex he'd had in New York.'[9] Bartlett had the impression that, in his life on the Île Saint-Louis, White was amusedly performing what was expected of him as an expatriate writer living in Paris, with both irony and pleasure. For Bartlett, who felt himself heavily anchored in place by being English, White was essentially itinerant and rootless, incessantly on the move within Paris itself, always planning journeys to other cities and islands, and never at home except in the sensations of the present moment. White himself was gratified that Bartlett viewed his work as being deviant and perverse, and at the same time as absolutely central to contemporary gay culture. Bartlett would later describe how formative White's work had been for him when, as a young gay student who had been entranced by Oscar Wilde's evocation of an illicit and decadent sexuality which insidiously 'tampered with' the reader's world, he was trying to find contemporary writings which also carried that impact of a forbidden but vitally disruptive sexuality: 'Edmund White's *Nocturnes for the King of Naples* was the first book by a contemporary writer that I bought because I knew he was a gay artist. I remember shaking with fear when I went and ordered the copy of this book from a bookshop in Bristol. The reason I did that was because I knew that this was an improper form of writing, that it was writing from a twilight world . . . It is all right if the author is dead, but it is really shaming if they are still alive to admit that you want to be exposed to this kind of writing.'[10] Bartlett believed that it was his experience of White's second novel – 'a beautiful, fantastical, bizarre, poisonous orchid', as he called it – which had inspired him to start writing himself for the first time: 'It was like a bell ringing.'[11]

In Bartlett's company, White would also experience the less welcoming side of London, with its homophobia and its paranoia about public demonstrations of gay friendship. On one occasion, after White had spoken at the Institute of Contemporary Arts, along The Mall from Buckingham Palace, he and Bartlett were arrested while walking and holding hands in nearby St James's Park. The arresting policeman told White: 'If you're capable of that, you're capable of blowing up Buckingham Palace.' White was appalled by the thin margin between approbation and oppression in a country which would invite him to speak at a state-funded cultural institution, and then immediately afterwards arrest him for publicly practising – even in such an innocuous form as holding hands with a lover – the gay sexuality which he had just been applauded for advocating.

In London, White also became close friends with the young gay novelist Adam Mars-Jones. At the time, Mars-Jones was in his late twenties and had published his first collection of stories, *Lantern Lecture*, in 1982. He had written one of the relatively few cool reviews of *A Boy's Own Story* on its British publication, for *Gay News*. The book's critics tended to go in for arcane domestic metaphors – where the composer Virgil Thomson had told White that the novel was 'a lot of wash and not much hang-out',[12] Mars-Jones noted that it was 'a cake that had been iced but not baked'.[13] But White obliviously absorbed the criticism and made friends with Mars-Jones anyway. White saw Bartlett and Mars-Jones as young gay men embodying many of the dilemmas and contradictions he faced within himself as a writer attempting to find creative forms to both represent and incite transformations in gay culture. Bartlett and Mars-Jones both perceived that gay culture thrived in an atmosphere of activism; however, where Bartlett's work spilled provocatively from writing to performance to an activism of anger and protest, Mars-Jones positioned himself firmly as a literary figure making reasoned arguments in favour of gay culture. Before his diagnosis as HIV-Positive, White occasionally contemplated the fantasy of fathering a child, and he had served as a kind of 'surrogate father' to his sister's teenage son during a stay he had made in White's New York apartment in the mid-1970s; now, White was fascinated by Mars-Jones' engagement as a gay man in investigating the potential for gay family structures (Mars-Jones would subsequently father a child with a lesbian mother). White and Mars-Jones remained close friends, and White would often stay at Mars-Jones' flat in Islington during his visits to London; three years later, they would formulate the project of writing a joint volume of stories about the impact of AIDS, with each writer contributing half of the book.

White also met and became fascinated by the English novelist and traveller Bruce Chatwin, who often lived an itinerant life, descending on friends for months at a time, before brusquely disappearing on another journey. Although White and Chatwin were exactly the same age, their personal histories and approaches to contemporary life were deeply different. The married but gay Chatwin presented himself to White as a conventional and reserved man, following in a long tradition of English explorers, and stubbornly documenting the few remaining unknown extremities of the world. But he never hid his sexuality from White, who knew that Chatwin's exploratory journeys were sexual as well as geographical. They were very briefly lovers – having sex immediately on their first meeting and never again – and when they ate in discreet Parisian restaurants, White often had to make Chatwin switch from English to French to make him lower the volume of his accounts of his sexual adventures, and of his versions of his novels' narratives studded with gay sex scenes; in French, to White's relief, Chatwin's 'voice would drop to a murmur'.[14] But White was aware that there was an immense subterranea to Chatwin's life, and believed that he had caught only glimpses of that complexity.

White frequently saw the novelist and historian Marina Warner, whom he had first met when he had invited her to speak at the New York Institute for the Humanities. Warner was the nearest British equivalent to Susan Sontag – a brilliant philosopher and researcher who could channel her findings both into meticulous histories and into baroque novels. In her dealings with the London cultural and artistic scene, Warner was adept but deeply tactful, and during the period of their closest friendship in the mid-1980s, she helped to guide White through the city's literary world, which to White appeared strangely tentative and oblique after the incessantly vocal self-promotion he had been used to among New York's writers. Warner had what White perceived to be an enormously hard-working approach to her own writing, which left him bemused: 'She was always in hyper-productivity, writing all the time – it made me feel tired to see all that activity.' As an atheist, White was particularly intrigued by Warner's intense creative engagement with religion; in books such as her study of the cult of the Virgin Mary, *Alone of All Her Sex*, she had critically interrogated the manipulations of history and its imageries by the Catholic Church, but she remained fascinated with the allure and attraction presented in their different, contradictory ways by world religions. White also found Warner to be an excellent confidante when his relationships with lovers became too fraught.

Marina Warner, together with all of White's friends, located the essential core of his character as a genius for friendship: an absolute openness towards absorbing the idiosyncrasies, aberrations and ecstasies of other people, and returning them fully from the resources of his own identity. The amplitude and diversity of White's friendships demonstrated the sheer vastness of that engagement with the ideal of friendship: as a human relationship to be executed with a total lack of duplicity, with an enduring empathy and solicitude, and a perpetual, candidly curious eye on what that friendship could transmit in tactile experience or in knowledge of sex. White's friends saw his character shot luxuriantly through with mischief and desire, oscillating between discipline and anarchism, and always receptively ready for the ludicrous and the hilarious aspects of a life spent existing primarily in the colliding worlds of sex and art.

After moving to Paris, White would often spend several weeks of the year – usually in late August and early September, and for the carnival in February – in the island city of Venice. He had been travelling to Venice with David Kalstone since the early 1970s, and in recent years, they had been renting one sumptuous floor of a fifteenth-century mansion, the Palazzo Barbaro, on the banks of the Canale Grande close to the point at which the wide boulevard of water was crossed by a wooden bridge, the Ponte dell' Accademia; the Accademia art museum itself lay just across the canal, and behind the Palazzo Barbaro, the imposing Santo Stefano church rose above the surrounding decrepit mansions. A needle-thin canal ran along the side of the Palazzo Barbaro, where, in other centuries, its owners had moored their gondolas. The Palazzo Barbaro had been owned since 1885 by a wealthy American family, the Curtises, and had long served as a base for visiting American writers and artists: the novelist Henry James had written *The Aspern Papers* there, and the painter John Singer Sargent had maintained a studio in what was now a kitchen; Claude Monet and Robert Browning had also stayed at the Palazzo Barbaro. White and

Kalstone's floor housed the mansion's vast library. There, White would become absorbed in looking through ancient volumes of memoirs that had been written by travellers and merchants in the Venetian dialect. Venice itself was at the same time both breathtakingly beautiful and decaying, stinking and terminally polluted; it came alive briefly during its carnival and film festival, and then fell back into its habitual semi-comatose sulk under the lead weight of its mass tourism. White held a deep affection for the city's atmosphere of morose imperial disintegration, which he would later encounter again on the Turkish island of Büyükada. The travel writer James Morris (who herself later metamorphosed into Jan Morris) evoked Venice's historical fall and its sexual consequences: 'And when at last she grew too old and weak for greatness, she spun towards her fall in a dizzy whirl of merry-making, a daze of perpetual masked carnival, when even the Papal Nuncio wore a domino, when "women were men, men were women, and all were monkeys".'[15] That quality of sexual oscillation and furore in Venice's carnival entranced White – together with its poignant sense of a deep emptiness and despair about the passing of time and human lives – and he fully participated in the carnival's excesses. White's preferred cruising place, around the Giardinetti Reali gardens, was a productive and idyllically situated location at night, with its view out over the lagoon to the island of San Giorgio Maggiore. Venice and the Palazzo Barbaro became a second home for White, although one too richly exacting in sensation to endure for extended periods of time. After Kalstone's death from AIDS in 1986, White would continue to spend part of each summer in Venice, but as the years went by, he would grow more and more oppressed by his awareness of the haunting presences in Venice of all the friends and lovers he had spent time with there, and who had since died.

White's fourth novel, *Caracole*, appeared in 1985; it was the last of his books to be published initially in the United States, with its British publication following later. With his subsequent books, the reverse was usually the case, and this reversal in priorities explicitly showed how White was increasingly beginning to view himself as a European rather than American writer, both in terms of his audience and his creative preoccupations. The writing of *Caracole* had been a long haul: White had begun the first chapter nine years earlier, in 1976, but it had been *A Boy's Own Story* – started later and partially written during the same period as *Caracole* – which had appeared first. Some elements of *Caracole*'s composition went back as far as 1974: the first chapter's lists of plants and its setting in a disintegrating mansion had been inspired by White's leisurely perusal of books on botany and English stately homes, such as Chatsworth House, during his time as an editor at *Horizon* magazine in New York. But most of the remaining chapters of the book had been written between the autumn of 1983 and the summer of 1984, after White's move to Europe. The novel's title evoked the half-turning movement of a horse and rider known as a 'caracole', combining elegance with waywardness. For the first and only time in his novels, White assumed the position of a third-person narrator. He commented: 'To my surprise, I found this more expressive than working in first-person fiction, because I could enter freely into the minds of all my characters and dramatize my own internal conflicts through the conflicts between the characters.'

Much of the novel had been inspired by White's stays at the Palazzo Barbaro, and the atmosphere of the imaginary island city of the book was saturated by the decay and revelry of Venice. White took elements for his city from the volumes of memoirs he had read in the library of the Palazzo Barbaro, in which his favourite accounts had been those describing the period in the first half of the nineteenth century when Venice had been unwillingly submerged into the Austrian Habsburg

Empire. However, in assembling his imaginary city, White had also drawn on 1940s Paris for his narrative of foreign occupation and revolution. The dilemma of capitulation or dangerous resistance which Paris's inhabitants had faced during the four years following the invasion of France by Hitler's troops still remained a hotly debated and divisive issue in the city, even forty years on. And White had also drawn on his experiences among the artistic factions of New York for his characters' brilliant acrimony and labyrinthine social intrigue; White's acrid portrait of that scene, although highly disguised – and partly imaginary – remained transparent enough to cause him considerable trouble on the book's publication. White intended the setting of the novel to be an amalgam representing a number of cities simultaneously, just as its timescale was simultaneously that of the eighteenth and twentieth centuries. He was intrigued while writing the novel by the idea that the intimate aspects of relationships between lovers and families became transformed rapidly and unrecognizably from century to century, whereas the exteriors of the cities those people inhabited often remained essentially the same (as was the case with Venice and Paris); his aim with *Caracole* was to make intimacy itself a strange and arcane human process, while placing those intimate relations within a setting composed of contemporary or clearly recognizable historical elements.

Caracole is about a boy's initiation into sex and revolution, and thereby acquiring adulthood; the unique rôle which is ultimately assigned to that boy, Gabriel, parallels the assumption by the narrator of *Forgetting Elena* of his special responsibility. And, as with White's first novel, the world of *Caracole* is hierarchical and insular, but arranged so as to give shifting, prismatic perspectives on the nature of society, as apparently solid and substantial, but in danger of evanescing instantly, in a riot of elation and violence. White noted that, despite its imaginary island setting, '*Caracole* was consciously about society and the individual's place in it.'[16] Every figure in the book is faced with their relationship to the oppressively dominant power structure imposed from above by the colonizers, with many characters happily absorbed into its comforts and others in open revolt against it. The character of Gabriel oscillates so fluidly through those social borders – largely as a result of his own avowed indifference to those borders – that the narrative is able to present the entire dynamics of a society which is powerless, and obsessed either with the loss of power or with the potential power of freedom. The individual's experience in society combines pleasure and nostalgia with either the avoidance or the adoption of activism against oppression. For White, the social preoccupations of the book (at least, the main part of it written after his move to France) came out of his own experience of entering a new society which was both bewildering and demanding: 'In New York, without even really noticing it, I had come to lead an almost exclusively gay life ... But, when I came to Europe, partly because there isn't such a strong gay ghetto in Paris, I began to lead a more ordinary life. *Caracole* represents that renewed participation in society.'[17] Paris, with its post-war history of artistic engagement with social issues (contemporary examples included philosophers such as Gilles Deleuze and Michel Foucault, and novelists such as Jean Genet and Pierre Guyotat), made the question of the rapport between creativity and activism compelling for White in a new way. His social preoccupations acquired an original, deceptive form. While *Caracole* appeared capricious on the surface, it possessed a deep cutting edge in its questioning of the concept of society. Similarly, while pointedly omitting any specific reference to gay sex, the novel explored issues such as mixed-race sex, sex between people of widely differing ages, and the dilemmas of an insular society determined entirely by its sexuality. For White, *Caracole* was broadly about 'the triumphs and humiliations of adult sexuality'.[18] The novel also concerned the experience of discovering Europe, and reacting to the imperatives for an outsider of creating a language for that experience. For the location of his novel, White compacted together elements from diverse cities to reinvent – and thereby inhabit an individual variant of – Europe.

In a decrepit mansion on an unkempt estate in the country-side, a boy named Gabriel is living an isolated childhood. He is the oldest of seven children: the rest are all half-wild and eager for Gabriel to feed them scraps of goose fat. His mother is too obese to get out of bed, and the boy has to pummel her flesh. Wandering the estate, he meets a black girl named Angelica who belongs to a community of migrant workers. They immediately have sex: 'They ended up grappling one another, rolling in the dust, teeth bared in grins, his loose buckle caught in her hair, her skirt trapped under his knee and ripping as the last spasm shook them. They were bewildered by what their bodies had done to them.'[19] Gabriel finds the experience strange and painful. He and Angelica are married in an orgiastic ritual ceremony of Angelica's 'tribe'. Gabriel's father oppresses and imprisons him. Almost starving to death, Gabriel hallucinates the erotic presence of an austere woman named Jane Castle; he prefers these sexual hallucinations to his actual bouts of sex with Angelica. Gabriel's mother sends Angelica to fetch her brother, Mateo, who lives in a city several days' walk away. Mateo – whose occupation is withheld, though it involves seduction, women and fashion – rescues Gabriel and takes him to the city, a once-magnificent island metropolis but now an array of decaying palaces, coursed by waterways. The city – though the site of endless carnivals – is under the rule of a dour foreign power whose aim is to ingratiate itself culturally with the city's intellectuals, in order to make its process of colonization secure.

Increasingly, the narrator describes his characters and their society at length, rather than narrating plot action; incidents from different time-frames intersect; sequences of action are repeated from different characters' viewpoints, investing the layers of narrative with accumulating, multiple textures. New elements of the narrative appear obliquely, often cryptically or abruptly, within the flood of images and sensations. Mateo installs Gabriel in his palace, which has revolutionary associations for the city's population; he introduces the awkward Gabriel to the city's leading cultural figure, Mathilda, and they begin an affair. Mateo and his friend Walter host a cultural symposium or 'chat-box', together with Mathilda. Although a lauded intellectual herself, Mathilda ludicrously despises the city's other intellectuals and complains to Gabriel: 'Is there anything more loathsome than an intellectual?'[20] Gabriel is more captivated by Mateo's mistress, a young actress named Edwige who collaborates with the occupying powers. They too start an affair. It transpires that Angelica has remained in the city and that Mateo has been looking after her, preparing her social initiation just as he has done with Gabriel. Eventually Mateo and Angelica become lovers, and Mateo – dispirited by his life in society – now experiences a kind of physical resuscitation through Angelica's body: 'It seemed that he could reach down through her mouth or up through her cunt to her winedark, richly bathed, majestically beating heart.'[21] Mateo has been preoccupied with his 'career in sex' and its accompanying rituals and language of seduction, but – now entering his mid-forties – he is becoming increasingly anxious about the signs of ageing and about death: 'He knew he'd be, a few days after death, a repulsive corpse, for without his false front teeth, without his fashionable coiffure, without the constant trimming and shaping of all these suffocating hairs and nails, without these tailored jackets that gave him shoulders and a waist, after a week of neglect in the grave he'd exhale at last the putrefaction he'd always known was within him.'[22] Mateo depends for reassurance on Angelica, but she is caught up in the sexual exhilaration of the city's carnival and in her contacts with resistance fighters. Gabriel, having been painfully inducted by Mateo into social life, is now able to determine his own idea of social identity, in independence from Mateo. Finally, at a masked costume ball where Angelica and Gabriel meet again for the first time since their respective arrivals in the city, Edwige is shot and killed by the wretchedly jealous Mathilda; this act is presented by the resistance fighters as the start of their revolution, and Gabriel is instructed by Angelica in his responsibilities as the revolution's appointed leader.

Caracole uses a highly intricate language, dense with imagery and formed of sentences with a Proustian tendency to elongate themselves endlessly, through clause after clause and image after image. The novel reconstitutes the gasped language of sex, composed of exclamations and urgent instructions. And the luxuriantly corporeal language of the entire novel is one that attempts to grasp hold of the body and translate it into a tangible material of words. Even the ominous evocations of physical decay and disease are rendered in a language of extreme, gestural beauty. White elegantly describes Gabriel's facial acne, which is miraculously cured by Angelica's tribe: 'And the pustules grew, reddened, broke, spread, became quilted on this disc of a face he was obliged to tilt up to every comer, push forward as if it were his finest wheel of cheese, ripe at last.'[23] In this language of multiple evocation and resonance, everything is open to revision and to the reader's imaginative input, as it had been in White's first two novels. Angelica's tribe, for instance, seem at first to have the character of American blacks from the Southern states or of Mexican migrant workers; then, they appear to be Islamic; next, they seem to have Haitian voodoo rituals. No final, definitive version of identity is ever established; everything is conveyed, raw and fresh, while still in the process of creation. Time reverses, contracts and expands, as it did in *A Boy's Own Story*; the language builds up layers of decrepit history as it evokes the island city, and then suddenly overrules that history by making the city in revolution vital and contemporary.

Although the writing of *Caracole* coincided in part with that of *A Boy's Own Story*, and the two books share a concern with childhood initiation, the language of *Caracole* is deeply divergent in its richness and its poetic inflections. Where the reader of *A Boy's Own Story* is directly approached and seduced, the reader of *Caracole* finally becomes overwhelmed, almost swamped with the book's sensations. The transformation of identity which the novel's language depicts is that of a decadent fairy-tale, in which the beauty of youth metamorphoses through sex and revolution into the form of a powerful but jaded maturity. The reader is not 'carried' through that fairy-tale by a comprehensible plot, but rather positioned within a space which is assailed from all sides by a stream of images. That sense of assailed perception induces vertigo, since the social concerns of the novel do not come to any logical resolution, and its ultimate preoccupations are with the lethal human dangers which the individual's attachments and experiences in society only temporarily disguise: 'If there were any wisdom (and there isn't – there's everything and nothing to be learned) it would consist of learning to fall freely. For we are in full, flaming descent, but we move so slowly we imagine we can hold on to certain things (at least this friend, at least this moment). If we fell faster we'd call out in panic. But our speed is slow if constant and some things and people are falling at the same rate; relative to them we don't seem to be moving at all. But then something we are holding (as Mateo was holding his sleeping nephew) accelerates and slides out of our grasp – and suddenly we glimpse blackest, rushing night through the gap.'[24]

The American publication of *Caracole* was marked by an extravagant costume party in a New York ballroom that had been decorated to emulate the setting of the novel's climactic scene. But, despite the high expectations for the novel after the success of *A Boy's Own Story*, its reception was very often negative. White was well aware of the novel's heavy proliferation of inter-bred locations and sources: 'Imagine if you had taken a course in world literature and then the night before the exam you fell asleep and had a nightmare – that would be *Caracole*.' The novelist Julian Barnes complained in a review that it didn't have enough dialogue or action. The novel's entirely heterosexual content baffled a large part of White's gay audience. When he made a tour of American gay bookshops to give readings from *Caracole*, the air of disinterest in the book was palpable – the huge crowds who had come to listen to White's follow-up to *A Boy's Own Story* simply 'glazed over', as he put it: 'It was not of interest to them in any immediate way.' However, some gay readers of the novel, such as Neil Bartlett, viewed *Caracole* conversely, seeing the very exclusion of any trace of gay existence from the novel as being an essentially gay act, both audacious and contradictory; and the narrative of a revolutionary struggle, conducted from silence, with communal courage, was also powerfully evocative. Being pointedly and capriciously emptied of homosexual content, *Caracole* was, in a perverse sense, full of it. White himself noted that he had been inspired in writing *Caracole* by his reading of the eighteenth-century Parisian novels of Claude Crébillon, where the male characters are preoccupied with heterosexual seduction and its vocabularies, and oblivious to everything else: 'The heterosexual characters seemed so gay in that they were interested only in promiscuity and con-quest.'[25] That compulsion resonated with the atmosphere of the gay sex scene of mid-1970s New York, where the book had its origins.

Other readers of *Caracole* were attracted by the novel's stylistic experiments; Marina Warner, whose novels – such as *Indigo* – made use of a similarly lush and non-linear style, found *Caracole* to be White's best work to date. She perceived a clear division between, on the one side, the elaborate styles of White's first two novels and *Caracole*, and on the other side, the sparer – and to her, less satisfactory – style of *A Boy's Own Story*. She commented: 'To me it was very exciting what he was doing with prose in *Caracole*: it was fabricated, ornate and fantastic. The characterization is particularly striking – he runs sex *through* character, not just within the erotic encounters. Whereas with most writers – heterosexual as well as gay – sex is a separate thing, done in set-pieces. He's probably so good at sexual writing because he's had such a lot of practice with sex himself, so much time to observe! With most people, their faculties are exploded in sex and they can't take anything in.'[26] Some of the novel's sex scenes, particularly the heated anal sex between Gabriel and Edwige, provoked a strong response, much to White's amusement: 'A number of heterosexual men told me they found it arousing. An English novelist said that he'd gotten very embarrassed reading *Caracole* in a train. A reviewer from *L'Express* was reportedly confused and disap-pointed to learn I was gay.'[27] White discovered – with a certain perverse pleasure, since he believed that an innovative writer should be oblivious to the notion of a linear career, and should aim to create a new audience and discard the existing one with each book – that he had managed to alienate much of his readership. However, his next novel, *The Beautiful Room is Empty* – the sequel to *A Boy's Own Story* – would recapture a great part of that bemused audience.

White had been concerned in *Caracole* to explore his own ageing body through the character of the middle-aged Mateo, and also the social initiation of the teenaged nephew he had looked after in New York in the mid-1970s in the character of Gabriel. But it was the book's use and combination of scattered character traits of his intellectual friends in New York that got White into deep trouble. One important element of the negative response to *Caracole* was that the book angered a number of those New York friends who saw themselves outrageously satirized and ridiculed in the novel; this tendency for New York writers to wholeheartedly 'read themselves into' the characters of other New York writers' work forms an enduring obsession of the city's literary scene. With *Caracole*, the manifestation of this tendency was all the more unfortunate for White in that it began indirectly, and by chance. While writing the book, he had invited an American fashion journalist named Kennedy Frasier to dinner on the Île Saint-Louis. John Purcell had been concerned that White was feeling isolated and dispirited that evening; so, to cheer him up, he had encouraged White after dinner to read aloud some pages from his work in progress to the journalist. White read some of the pages about the intellectual 'chat-box'. The journalist listened intently. White remembered: 'She then made a bee-line back for America to tell all the people involved that they were being mercilessly pilloried in my book.'

As a result of those reports, several of White's friends in New York, such as Susan Sontag and the translator Richard Howard, were already hostile to the book in advance of its publication in the following year. Howard believed that the character of Mateo, in which White had been attempting to satirize himself and his own body, was a malicious attack on him. The character of Mathilda – which White saw as being based primarily on the persona of the novelist and essayist

Madame de Staël, whose work from the era of the French
Revolution he had been reading in Paris while writing his book
– angered Sontag. Alongside its basis in the passionate persona
of Madame de Staël, the character of Mathilda was a mischievous concoction of what White perceived to be Sontag's manipulation of her social and intellectual power, together with more
imaginary character elements, and aspects from his own character. Although White and Sontag never discussed the character together, it generated a permanent rift between them.
Ironically, it had been Sontag's powerful recommendation of
White to the Guggenheim Foundation that had enabled him in
the first place to travel to Paris and complete *Caracole* there.
To White's dismay, he and Sontag never spoke again, although
Sontag would become increasingly preoccupied over the next
few years with exploring the representation of AIDS, publishing a short story about the anxieties of an AIDS sufferer's
circle of friends, entitled 'The Way We Live Now', in the *New
Yorker* magazine in 1986 (the story was published five years
later in Britain in the form of a collaborative book with the
painter Howard Hodgkin); she also wrote a book of theory,
AIDS and its Metaphors, which appeared in 1989. In *AIDS and
its Metaphors*, Sontag argued that the media vocabulary of
AIDS – such as the discussion of a 'plague' – was being used
to foment a bogus social panic out of individual lives, and that
the emphasis on the virus's alleged African origins was deeply
racist. White did see Sontag one more time, a decade after
their break. One autumn day in 1995, he was walking past La
Hune bookshop on the Boulevard Saint-Germain in Paris, and,
looking through the window, noticed a crowd of people congregated around a woman with a shock of white hair who was
signing books. He looked closer, like a guilty voyeur, and saw
that it was Susan Sontag, signing copies of her newly translated
novel *The Volcano Lover* (which, by an ultimate irony, had

been compared to *Caracole* in one of its negative American newspaper reviews). White kept on walking.

While staying at the Palazzo Barbaro in Venice during the late summer of 1984, White had met a Swiss man in his early forties named Matthias Brunner, with whom he became lovers. Brunner managed a chain of twelve cinemas in the Zürich area. He was very unlike Purcell in temperament – calm and tentative, with a deeply studious attitude to whatever he was discussing. He had been married and had had only one gay lover before White, a celebrated art collector and curator named Thomas Amman. Brunner and Amman formed part of a fashionable and wealthy Zürich circle that encompassed the worlds of cinema, fashion and art. One of their close friends in the city was the celebrated art gallery owner Bruno Bischofberger, who was successfully promoting the work of Jean-Michel Basquiat and other figurative painters. Brunner was himself deeply interested in contemporary art and owned a large collection of works. During the following two years, White began to make frequent trips from Paris to see Brunner at his home in Zürich. He found Zürich a strange and beautiful city, saturated with drugs – especially heroin – because of the liberal Swiss drugs laws, and possessing a strong gay community. He and Brunner began to travel together to the principal European film festivals. They also went together to Egypt in November of the year they met; White had been commissioned to write a travel article about the country, and was able to invite Brunner along to take the accompanying photographs.

Brunner was always fearful of contracting AIDS – it appeared that many people in Zürich were falling ill with AIDS at the time because of the presence both of the extensive gay community and of the many heroin addicts who shared needles – and in the spring of 1985 he insisted that both he and White should take blood tests to discover whether they were HIV-Positive. Although White knew – from his sheer number of sexual encounters, and from the evidence of his former lovers in New York who had the virus – that it was probable that he was indeed HIV-Positive, this was the moment he had been dreading. Purcell had never put him under any pressure to take the test (which had only recently become available), since he was sure he would himself be HIV-Positive – as, in fact, he was – and he found it hard to face the unequivocal confirmation of a brutal medical diagnosis, which would leave no margin for wilful naïveté or for unexpectedly fortunate luck. White and Brunner took the test together in Zürich in May: Brunner was Negative, and White was Positive, as he had expected. Immediately after the diagnoses, he and Brunner travelled to Vienna for a holiday which they had arranged before deciding to take the test, and White found himself weeping uncontrollably, wherever they walked in the city; everything he saw moved him, filled him with human longing and sadness, and he cried incessantly. He began to feel that he must be seeing every friend and place for the very last time. But, once that initial reaction was over, White gradually became calmer. The sensation that it was very likely he had only a limited time left to live made him aware that the crucial imperative now was to live that time fully and creatively; any despair or lethargy would only impede that determination.

One of the ways in which White began to develop his creative engagement with and resistance against AIDS was through his writings on art. He had begun to contribute occasional essays and articles about contemporary art to magazines from 1977, but his passion for contemporary art had first taken off in the 1960s, when he had been working for Time-Life; his workplace's proximity to the New York Museum of

Modern Art and the expanding gallery district around 57th Street had made it easy for him over the years to view innumerable gallery and museum exhibitions of contemporary art. On his arrival in New York in 1962, he had still been absorbed with the Abstract Expressionist style which he had first seen in the work of the painting students he had met at the art school in Detroit that Marilyn Schaefer had attended; over the course of the 1960s, he had seen Abstract Expressionism become completely supplanted in New York by the then-startling imageries of Pop Art (and by the more ephemeral ascendance of Op Art). However, for much of the 1970s and early 1980s, White had been more preoccupied with experiments in performance and poetry rather than in art, and his engagement with the current developments in art had lapsed. Now, with Matthias Brunner's influence, he experienced a new engagement with contemporary art and its potential to represent the dilemmas of AIDS. He wrote an essay for the New York magazine *Artforum* entitled 'Aesthetics and Loss', in which he explored the necessity for contemporary artists to document the spread of the disease. He believed that the negative impact of the hostile media coverage of the subject, with its huge popular sway in stigmatizing AIDS sufferers (White was particularly appalled by the tabloid frenzy surrounding the death of Rock Hudson), had to be resisted through an art which could be lucid and accessible, in order to reach a wide audience. And for White, only art could form an authentic and dignified memorial for those dying of AIDS during the period it would take for medicine to find a means of arresting the disease.

In 'Aesthetics and Loss', White discussed the issue of whether gay artists and writers should focus solely on AIDS. He noted that: 'If sex and death are the only two topics worthy of adult consideration, then AIDS wins hands down as subject matter.'[28] In this context, he highlighted the work of painters such as Ross Bleckner and video artists such as Gregg Bordowitz. But he was concerned that an exclusive preoccupation with AIDS involved a surrender, allowing the disease and its accompanying media furore to determine the agenda, and potentially to swamp the gains of gay liberation and gay culture entirely. He himself, in his fiction and non-fiction of the following years, would attempt to consolidate and open out that culture, leading to accusations that he had neglected the urgent issue of AIDS. A further pressing concern for him at the time of writing 'Aesthetics and Loss' was the then hotly contested question of whether or not AIDS should be reacted to with humour, either through a defiant black ridicule or through a softer kind of humour that would make the subject more familiar and assimilable; he decided in the end that AIDS was no subject for humour, at least in the area of culture: 'Humour then was just reducing AIDS to one more comic mishap,' he remembered. Published at a critical moment in the response to AIDS, 'Aesthetics and Loss' became a seminally influential article in the cultural debate that surrounded art, AIDS and the media. White's emphasis in the essay was on the power of anger, both in a strategic response to the media and as a true expression of human devastation: 'If art is to confront AIDS more honestly than the media have done, it must begin in tact, avoid humour, and end in anger.'[29]

On the journeys around Europe which absorbed White in the years following his arrival in Paris, he travelled several times to Greece, where he found a living culture of the human body alongside the remnants of ancient cultures which had prized male beauty and action, and had intricately ritualized the world of the dead. White spent most of the summer of 1985 staying with John Purcell in the port town of Xania, on the northern coast of Crete, in a beautiful fifteenth-century Venetian palace; he had rented the top floor of the palace – which had formerly housed the town's archives – from an American painter named Dorothy Andrews, who had lived in Xania since the 1950s. He had also spent part of the spring of the previous year in Xania, when he was still working to complete *Caracole*, and had written many pages of the novel there. Xania wasn't exactly the idyllic setting he had been expecting before first seeing the town. It had been partly destroyed in heavy fighting during the Second World War, leaving many patches of waste ground and half-ruined buildings. The remnants of the 1960s hippie culture which had chosen Crete as its paradise were almost all gone. But White loved the area around the harbour, with its pink and blue houses and arcades against a background of austere white mountains. From the palace's twenty-two windows, he could look out on the town's Venetian harbour, with its lighthouse; immediately below him on the quay-side was the derelict Mosque of the Janissaries whose minaret had been partly sliced off by the town's jubilant inhabitants at the end of the Turkish colonization of the island. White was fascinated by the way in which the town presented an intricate visual concoction of supplanted historical moments, while simultaneously exuding its contemporary life: 'It had layers of Byzantine, Venetian, Turkish and modern Greek civilizations – it was really a palimpsest.' He also travelled around the island, visiting the surreal Minoan archaeological site of Knossos, where an unstoppable Edwardian digger, Sir Arthur Evans, had erected an arrangement of fetchingly ruined temples for the edification of tourists, producing what White called an 'absurdly over-restored' spectacle of concrete and garish colours. He also travelled into the island's interior, where he saw the curiously clone-like Cretan men, uniformly muscular and moustached, working on their olive and banana plantations.

White spent his evenings in Xania sitting at the harbour cafés, where the salt-smelling turquoise water lapped the sides of the narrow stone promenade, watching the parade of young townspeople showing off their best clothes and elaborately flirting with one another. He was often joined in watching this ritual by other expatriates, including an aged American surreal-ist poet named Charles Henri Ford and a British painter, John Craxton. Xania was close to the huge NATO naval base at Souda, and the promenading Xanians were mixed with hordes of young sailors from everywhere in Europe and North America, on the look-out for both gay and heterosexual sex. The Greek sailors from the base were mostly impoverished con-scripts in their late teens, and White discovered they were often ready to supplement their meagre earnings by having sex with visitors to the town. Brawls between the sailors often broke out, and they were banned from many of the town's bars and nightclubs. The atmosphere of Xania was a strange com-bination of elements of gravity and levity, with the islanders' natural reserve and pride juxtaposed with the very visible working-through of complex permutations of sexual desire. The beauty of the human body was the force which connected those two contradictory elements. White had invited an old friend from New York to stay with him in Xania, a former publisher of comic books named Herb Spiers, who spoke to White about how he had been living in the shadow of a domineering older lover, now dead from AIDS.

White's time on Xania and his encounter there with Herb Spiers inspired a short story, *An Oracle*, which he wrote on his return to Paris. Matthias Brunner had invited White to stay with him at the Swiss skiing resort of Gstaad. Although White couldn't ski (and had no intention of learning), he decided that he would go in order to be able to spend time with Brunner. On the train from Paris, he started to write the story, and continued to work on it when he arrived in Gstaad. He was so immersed in his work that he refused to participate in any of the parties and gatherings that were taking place in the fashionable resort, even turning down an invitation to dinner with the actress Elizabeth Taylor, who was staying in the adjacent chalet to his and Brunner's. White continued writing on the train back to Paris, and completed the story shortly after arriving back at the Rue Poulletier. *An Oracle* would appear first in the New York gay magazine *Christopher Street*, and was then collected in the volume of stories about the impact of AIDS which White collaborated on with Adam Mars-Jones. Set mainly in Xania itself, the story is about responding to loss and mourning, and its writing served White as a kind of preparation for the experiences which were soon to become an intimate part of his own life. The language of the story mixes an aura of almost terminal sadness and nostalgia with a deep, lush evocation of its characters' bodies and surroundings. Where White's non-fiction writing of the time on AIDS emphasized the positive necessity for anger, in his fiction the tone was more insolubly hopeless and elegiac, hinged on the desire for a momentary miracle.

In *An Oracle*, Ray, a New York corporate businessman, has lost his older lover, George, through AIDS. George has dominated Ray's life and determined every aspect of his appearance and attitudes, but has simultaneously insisted that Ray must 'look out for himself' and make his own life. Ray is numbed by George's death, and feels the need to shake off his overpowering influence in order not to sink into death himself; he does not know for certain whether he himself carries the virus. He travels to Xania at the invitation of a friend and once there,

Edmund White aged 5
in Cincinnati, 1945

Edmund White aged 7 in
Cincinnati, 1947

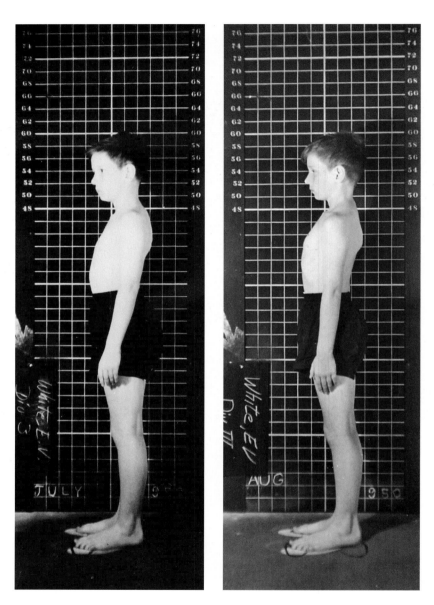

Edmund White at Summer Camp, aged 10, 1950

Edmund White at the time of the publication of *Forgetting Elena*,
New York, 1973

Robert Mapplethorpe's portrait of Edmund White with Truman Capote,
New York, 1980

Edmund White with Gilles Barbedette, Paris, 1984

Edmund White with John Purcell at the grave of Jean Genet,
Larache, Morocco, 1989

Hubert Sorin, Deauville, 1989

Photo booth portraits
of Hubert Sorin

Hubert Sorin on his last journey,
Marrakesh, Morocco, March, 1994

Edmund White with Felice Picano, Andrew Holleran and David Bergman,
Florida, 1997

Portrait photo from
Edmund White's passport

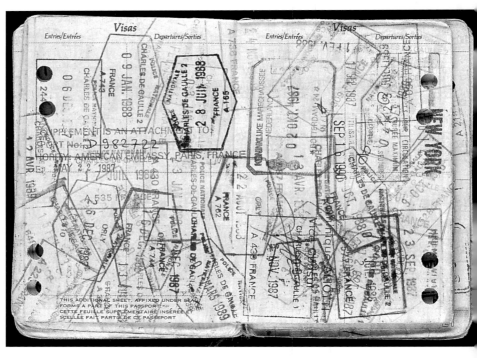

Visa pages from Edmund White's passport

he becomes haunted by a book of Greek death rituals which invoke the entangled proximity of life, sex and death. He meets several other gay Americans around the harbour, and they assess the sexual possibilities the town presents. The men are troubled but baffled by AIDS – one of them asks: 'What *is* safe sex, exactly?' and a schematic discussion follows. One night, Ray meets a sullen youth from the town and pays to have sex with him in the toilets of a deserted school. Ray is surprised when the youth, Marco, insists that Ray should buy condoms: 'Why rubbers? Ray wondered. Has he heard of our deadly disease way out here at the end of the world, in a country where there are only two recorded cases, both of whom were visitors to New York?'[30] He decides that Marco is concerned not with AIDS, but with maintaining a token physical barrier from a sexual act which is stigmatized in his country. They meet every night, and Ray falls in love with Marco, who seems increasingly receptive. Ray dreams of staying on in Xania and buying a house for himself and Marco to live in. But when he finally proposes this to Marco, he is devastated by Marco's refusal, which uses exactly the same words as George's demand that Ray 'look out for himself'. Even in his acute pain, Ray experiences elation at the way his revived emotions have suddenly released him from the world of death: 'He was blown back onto the bed, and he smiled and cried as he'd never yet allowed himself to cry over George, who'd just spoken to him once again through the least likely oracle.'[31]

In the autumn of 1985, White travelled to West Berlin, together with the photographer Dominique Nabokov (a distant relative by marriage of the writer), to research an article for *Vogue* entitled 'Berlin: Bright Lights, Black Leather', about the city's contemporary culture and its sex scene. Dominique Nabokov knew the city's culture well and introduced White to its leading figures, notably the most celebrated living gay film-maker in Germany, Frank Ripploh, whose films followed the sexual adventures of Ripploh himself as he cruised Berlin's streets and explored its public toilets. The city of West Berlin itself – then still divided by the Wall from its Communist eastern half, and isolated from the remainder of West Germany – struck White as the most exhilarating and ephemeral city he had visited in Europe. Part of his assignment for *Vogue* was to speak to a number of politicians from the ascendant Green Party, who told him categorically that the city could not continue in its present divided form, and that one side or the other would soon take over. The city had a thriving and well-organized gay scene, and a unique contemporary culture of experimentation under the threatening geographical pressure of the Cold War's last days. Berlin's culture was the reverse of Paris's reliance upon its eminent cultural history to camouflage its largely moribund contemporary art scene. In Berlin, White met the art historian Heiner Bastien, who was a close associate of the legendary German artist Joseph Beuys, as well as the leading European authority on Cy Twombly's work. White was particularly fascinated by a group of young gay figurative painters based in Berlin, whose work Matthias Brunner had introduced him to. They were then widely regarded as the most exciting artists in Europe, and had single-handedly re-launched figurative painting after a decade in which it had been eclipsed by the dominant conceptual art of the 1970s. This group of artists were known as the 'Neuen Wilden' – the 'New Wild Ones' – and their obsessions were with violent sex, nightclubs, and punk music. One artist, Salomé, enjoyed painting his body white with black spots and being led around the Berlin streets and department stores on a dog leash. Another artist, Rainer Fetting, fronted a punk band, 'The Horny Animals', who performed in an ear-splitting naked frenzy of spilt semen and paint. The artists' painfully vibrant paintings showed angelic figures crashing to earth and contorting with ecstasy. Both Salomé and Fetting had spent time immersed in the New York gay sex scene at the end of the 1970s (with travelling grants from the West Berlin local government), and they had both read White's *States of Desire*. Fetting executed many hallucinatory paintings of the Manhattan piers at night, which he knew from White's evocation of them in *Nocturnes for the King of Naples*; he had done these paintings after he had returned to Berlin, since he had been too busy exploring the bath-houses and piers themselves during his year living in New York, and hadn't found time to do a single painting there.[32] Salomé was to become one of the leading German artists documenting the impact of AIDS, in contrast to Fetting, who was to disown his gay past.

White returned to Berlin a few months later, in February 1986, together with Matthias Brunner, for the city's yearly film festival. It was the coldest month in Berlin for decades, and huge flurries of snow whipped around the frozen streets as White trudged through the city centre from one film screening to another. He was astonished by Derek Jarman's new film, *Caravaggio*, which was premièred at the festival and won the prize for best film. On meeting Jarman, White suggested that he should consider making films of Christopher Marlowe's play *Edward II*, and of the life of the philosopher Ludwig Wittgenstein; Jarman would eventually follow up on both suggestions, with his films *Edward II* and *Wittgenstein*, although the latter film eventually took the form of a commissioned project that Jarman himself did not instigate. In person, White found Jarman offhand and elusive, and he viewed much of Jarman's later work as excessively convoluted and over-layered (Jarman would become increasingly preoccupied with finding the exact visual means to represent his anger and his suffering from AIDS, which left him blind for a period and resulted in his death in 1994). But *Caravaggio* impressed White deeply as a film with extreme dignity and stark beauty; the film – in which the artist Caravaggio, on his death-bed, remembers incidents from his life – evoked the imminence of death, and the intense imageries of memory and desire that surged out from that moment. Over the next few years, White would often return to Berlin, particularly at the time of its film festival, and he viewed it as the only European city apart from Paris which he would find thrilling to live in.

White spent much of the summer of 1986 with John Purcell on the Turkish island of Büyükada, in the Sea of Marmara, working on *The Beautiful Room is Empty*; a large proportion of the book would be completed there. Büyükada, which White had also visited in the previous summer, was a bizarre and atmospheric place: the island's town was dotted with enormous wooden villas, connected by rotten, decrepit alleyways; cats prowled everywhere. The rest of the tiny island was covered by a thick forest, with a derelict monastery on each of its two hills. White believed that the island would form an ideal location for a film version of *Caracole*. He saw his novel's imaginary city setting, existing simultaneously in different centuries, as being mirrored by the convergence of periods, influences and languages in Büyükada: 'The place has these big white wooden houses and everything is blazing with electricity, very modern in one sense, and yet the houses are all turn-of-the-century, leading down to the ocean, and there are only horses and carriages on the island; half the women are veiled but the other half are dressed-up in very chic clothes – and you really don't know where you are or what century you're in.' For White, it was also a perfect writing environment for his work in progress; the island's aura of ambiguity and fragility gave him an appropriate sense of distance with which to excavate his memories of the over-solid American Mid-West society of the 1950s, which was the setting for much of *The Beautiful Room is Empty*. The lavish villas of Büyükada (which White saw as the more extravagant twins of the foursquare lakeside houses of the Mid-West) had been built as summer retreats for the Jewish merchants of the nearby city of Istanbul, and they were still largely owned by the city's Jewish community, with the addition of a small international element of aristocrats, artists and writers (the American novelist James Baldwin had lived there in the early 1960s). Every European language could be heard there. The island's inhabitants spent their evenings strolling through the town's avenues in the kind of hierarchical display of idiosyncrasy, wealth and beauty that White found infinitely fascinating. The island's aura of imperial decay was tangible. Some of the more neglected villas had simply given up the ghost and fallen in on themselves.

As with Fire Island, Büyükada was completely silent except for the cries of seagulls. All cars were banned, and journeys around the island were made in horse-drawn carriages manned by taciturn drivers who assembled in the island's main square, which stank and steamed with horse excrement. Unlike Fire Island, the possibilities for gay sex were near zero. But White was captivated by Büyükada; it had the dual attraction of its anachronistic island society, and of its proximity to the overwhelmingly contemporary cacophony of Istanbul, which was reached by an hour-and-a-half's ride in an ancient ferry-boat that departed from the collapsing pier, its domed customs house emblazoned with a faded imperial insignia. White loved to cross to Istanbul to walk through the city streets and lose himself in the incessantly teeming mass of human bodies that made up the city's vast population. He was also attracted by Istanbul's atmosphere of colossal power having long since disintegrated into poignant decline; he saw the city's evidence of its lost imperial and religious eminence everywhere, 'with its palaces and mosques stepping away from the Golden Horn and its melancholy cemeteries, the tombs of virgins covered with a carved marble veil and those of notables topped with a stone turban'.[33] White would make further summer visits to

Büyükada in the following decade; but then the chaos that resulted from a botched Turkish general election in December 1995 led to the establishment of an Islamic-dominated coalition government with anti-Semitic overtones, and White decided that the time had come to leave Büyükada to its exquisite slow decay.

Adam Mars-Jones had read White's short story, *An Oracle*, when it first appeared in the American gay magazine *Christopher Street* in 1985. Mars-Jones had himself lived for three years in the United States, in Virginia, from 1978 to 1981, and had become a regular reader of the magazine there. An extract from *An Oracle* was also published in the New York gay magazine *Out* in the autumn of 1986. Towards the end of 1986, Mars-Jones (who was not himself HIV-Positive, but was beginning to lose friends from AIDS) proposed to White that, between them, they should put together a volume of stories about the onset of AIDS. White felt that virtually everything he had read about AIDS up until this point had been written with clinical objectivity by people in the medical profession, and usually by heterosexuals; his exasperation about this led him to welcome Mars-Jones' project as one that would allow the subject to be approached more intimately, and which would enable a range of subjective and emotional responses to AIDS to be articulated. Mars-Jones convinced the editor Robert McCrum at his publishers, Faber and Faber, of the urgency of the project, and McCrum readily agreed to publish the book quickly, as a paperback, in June of the following year. White's intention was that the volume should be relevant to the unique needs of that time, serving as a kind of immediate documentation of a particular moment in the history of gay life, under the impact of AIDS. He suggested the title *The Darker Proof* for the book; the title came from the diaries of the French writer Jean Cocteau, who had told the cast of one of his plays that they needed to 'draw a darker proof' – a more authentic and solemn interpretation – of his text, in the way that a print-maker adds more ink to darken the image. For White, the title also had resonances of the extreme challenges and demands which AIDS precipitated in friendships or relationships.

The collaboration between Mars-Jones and White was extremely loose, not least because they were living in different countries. 'We hardly had any contact at all during those months, we weren't working at all closely,' Mars-Jones remembered.[34] While Mars-Jones was writing his own stories for the book in London, White worked during the first months of 1987 in Paris on a long story entitled *Palace Days*. The narrative of the story – about a conservative business entrepreneur and would-be gay activist who migrates from the AIDS-stricken New York of the early 1980s to Paris with his younger lover – drew in some of its elements on White's relationships with John Purcell and Matthias Brunner, and on his own diagnosis as being HIV-Positive and on David Kalstone's recent death from AIDS. But White believed he was describing a situation that was far from being unique to his own experience. Over his years in Paris, he had met many wealthy gay New Yorkers (and expatriates from other cities around the world) who were HIV-Positive and had arrived in Paris to spend up their remaining money; soon, they would become lost and disillusioned in the alien culture of Paris, but unable to face returning to the desolation of New York. Like *An Oracle*, the story is a response to AIDS that explores the depths of the disease's emotional as well as physical devastation. But the second story is more intricate in its scope, with an encompassing structure of a long individual journey over years and continents, spanning intense and fragmentary sequences of sex, friendship and loss.

Palace Days evokes both the New York of the 1970s and early 1980s, and the Europe of the mid-1980s. The principal character, Mark, is a self-defined 'gay leader' whose business involves organizing dating services and riotous holidays for New York gays. He believes that the more crass business aspects of his life are redeemed by his friendship with an intellectual professor, Joshua, with whom he regularly spends holidays in a Venetian palace. Suddenly, Mark's life of bathhouse sex and drugs in New York is overturned by the onset of AIDS, and he finds himself oppressively surrounded by his former clientele, who have mutated from a community of powerful body-builders to a horde of deathly, emaciated figures. Mark feels guilty: 'He feared that he'd misled all those guys who, imitating him, had worn madras, sniffed ethyl and voted Republican – and had had sex with hundreds and hundreds of partners. All those hot athletic men came now to haunt him with their skin hung like a wet shirt on a hanger.'[35] Mark moves to Paris with his young lover, Ned. Though they are intensely dependent on one another, their relationship is largely asexual and, while living together, they both take new lovers. Mark meets a German film producer, Hajo, and they carefully practise safe sex: 'In bed they were passionate but cautious – ardent in their kisses but afraid to exchange those fluids that had once been the gush of life but that now seemed the liquid drained off a fatal infection.'[36] Hajo insists that they take an AIDS test, and when the results show that Mark is Positive and Hajo is Negative, their relationship rapidly crumbles away through Hajo's fear of infection. Mark visits his friend Joshua in Venice; Joshua is clearly dying from AIDS and Mark is struck by the way that, while the city possesses a permanent existence, their own lives are vanishing into air. Mark realizes that – however fragile and ephemeral it may be – all that he has left now is his loving relationship with Ned.

As a collaborative project, *The Darker Proof* was slightly unequal, since Mars-Jones contributed four stories and White only two. (Over subsequent years, Mars-Jones wrote four more stories about the evolving impact of AIDS, and published them all together in 1992 as a book of his own entitled *Monopolies of Loss* – he felt with some irony that he had 'monopolized' the losses of AIDS with his stories, just as the Violet Quill's members had haphazardly carved out territories of gay subject matter among themselves, ten years earlier; White would include his own contributions to *The Darker Proof* in his collection of short stories, *Skinned Alive*, in 1995.) Where Mars-Jones concentrated in his methodical style on the minute details of the lives of individual characters with AIDS in London, White's stories were more expansive both in their vivid, nuanced style and in their scope, with multiple characters and locations. The two writers delivered their stories to the publisher in April, and *The Darker Proof* appeared only two months later (it was left to Mars-Jones to check the final text of the edition). French and German editions soon followed. On its British publication, the book was received as a crucial and formative contribution to the literature about AIDS (a literature which at that point was virtually non-existent), but White was criticized for writing only about the experiences and travels of rich gays – the principal characters in both of his stories were wealthy Americans who made journeys to Europe. Mars-Jones commented: 'It was a valid criticism to the extent that we were involved in a public document with an element of agit-prop and consciousness-raising to it – using literature to make people think more clearly than they do in other contexts.'[37] White took the criticism to heart, and when a second edition of *The Darker Proof* was being prepared in the following year, he added a third story, *Running on Empty*; this time, the protagonist was a poverty-stricken gay Texan with AIDS who travels from Paris back to the United States to visit his family for the last time, and whose main preoccupation is his lack of money to pay for his imminent medical treatment in New York. Details for the setting of the story were drawn by White from a journey he made that year with his mother to visit her family in Texas, where he encountered his religious cousin, Dorothy Jean Teddlie (Teddlie was also White's mother's maiden name), a 'fire-breathing Baptist' – as he described her – with apocalyptic preoccupations.

Running on Empty presents the defiant gesture of survival of a young man who is both slowly dying of AIDS and being suffocated by his attentive but oblivious family. Luke is a translator who has been living a life of quiet poverty in Paris, where his relationships have been with 'chumps too broke or too dumb to get chicks, guys with girlie calendars tacked on the inner side of the closet doors, guys who practised karate chops as they talked on the telephone to their mothers'.[38] Luke is the antithesis of the suave characters in *An Oracle* and *Palace Days* – a marginal, idiosyncratic figure who is deeply uncomfortable with New York gay life and clone culture, and who perceives himself to be outside any accepted definition of a gay man. Ill with AIDS and unable to work, Luke has to return to the United States; the narrative of the story is incessantly punctuated with his worries over money and the possibility that he may become helplessly dependent on his fundamentalist religious family. In Dallas, Luke meets his cousin Beth – though they are close friends, he is aware that an abyss of religion separates them: 'Luke realized she probably saw his disease as another proof of Satan's reign or God's punishment. He knew the Texas legislature was considering imprisoning diseased homosexuals who continued having sex.'[39] They travel to a small Texan town where Luke visits his aged relatives, who do not realize that he is ill. Walking in a park with Beth, Luke sees a gang of drunken, rowdy boys, one of whom urinates from the back of a truck. Luke is sexually excited and Beth is outraged. That night, Luke returns to lick the dirt where the urine fell, to try and swallow it down. It is his gesture of resistance to his family's hold, and of his determined attachment to the last traces of a sexuality which he believes is all that may miraculously save him now.

Over the winter of 1986, White had continued to work on *The Beautiful Room is Empty* in Paris, and the book was completed early in 1987. White found that the writing of the book went much more quickly and fluently than that of the novel to which it formed a sequel, *A Boy's Own Story*. After completing a hand-written draft in his notebooks, he dictated the novel in night-long sessions – revising spontaneously as he went along – to his friend Rachel Stella, who produced a typescript of it. White dedicated the book to his lover of the early 1960s, Stanley Redfern. Following the largely negative response to the capricious social and sexual explorations of *Caracole*, it had been clear to White that he needed to publish a novel that would be both accessible and successful. He commented: 'After the excesses of *Caracole*, the main thing I needed to show was that I could write a good story – a page-turner!' And he was also aware of the pressure in the gay community for him to write a novel which engaged with the now-critical AIDS crisis. But at the same time, he was determined to express his preoccupations with memory and sexuality in the form that transmitted them most tangibly; *The Beautiful Room is Empty* would be a novel that traced the origins of the gay liberation which AIDS was now threatening, and the opposition of that movement to an intolerant society which had now come to form the site of the media frenzy levelled against AIDS sufferers. In his novel, White was especially concerned to deal directly with the corrosive impact of psychotherapy on his identity as a gay man – a concern which he had begun to formulate in *A Boy's Own Story*: 'What

I wanted to show was the harm psychotherapy had done to homosexuals and the self-hatred that was forced on a young gay man by a society that could conceive of homosexuality only as a sickness, sin or crime.'[40]

White had originally planned that the book would conclude with his character's participation in the Stonewall uprising in 1969, but when he came to start writing about the event, he had doubts, believing that it was 'too much like agit-prop'. He decided instead that he would emphasize the book's preoccupation with therapy by abruptly ending it with a scene in which his character is driven to violent anger by his experience at a group-therapy session, where another member of the group instructs him to stop agonizing about his homosexuality and start talking about 'goils' instead; the character leaps up and tries to strangle his tormentor. White remembered: 'I wanted the ending of the book to feel like a release from all that exasperation.' But in reading his work-in-progress out loud to John Purcell, as he always did, White found that Purcell thought this was an unsatisfactory ending. He convinced White that he should go back to his original plan, and write about Stonewall. In the course of one day's writing, White added another six pages to the novel, narrating the Stonewall riot as another kind of liberation – more political and communal – alongside that of the final therapy scene; he then read out what he had written to Purcell. At the end, he saw that Purcell had tears in his eyes, and decided he would keep the novel's new ending.

With *The Beautiful Room is Empty*, White had intended to develop a human narrative which could confront and document the oppressive social climate towards gays in the 1950s and 1960s, articulating that oppression through the experiences of an individual life. Again, as with *A Boy's Own Story*, this necessitated the construction of a character able to reflect that society, but whose own idiosyncrasies would not prove too obtrusive. Where the narrative of *A Boy's Own Story* had caught its readers' empathy by its character's sensitized trajectory through the universal terrain of childhood, with its resonantly mythic texture, White now took his same character through the formative and similarly resonant years of the late teens and early twenties. The essential difference between the strategies of the two books was that White – having gauged the positive response to *A Boy's Own Story* – now believed that his own youth had been exactly representative of the sexual repression of the period, rather than bizarre or potentially repulsive. As a result of that conviction (and of White's new sobriety), the new novel had a calm, reporting tone, devoid of the sudden emotional eruptions that had constellated *A Boy's Own Story*. White's narrative would be deeply infused with sadness and frustration, despite its account of sustained sexual experimentation, and the conclusion of the novel at a revolutionary moment in gay history. The title of the book – a phrase from a letter by Franz Kafka to his lover Milena Jesenská – had been recycled by White from the title of an unpublished novel he had written between 1966 and 1967; he had also used the same title for one of his unproduced plays, and for a short story he had written in 1977. In the context of the published novel, the title articulated the impossibility of two perfect but fearful lovers remaining together, for more than an instant, in the same shared space of happiness.

In *The Beautiful Room is Empty*, the narrator of *A Boy's Own Story* takes up his youthful character again at a slightly older age – around seventeen – than he left him. The boy is still at boarding school, but now makes friends with an older group of bohemian painters from a nearby art academy. In particular, he is befriended by a young painter named Maria. The narrator's grip on the immediate presence of memory which propelled the narrative of *A Boy's Own Story* is still strong: 'It's terribly cold, snow is excitingly in the air like the promise of Christmas, we're hurrying up the steps leading to the academy's museum, and she has a cigarette dangling from her small blue hand purely for ornamental effect, since she doesn't know how to inhale.'[41] Another student, Ivan, introduces the boy to surreal French writing such as the work of Lautréamont. The narrator lucidly spells out the social world of the American Mid-West in the late 1950s: 'The three most heinous crimes known to man were Communism, heroin addiction and homosexuality.'[42] The atmosphere of the provincial city – Detroit – is evoked with an explicit visual force. But the narrator occasionally shatters that vividly evoked world to refer to his own presence – and to the sensations emanating from the book which his reader is holding – in a way that never occurred in *A Boy's Own Story*. The boy is in Maria's room: 'Like everything else in the art academy, her room had a distinctive odour I've never encountered since except once, recently, in the Chanel boutique of a Paris department store. I almost asked the saleswoman what the smell could be, but the most important things in our intimate lives can't be discussed with strangers, except in books.'[43] At another point, the narrator refers to his 'solitary lunch in a Paris café' over which he dispassionately observes a family of garish American tourists; his life in memory is as vital as his life in the contemporary world. The narrative resumes with sequences of scattered incidents revolving around sex and power: the boy meets a gay man who runs a bookshop in Chicago, and they have sex. He goes to stay with his father, who gives him strict instructions for work to be done at their holiday home, including the futile raking of pine needles: 'He put me on a strict regime of yardwork, mainly raking the pine needles that formed a thick carpet from top to bottom of the slope on which the house was built. When I asked him what possible reason there could be for removing the needles, he turned red, his already thin lips grew thinner, and he said, "Goddamn it, you'll do what the hell I goddam well tell you to do." '[44]

The boy goes to university, where he haunts the toilets in order to anonymously suck the penises of other students through gaps between the toilet stalls. His sexuality makes him anguished, and he is still seeing the incompetent psychiatrist from *A Boy's Own Story*, Dr O'Reilly, who is now a drug-addled wreck and plays intricate power games of humiliation and dependence with the boy. Once, when Maria visits the boy, they have sex almost inadvertently: 'Now we sprawled on the bed, smoking and reading and listening to Bartók. One afternoon we started kissing. In a second we'd undressed. Maria thrashed with shocking passion in my arms and in my ear her smoky mouth breathed with short, voiced gasps. She was so fragile, so supple in contrast to all the big, clumsy men I'd known.'[45] But the boy is beginning to believe his gay identity is not the curse he has been induced to think it is, and he speculates that he may discover or create a life for himself in which all the negativity he has absorbed from his therapy, family and society will be swept aside: 'Was there a secret fraternity that linked homosexuals across the states, countries, centuries?'[46] He meets an older man named Lou, who gives him a name: Bunny. Even on the point of orgasm with Lou, Bunny is still desperately preoccupied with the dynamics of power that have governed his life up to this point: 'The moment I looked at what I was doing to him, I could feel myself ready to explode. My come wanted to enter him in order to stake even the smallest claim on someone who seemed superior to me in every way.'[47] Together, they move to New York, and Bunny experiences the elation of seeing the visible gay community of Greenwich Village; soon, he is part of that community. He meets and falls in love with a young gay man named Sean, who is so tortured by the social pressure over his sexuality that he cracks up and is put in an asylum. Bunny is himself still receiving therapy. There is a blackout of time. Then, suddenly, Bunny is spending an evening at the

Stonewall Inn. A friend tells him that Judy Garland has died that day, then the police abruptly raid the bar and eject the customers onto the street. For the first time, the gays resist the harassment, and a riot starts; the police barricade themselves back into the bar: 'The double wooden doors to the Stonewall cracked open. I could hear the cops inside shouting over their walkie-talkies. One of them stepped out with a raised hand to calm the crowd, but everyone booed him and started shoving and he retreated back into Fort Disco.'[48] Despite the confusion and the participants' ironic attempts to find a name for their revolution, Bunny knows that something momentous has happened, that will transform his future as a gay man. He is dismayed to see the event unreported in the media.

The Beautiful Room is Empty intimately charts the formative moments in an individual life, and their potential to reveal the essential substance of a unique time of upheaval, in which the identity of the New York gay population began to coalesce and strengthen (at the same time that the surrounding counterculture started to fall apart). The identity of White's character is insistently transformed both by external events and by the power of the narrator's memory. The presence of memory in the book's creation of time and space is so strong that the narrator is occasionally compelled to burst though physically into it, in sudden evocations of his current life in Paris. In *The Farewell Symphony* – the novel which succeeded *The Beautiful Room is Empty*, and whose timescale overlaps with it to some extent – this movement towards transparency would be more fully accomplished, with the book aiming to encompass the presences of the narrator, the reader and the entire process of narration. But, in *The Beautiful Room is Empty*, the narrator's presence is more erratically and irrationally included, rather than as the result of a wholly intentional strategy – the force of memory is so beguiling that it carries the narrator in his everyday life irresistibly into the flood of memory, and so into his own book.

The Beautiful Room is Empty was conceived as an attack, and it stands far more as an angry settling of scores – with psychotherapy and with an oppressive, homophobic society in general – than its predecessor. The myth of childhood in *A Boy's Own Story* is supplanted by the myth of youthful rebellion, equally illusory but equally powerful. The novel possesses its deep sense of intimacy in its revelation of the narrator's youthful self, but it remains a novel with invented or transfigured characters and incidents, alongside its sources in a number of autobiographical incidents, such as White's participation in the Stonewall uprising. (However, the central elements of White's own life in the 1960s are absent from the novel. Notably, no character corresponding to Stanley Redfern, White's own lover during the period of much of the novel's timescale, appears; the novel was dedicated to Redfern as White's compensation to him for his absence.) White is ready to manipulate historical events to transmit the dynamic impact on individual lives of his narrated events. Although the novel ends with Bunny and Lou eagerly scanning the newspapers on the morning after the Stonewall riot and finding not a single word about it, the gay historian Martin Duberman has established that the uprising was widely documented in the New York media, noting that: 'all three of the dailies wrote about the riot (the *News* put the story on page one), and local television and radio reported it as well'.[49] The night of the Stonewall riot had actually followed the day of Judy Garland's funeral, rather than her death. The language of *The Beautiful Room is Empty* works by evocative captivation – as well as by documentation – and such historical alterations serve to promote the intimate hold of the novel on its reader, in order to engender what White called a 'shared experience, a clumsy but sometimes funny conversation between two people in which one of them is doing all the talking'.[50]

That evocative fluency is vitally necessary, since the book – as with all of White's novels – subordinates realistic plot to the majesty of the image, as articulating the pre-eminent sensations of ecstasy, beauty and sadness. The language of the novel works to project a filmic sequence of such images, vividly isolated but always interrelated with one another. At a key moment in his novel, White develops a haunting human image and then goes on to emphasize the way in which it exists outside and even *against* narrative: 'Nothing happened. There's no pay-off to this story and I repeat it only because the snapshot of Lou, so lost and so remote, impeccable despite the chaos in his apartment, still speaks to me with the force of an event (my plots are all scrapbooks).'[51] That sense of the immediacy of the image, which had been present in *A Boy's Own Story*, is now more charged, edged with the note of livid reproach which culminates in the brief, ironical furore of the Stonewall uprising. White's anger is always calmly controlled in *The Beautiful Room is Empty*, but that relentless, determined calm is what ultimately makes the language of the novel – in its evocation of a gay individual life under pressure – so enveloping and also so provocative in its effect. As White noted: 'My strategy in *The Beautiful Room is Empty* was to present a gay hero so self-hating that even the most retrograde reader would become impatient with his inner torment and welcome with relief the Stonewall uprising ... I felt my strategy had worked when Christopher Lehmann-Haupt, an avowed heterosexual, wrote in his *New York Times* review that he found himself longing for the hero to settle down and get on with his life, even if it was gay.'[52]

The novel was in fact overwhelmingly successful and critically well-received, both in the United States and in Britain. White commented: 'It was exhilarating, after what had happened to *Caracole*.' The novel's British publication, in January 1988, was marked with a party in the upstairs room of L'Escargot restaurant in Soho. It would be White's last novel for over nine years, until the concluding novel in his trilogy (a trilogy which White was only beginning to formulate at the time of the publication of *The Beautiful Room is Empty*) appeared in May 1997 as *The Farewell Symphony*. Although he would write a small number of short stories in the intervening years, White's work in fiction was about to undergo a sustained interruption, in the form of a vastly challenging project that would preoccupy him over the next seven years.

On the night of 14 April 1986, the legendary French novelist and criminal Jean Genet collapsed in the bathroom of his hotel room in the Place d'Italie district of Paris, half an hour's walk away from White's apartment on the Île Saint-Louis. Weak from cancer, Genet cracked his head on the bathroom floor and died, aged seventy-five. His novels written during the 1940s had appeared in translation in Britain and the United States in the years leading up to gay liberation, and had been inspirational for innumerable young writers, including White. In such novels as *Our Lady of the Flowers*, Genet's fictional characters, with their enormous penises and hierarchical obsession with power and style, acted entirely without shame on their desire and lust for male beauty, whether they were confined in prisons or formed into fabulously self-created groups in Paris. His work had immense resonance for an emerging gay community that was oppressed and criminalized, but was developing an extravagant and vividly oppositional sense of individual identity. Genet's novels also charted the delicate but wild sexual terrain of male childhood. Although Genet's relationship with the gay liberation movement was always oblique, he had covertly visited the United States in 1970 to speak at a rally in support of the militant Black Panther movement, and had been instrumental in forging a short-lived attempt at an alliance between black revolutionaries and gay revolutionaries. In the fifteen years leading up to his death, Genet had been an ardent supporter of the exiled Palestinians, and had spent his last months completing a vast book about his political and erotic attraction to the Palestinians, entitled *Prisoner of Love*. Genet had become a mythical but unseen figure in the United States and France in his final years, although he had been interviewed for British television in the year before his death. For White, Genet's death represented the loss of a figure who had been spectacularly influential in the two seemingly contradictory fields which he himself had spent his life exploring and connecting: imaginative fiction and activism.

That summer, White's American editor Bill Whitehead came to Paris and discussed with White his plan to commission an English-language biography of Genet. Whitehead had been White's editor for seven years and they had become close friends; he had first worked with White on *States of Desire*, and then on *A Boy's Own Story* and *Caracole*. He was suffering from AIDS and would shortly have to retire as an editor. Although Whitehead was hoping to persuade White himself to take on the Genet biography, he chose a circuitous approach and instead asked White for his suggestions about a suitable author. Although the project came out of the blue, White immediately proposed himself. His response had an element of effusive spontaneity to it, but having contemplated the idea, he knew that it was an ideal project for him at that moment. White knew Genet's work well, and reading his novels for the first time in the mid-1960s had been a seminal experience for him; he had first written about Genet's work in *States of Desire* at the end of the 1970s. Crucially, White was becoming increasingly absorbed with the culture of Paris, and researching Genet's life would take him into both the prominent and subterranean areas of the city's cultural life over the past fifty years. It would also reveal an entirely different conception of gay identity to the one he had helped to forge in New York City. White was also influenced by the idea that, as he grew older, he needed to undertake a large, scholarly project that would dispel what he called the 'louche and sleazy' reputation which he felt the American press had attached to his work and its subject matter. In practical terms, he knew the book would take a number of years to write (he originally expected it to demand two or three years of work, although a total of seven years would in fact pass between the book being commissioned and published); after decades of working in fragments and short bursts, such a sustained project was an enticing and challenging prospect for White. He also believed that the project would help him to survive: working on such a vital and compelling book would certainly leave him no time to become ill and die.

White bought copies of Genet's books and all the critical studies he could find. He wrote an outline sketch of Genet's life, which appeared in the *Literary Review* in September. After that, he came to a grinding halt. As he read through the books and became aware of the complexity of Genet's life, the project began to appear more and more vast and overwhelming, and he had no idea how to proceed. His research work at Time-Life, which he had thought would stand him in good stead for this project, had mainly consisted of assimilating and summarizing work from readily-available books which were brought to him by the junior office staff. In approaching Genet's life, he now saw that much of the essential material he needed to read was hidden, and most of the people he needed to talk to were secretive. Although his command of French was now fairly good, he found the prospect of making contacts and conducting interviews in French daunting. He asked his American acquaintances in Paris if they knew of anyone who was fluent in both English and French and could help him. As a result, he received a call from a gay American man in his late twenties named Gregory Rowe, who had come to live in Paris several years before White. Rowe lived with his French lover in a magnificent old artist's studio on the Boulevard de Clichy in Montmartre; he always spoke in French with his lover, and as a result his command of the language was so perfect that Parisians invariably assumed that he was a native speaker. Rowe enthusiastically told White that he knew Genet's work well and would be happy to work with him. White liked Rowe immensely – his style was a bizarre but charming combination of American college boy and sophisticated Parisian urbanite – and promptly hired him as his assistant, despite the fact that Rowe had no experience as a researcher. White commented: 'I thought he was so cute that he would definitely be fun to work with.' Rowe soon managed to uncover the name of the village where Genet had spent his childhood; although Genet had written extensively about the village, he had never named it. White watched in awe as Rowe made endless telephone calls in his gabbling French, frantically gathering information and setting up interviews. But as the months went by, they seemed to be making only very superficial progress. When Rowe delivered the transcripts of his interviews to White, they seemed strangely vague and confused, as though Rowe and his interviewees were talking at cross-purposes. With dismay, White now came to suspect that Rowe had never read a word of Genet.

By the beginning of 1987, White was beginning to despair about the Genet project, and knew that he badly needed more expert assistance than Rowe could provide. At the end of

February, a young woman named Jane Giles came to see him on the Île Saint-Louis. Giles was only twenty-two, but had already completed most of her research for a book on Genet's many filmscripts and his one completed film, *Un Chant d'Amour*. White was captivated by Giles, who had vivid orange hair and a candid, caustic view of Paris. Andy Warhol had died suddenly on the day before, and White – who occasionally chatted and gossiped with Warhol on the telephone and had last spoken to him only a few days before – was still taken aback by the news, though eagerly curious to know if the death had been AIDS-related; Warhol's death marked the closure of the New York artistic scene of cultural icons, drug use and exploratory sexuality that had flared up in the mid-1960s from Warhol's studio, The Factory, and had proved vastly influential. White was completely open with Giles about the material he had so far collected on Genet's life, and happy to share it. He also confided in her about his impasse with his own book, and she told him about her encounter in the previous week with an expert on Genet's work whom White had heard of through his friend Marie-Claude de Brunhoff, named Albert Dichy, who worked at a small archive of manuscripts on the Jussieu campus of Paris University, just across the river from the Île Saint-Louis. Although Dichy guarded his Genet research jealously, and had been almost obsessively cautious with Giles – refusing to confirm or deny the existence of films which Giles had herself already seen – she told White that he was clearly the one person who could help him. White invited Dichy to come to lunch at the Rue Poulletier.

Albert Dichy was a tiny Lebanese Jew in his mid-thirties, with a balding dome of a head and a calm but incisive manner. He had arrived in France from Beirut as a refugee from the Lebanese Civil War, in which his family had lost all of its money. His position at the archive paid very badly, and he had to combine it with work as an advertising salesman. He had spent years researching Genet's work and had briefly met Genet shortly before his death; as a displaced individual himself, Dichy was particularly preoccupied with Genet's incessant wanderings around Europe in the years before he had started writing his novels. The archive Dichy worked at had been bequeathed many of Genet's manuscripts, and he was to be in charge of this collection; with funding from the French publishing house Gallimard, the archive was moved from its cramped alcove in a concrete university tower to a beautiful courtyard building further along the river, in the Rue de Lille. It specialized in collections of manuscripts and works by recently deceased contemporary writers, and acquired the illustrious title of the 'Institut Mémoires de l'Édition Contemporaine' (IMEC). White befriended the initially suspicious Dichy, who was seduced by White's status as a celebrated writer, and by his frank admission that he needed Dichy's help desperately. In turn, White was intrigued by Dichy's tumultuous personal history of exile, and amused by his extraordinary heterosexual appetite – although happily married, Dichy pursued other women relentlessly, and had a crowded schedule of assignations with lovers whom he attempted with little success to keep separate from one another. While many Genet scholars such as Jane Giles regarded Dichy as excruciating to deal with, others found him irresistibly charming. His friend Pierre Guyotat – whose manuscripts were also stored at the IMEC archives, despite the fact that he was still alive – liked to exclaim: 'Albert is delicious! He's like a juicy little mouse!'[53]

White now had the idea of formally employing Dichy on a long-term basis as his collaborator on the book. This would enable him to make use of all the research material Dichy had collected on Genet. Since Dichy's research was his one and only prized possession, he was at first reluctant to share it with White. He was already preparing to publish a book of his own – a meticulous chronology of Genet's early life which he had researched with a criminologist named Pascal Fouché. The crucial factor that made him capitulate was that White was able to offer Dichy enough money to enable him to give up his part-time work in advertising; a decade later, Dichy would be the acknowledged world authority on Genet. Dichy commented: 'Edmund White gave me my freedom and changed my life. He allowed me to devote myself entirely to my Genet research.'[54] White arranged to give Dichy 15 per cent of his earnings from the book (apart from the American edition) and an assistant's salary of around 5,000 francs each month for the next two years. He also promised that Dichy's name would feature prominently on the title page of his completed book. Once the financial aspect of their collaboration was concluded, White and Dichy became very close friends. Their characters were so dissimilar – White candid and outgoing, Dichy secretive and wounded – that, as professionally curious men, they found endless scope for exploring one other. Dichy usually didn't develop friendships with men, but saw that White would be no potential rival in his world of heterosexual seduction. 'Our marriage was a perfect one,' White commented. White and Dichy began to work regularly together over the course of 1988, and the form of the book started to crystallize in White's mind at the same time. Dichy also spent holidays in the villa which White often rented for part of the summer in these years on the island of Büyükada.

With his ingratiating charm, Dichy was able to disarm friends of Genet whom White and Rowe had been unable to approach. Often Genet's friends were secretive, either because he had sworn them to silence or because their friendships had ended with a degree of acrimony which still made them feel injured and unwilling to talk about him. One of the most important figures in Genet's later life was a loyal but savagely tempered woman named Paule Thévenin, who had been the assistant of the writer Antonin Artaud in the late 1940s, before becoming one of Genet's closest friends and collaborators in the twenty years leading up to his death; it was Thévenin who had shaped Genet's involvements with extremist revolutionary groups such as the German Red Army Faction. Genet had abruptly ended their friendship a few years before his death. When Rowe had attempted on White's behalf to persuade Thévenin to talk about Genet, she had been sardonically dismissive: 'An American wants to write about Genet. An *American*!!'[55] Trying to find a way around her reluctance, White had engaged another assistant in addition to Gregory Rowe, a young American woman named Roberta Fineberg, who arranged to take French lessons from Paule Thévenin (secretly paid for by White) in an effort to gradually accustom her to the prospect of speaking to White; even this intricate subterfuge failed to work. But when Dichy approached Thévenin, the response was radically different. Thévenin's mother had been Algerian, and she was receptive to Dichy's aura of being a wounded outsider, often subjected to French racism for his dark skin. Once Thévenin had befriended Dichy, she was prepared to meet White and share her memories with him. She had a huge collection of material relating to Genet's life, including even the X-rays from his illnesses. White remembered: 'She had a will of iron – she was terrifying.' Although Dichy often met with initial resistance, he was able to interview virtually all of Genet's friends and associates (although one or two, such as the reclusive painter Leonor Fini, kept refusing to see either him or White), and White himself met the most crucial figures in Genet's life. He found that almost every person he encountered was bitter and wounded from having their friendship with Genet abruptly ended by him, often inexplicably. White commented: 'The first layer I always had to remove was the wound.' Once he had Dichy's expert support, White was sure he would be able eventually to finish his book. A further factor compelled him to complete the project: to White's deep misery, Bill Whitehead had died from AIDS in September 1987, and White had decided that the book would be dedicated to his memory.

In the summer of 1988, White spent much of his time with Jane Giles, who was in Paris to complete her book on Genet's film projects, for which White would write an Introduction. White loved Giles' fiery personality and her extraordinary sullen beauty. She had just the combination of individuality and ferocity he liked in his women friends. On one occasion, in September, they decided to travel down to Cannes together to interview Lucien Sénémaud, Genet's favourite boyfriend of the late 1940s, whom Dichy had located. Although White often asked Dichy or Rowe to do the interviews for the Genet biography for him – he hated 'banging on people's doors', as he put it – he was eagerly curious to meet Sénémaud, who had been strikingly handsome as a young man. Sénémaud had acted in Genet's film, *Un Chant d'Amour*, as one of two convicts who communicate their desire by erotically blowing cigarette smoke into one another's mouths through a straw inserted into a hole in the wall that divides them. Genet's lovers were almost always heterosexual men, and when his affair with Sénémaud was over, he had married him off and set him up with a garage in the suburbs of Cannes. White asked Marie-Claude de Brunhoff – who had a persuasive, aristocratic voice – to call and arrange a meeting for White and Giles with Sénémaud, by claiming she was from the publishing house Gallimard, which was Genet's own publisher. White and Giles met up at the Gare de Lyon railway station in Paris at six in the morning to take the early high-speed train to Cannes. Although White greeted Giles with the news that he had been up all night smoking dope, she found him amazingly alert for that early hour. He spent the journey chatting up the young businessman who was sitting opposite them. Once in Cannes, they took a taxi to the 'Saint-Genet' garage. Although White had brought along a bottle of whisky for the oil-spattered Sénémaud, he was reluctant to talk, grumpily and monosyllabically answering a few questions in between noisily revving up his cars and banging his tools around. He only showed any interest at all when Giles produced some stills from Genet's film. Sénémaud's friendly wife Ginette told White and Giles that her husband particularly liked the film 'because he's in it'.[56]

Once the serious business of the interview was over, Giles felt the atmosphere of the day instantly change from one of work to one of gratuitous indulgence. Giles commented: 'It was like being on holiday with your very badly behaved but extremely charming favourite uncle.'[57] White immediately called in at a seafront boutique and bought a swimming costume, then they spent the afternoon at an exclusive beach club, the Plage Sportive. Giles – who had never been to the South of France before – happily splashed around in the sea, while White was preoccupied with tanning himself, performing cursory gym exercises, and scanning the beach for desirable men. In the evening, they went to the Carlton Hotel to drink kir royales on the terrace. Then, after taking Giles out to dinner, White led her to the Xanadu gay bar, where she watched him enthusiastically dancing to Kylie Minogue's 'I Should be so Lucky' while intently surveying the somewhat furtive men dotted around the pitch-dark bar. Giles was feeling tired after the long day, so White walked her back to the hotel, before deciding to head back to the Xanadu, remarking that he 'felt like having another drink'. The following year, White and Giles would meet up again in the Italian town of Reggio Emilia, where they took part in a conference on Genet's work and encountered another of Genet's boyfriends of the late 1940s, the still-handsome Java, who was a far more expansive character than the monosyllabic Sénémaud. Java had also been the recipient of Genet's generosity when their sexual relationship was over; where Genet had bought Sénémaud a garage, he had set Java up as the owner of a laundrette. White took Giles on an excursion by train one evening to the nearby town of Parma to see the magnificent opera house, the Teatro Regio, but insisted that they travel on the train without paying, so that hopefully they would have the thrill of hiding from the ticket collector (or, if they were caught, he would protest in English that he was just an innocent American tourist travelling with his daughter). 'This was his idea of a good wheeze,' Giles commented.[58]

White worked every day on researching the biography, for which he had selected the simple title *Genet*. He was having to work much longer days than he habitually did on his novels, when he was usually finished by ten or eleven in the morning after an hour's writing in bed. Now, he often had to work all day, fully clothed. At the same time, he enjoyed the clearly defined sense of undertaking an assignment which writing non-fiction offered, after the constant inventions and uncertainties of writing fiction. When he felt too isolated in the Rue Poulletier apartment (John Purcell had by this time returned to New York), White would walk over to see Dichy at the IMEC archives, where he would sit in the reading room alongside the industrious postgraduate students who worked in reverential silence on the collections of manuscripts. White's research was intricate, since he was planning a book of over seven hundred pages, and was eager to present a complete sociological account of the Parisian world that had surrounded Genet from the 1940s to the 1980s. He researched in depth the social living conditions of Paris and the city's visual appearance during those years. And he spent days searching through the labyrinthine basement archives at the Gallimard publishing house, to locate their collection of the mass-market detective magazines which they had published in the 1920s and 1930s – a major source of Genet's inspiration.

As White had anticipated, he found himself exploring with

fascination into every layer of Parisian society, from the aristocrats and intellectuals who had been Genet's close but usually
short-term friends, to the petty criminals, pimps and nightclub
owners who had accompanied Genet on his burglary
expeditions and on his journeys through the sexual subterranea
of Paris, with its rent-boys and drag queens. White met
everyone from the eminent philosopher Jacques Derrida to the
lowliest accomplice from Genet's days of crime. The encounters he found most compelling were those with the legendary
Spanish novelist Juan Goytisolo, who had befriended Genet in
the 1950s, and the wealthy collector of manuscripts, Jacques
Guérin, who owned an eighteenth-century mansion outside
Paris in the town of Luzarches. The suave Guérin (who owned
the contents and walls of Proust's bedroom as well as many of
Genet's original manuscripts) was already in his late eighties,
and living with a young Italian researcher, when White and
Dichy visited him at his opulent mansion. Guérin had played
a key rôle in Parisian gay life since the 1920s. White realized
that he was a racist and arrogantly sadistic figure; but he was
conscious too that, in working on his Genet biography and
meeting such archaic figures as Guérin, he was experiencing at
close range the traces of a rapidly disappearing French gay
society that would never otherwise have been visible to an
American of his age. Guérin ostentatiously read out extracts to
White from the precious original manuscript of Genet's novel
The Thief's Journal, which included substantial passages that
Genet had later cut out; meanwhile, White was surreptitiously
taping the reading with a small dictaphone concealed under his
coat. Guérin was too absorbed in his reading to spot this
strategy, but the Italian researcher had soon rumbled White
and, after his departure, told Guérin, who furiously demanded
that White send him the recording. Before mailing it off to
Guérin, White was careful to transcribe it all.

White also began to travel extensively, following Genet's life from his childhood as an adopted orphan in the isolated mountainous region of the Morvan in eastern France, to his youth as a colonial soldier in the city of Damascus in Syria, to his spell as an impoverished prostitute in the slum areas of Barcelona, and to his years as an old man living with the Palestinian exiles in Jordan. In most of these places, White's research consisted largely of visiting antiquarian bookshops to amass books and images from the period in which Genet had been there, in order to give himself a precisely detailed conception of how the places had looked then. In Damascus, he located the site of a fort which Genet had helped to construct in 1930, and which had collapsed immediately after its completion. In Alligny-en-Morvan, he observed in bemusement the drunken rural population whose parents or grandparents Genet had grown up among; he met Genet's one-hundred-year-old godmother, who spoke in the Morvan dialect which had to be translated into French for White. He also travelled to the town of Larache in Morocco, to see Genet's house and his grave there on a hillside beside the Atlantic ocean. He found that by tracking Genet's steps through so many diverse locations, he was absorbing the intricate trajectory of his life.

While the research for *Genet* consumed most of his time, White managed to maintain his Parisian friendships, and he remained avid for new encounters. In July 1988 he met the American short-story writer Raymond Carver, who was visiting Paris with his wife, the poetess Tess Gallagher. Like White, Carver had overcome acute alcohol abuse and now appeared to be writing unstoppably. His short stories and essays were beginning to give him the esteem and recognition which had been denied him for decades. On his return to the United

States, Carver died suddenly. Their meeting had been inspirational for White, who had been deeply impressed by Carver's creative determination and his belatedly emerging happiness; in November, White travelled to London to take part in a memorial event for Carver. The evening was bizarrely held at an up-market nightclub called Legend in Old Burlington Street; Salman Rushdie also took part, and read extracts from Carver's work in what was to be his final public reading before the Iranian Ayatollah Khomeini's edict calling for him to be murdered sent him into hiding. White felt increasingly surrounded by death and oppression, and he was developing a survivalist attitude of calm nonchalance towards the course of events, together with a macabre sense of humour; after the reading, he invited Jane Giles to dinner, and since the evening had been dedicated to Carver, he insisted that they should go and eat bloody steaks at a nearby 'carvery'.[59]

During the two years 1987 and 1988, White had been having a relationship with a young French artist, Hubert Le Gall; Le Gall was preoccupied with the element of power in his relationship with White, and oscillated between treating him with cutting cruelty and with sudden bursts of adoration. Since Le Gall was very young and unsure whether he wanted to have an older lover – or even to be gay at all – White attempted to put him at his ease in their relationship by regularly hosting large dinner parties that were entirely composed of boisterous young guests. Then, at the end of 1988, Le Gall abandoned White for a rich lover with a luxurious mansion on the Boulevard Beaumarchais, and White – who had been captivated by the emotional intricacy and sexual violence of their power struggle – was momentarily devastated. He confided in Marina Warner his feelings of abandonment and injustice: Le Gall had always accused White of making their affair too public, but now he was himself openly living with another man. Marina Warner remembered: 'Hubert was the kind of boy Edmund liked at that time: he presented himself on the surface as being straight, quiet and well-behaved – almost parodically so. Edmund was hurt by his defection because Hubert left him for a richer man – Edmund didn't like seeing their relationship put on the footing of some kind of social transaction, rather than as a reciprocity of feeling between two people, as he wanted.'[60] But even with this betrayal, White and Le Gall would remain friends.

At around the same time as Le Gall abandoned him, White fell in love with a young American student living in Paris, named David Stevenson. Stevenson was HIV-Positive, and would eventually die from AIDS in the summer of 1993. Almost the antithesis in appearance of the slim and habitually dishevelled Le Gall, Stevenson was a broad-shouldered, squat body-builder, with vivid red hair and freckles; he wore designer clothes and was fiercely proud of his physical appearance. In addition to his university studies at the Sorbonne, Stevenson worked as a doorman at the fashionable 'Bains Douches' nightclub in Paris. Marina Warner watched the relationship unfold: 'It was a very disastrous affair, in my view. David was astonishing – a squarely-built bouncer and body-builder who was also a rhetorician. He had a cruel streak, emotionally as well as physically, and he carried with him a lot of redneck baggage which was not at all Edmund's scene.'[61] Adam Mars-Jones, too, was disturbed by his encounters with Stevenson: 'David was an alarming creature who used to be a queer-basher. He was distinctly prissy and fastidious, but also savage with a potentially very destructive side to him. I thought Edmund was playing with fire and was out of his depth.'[62] Mars-Jones vividly recalled Stevenson's horror when he realized, during a stay with White at Mars-Jones' unkempt flat in London, that his host didn't possess an iron. In December, White and Stevenson flew together to Agadir, on the Atlantic coast of Morocco, then travelled on to the town of Taroudannt and the Saharan desert. It was there that they had their one and only sexual encounter, though their relationship continued in its state of intense sexual tension. Stevenson was completing his master of arts thesis on the work of Marcel Proust and John Ruskin, and White was eager to encourage him. On a visit to London in February 1989 to discuss a proposed film version of *A Boy's Own Story*, White bought Stevenson a set of the Oxford English Dictionary, in the complete edition which had to be read with a magnifying glass, since the print was so small; the heavy package containing the volumes was impossible for White to carry in his arms, so he held it balanced on top of his head as he walked through the London streets. He was happy when Stevenson successfully submitted his thesis that summer and received the accolade of a 'mention très bien' from the university. But over the spring months, their mutually exhausting relationship had gone into decline.

White spent the summer of 1989 in an apartment situated on the Canale Grande in Venice. That summer was to mark a transformation in his emotional life, and a point of juncture between his past and future. As well as Stevenson, he had also invited John Purcell to stay; Purcell was still living in White's apartment in Lafayette Street in New York and had been growing increasingly ill with AIDS. White observed the disintegration of Purcell's health with dismay. Two years ago in Paris, he had been radiantly youthful and active; now, he was weakened, aged, and in constant pain, suffering coughing spasms that went on for hours. In addition to Stevenson and Purcell, a new lover of White's came to stay with him in Venice that summer: Hubert Sorin. Although White amusedly numbered him 'the second Hubert', Sorin would become the most important lover in White's life. While Stevenson and Purcell were already receding into his past, his relationship with Sorin was to form a vitally enduring and haunting part of White's future.

During the spring of 1989, a young American film-maker, Bill Cory, had made a thirty-minute black-and-white film following White around Paris during the course of one day. White was seen visiting men he had contacted through the Minitel, wandering around the Paris streets, and having lunch with Marie-Claude de Brunhoff. White found the film-maker's intentions to be confused, but he attempted to keep him entertained: at lunch with Marie-Claude, he bemoaned his own chronic alcoholism, despite the fact that it was now six years since he had stopped drinking. He also told a story about a German boy who had recently come to stay with him in Paris; White had belatedly discovered that the boy was deranged, obsessed with the idea that he should be Jewish rather than German. White had finally thrown the boy out, and was rewarded with a parcel of the boy's excrement sent through the post. The incident gave the film its title: *The Day the Shit Happened* (although when the film was eventually shown at festivals, it acquired the more innocuous title of *A Day in the Life of Edmund White*). The film was notable only for a short sequence in which White watched an extraordinarily handsome man in his late twenties, with short black hair and a shy but smiling manner, walking in the gardens behind the Notre Dame cathedral, wearing an elegant suit and overcoat. On the film's soundtrack, White commented that he had often seen this beautiful, enigmatic young man on his walks around the Île Saint-Louis, and had managed to talk to him; he had discovered that he was married, but gay. In fact, White had met him at a gym he went to that was located nearby, underneath an old swimming-pool in the Rue de Pontoise. This young man was Sorin, and he and White became lovers. After White's return from Venice, they began living together in the Rue Poulletier apartment, although Sorin kept on an apartment of his own in Paris; White believed he had finally found the unique lover he had been looking for and imagining since his childhood.

Hubert Sorin had spent several years living in North Africa, teaching architecture and designing building projects in Ethiopia, Tunisia and Morocco. His time there had deeply marked his visual sense of landscape and architecture, and he loved to talk about the North African desert and the urban landscapes of Addis Ababa and Fes. He now worked in an architect's office in Paris. His wife, Fabienne, knew that he was gay and was unsurprised when he moved in with White; she remained friends with Sorin and would also get on well with White. From the window of the Rue Poulletier apartment, Sorin made an intricate drawing for White of the design of the beautiful church across the street. Like many young Parisians, Sorin spent much of his time absorbed in reading the kind of elaborate strip-cartoon book known as a 'bande dessinée'; these immensely popular books had a vast range of visual styles and contents, extending from low-key depictions of contemporary Parisian street life to extravagantly surreal science-fiction adventures. In addition to his architectural drawings, Sorin drew caricatures and strip-cartoons with a meticulous but gestural style, and had often dreamed about becoming a *bande dessinée* artist himself.

Several months after Sorin came to live with him, White insisted he take an AIDS test, although it seemed certain that it would be negative. Sorin had been living with his wife up until the time he moved in with White, and he had told White that he had had very few gay lovers. He appeared to be in perfect health. They were both astonished when the test proved positive: Sorin had full-blown AIDS. The disease was so advanced that the doctors believed Sorin must have contracted it five or six years previously. It was a momentous time for Sorin. He was now openly living with another man (a radical step for a formerly married man) with whom he was deeply in love; simultaneously, he had discovered that he was seriously ill and might well have only a short time to live. For White too, the moment was one of intense and contradictory sensations. The elation of his new relationship with Sorin was overlayered by a feeling of extreme upheaval in his life, and by the painful sensation that the first glorious moments of their relationship had now irretrievably vanished, to be replaced by the unremitting future schedule of Sorin's decline.

During the period when Sorin came to live with him, White was offered a university professorship in the United States. It was a position which would involve teaching both creative writing classes and courses in English and American literature (especially gay and lesbian fiction), at the prestigious Brown University, located in the East Coast state of Rhode Island, between New York City and Boston. Although he had grown tired with his experience of university teaching a decade earlier, White now saw an opportunity to begin a new life with Sorin, away from the complexity of his emotional and sexual entanglements in Paris. He knew by now that he would always regard Paris as his permanent adopted home, but the prospect of returning to the United States for several years appealed to him. He told friends that he was disturbed by the thought of developing AIDS and dying in Paris, away from his native country, although he realized too that it would be equally as horrific in the United States. He hoped to renew old friendships in New York and, for the first time in many years, to thoroughly explore the contemporary culture of the United States and the attitudes to AIDS across the country. Sorin liked the idea of spending a long period of time in the United States, but paramount for him was his desire to be with White, wherever that would take him; he was used to a rootless life from his years in North Africa. Since he could speak English well, the possibility existed that he could find work as an architect in Boston, the nearest big city to Brown University. White decided to accept the appointment. He intended to use the time at Brown to work on *Genet*, and at this point, he was hoping to be able to complete the book in the spring of 1991. Since he and Sorin planned to be away from Paris for a long period, they gave away many of their books and possessions to friends; White sold the remainder of his collection of books to the dealers who ran the open-air stalls on the banks of the Seine. And he finally had to give up the apartment on the Île Saint-Louis where he had lived for the past seven years. In the final days before his departure, White felt torn between his attachment to Paris and starting his new life with Sorin in the United States. The month before his departure, December 1989, was one of brilliantly blue skies and glacial air, and Paris looked uniquely beautiful; he wondered why he was leaving. Europe suddenly seemed an exciting and vital place to be, with the exhilarating collapse of the Berlin Wall in the previous month and the sense of ongoing, revolutionary transformations.

White's time at Brown University was a disaster from the very start. When he and Sorin arrived at Boston airport, the immigration officers meticulously searched Sorin's baggage. Sorin had applied for a professional visa before leaving for the United States, but had not yet received it; as a result, he had decided to enter the country on a tourist visa. At the bottom of his suitcase, the immigration officers found a copy of his application form for a professional visa. They refused him entry to the United States and sent him back to Paris on the next plane, on the grounds that he had misled them about being a tourist when, in fact, he was awaiting a long-term professional visa. White watched Sorin leave, devastated. He had to go on by himself to Providence, the small campus city where the university was situated: 'I was never so depressed in my life, arriving in grim Providence alone and in the rain.' The following week, oblivious to his new commitments at the university, he flew back to Paris. He had called the landlady of the Île Saint-Louis flat, and since she hadn't yet let it to anyone else, she had no objection to White and Sorin moving back in temporarily. They returned to the Rue Poulletier apartment. The rooms were now completely empty; the landlady had moved out all the furniture in preparation for renovating the apartment, and the walls of the rooms were marked with the lines from where pieces of furniture had been placed against them for many decades. It was a strange, almost hallucinatory time for White and Sorin. They saw none of their friends, since everyone believed they were in the United States and their misadventure was too painful for them to have to recount. They wandered endlessly around the city streets, without any purpose at all, returning at night to the denuded apartment. White remembered: 'We were always like ghosts and it was like coming back to a ghost's version of our own apartment.' It was an ecstatic time of suspension for White and Sorin: a moment outside life.

White finally had to return to the United States to begin his teaching. He and Sorin agreed that Sorin would stay over the Canadian border, in Montreal, and White would fly there to see him at weekends until Sorin's professional visa came through. White returned with some trepidation to the United States and moved into a large house in Angell Street in Providence. The city – founded in 1635 by dissident Puritans who had broken away from the more fanatical religious community in Salem – was a relaxed place scattered over a group of hills; it had an art college, the Rhode Island School of Design, as well as the university. The founder of the university, John Brown, had been a slave trader. The furnished house which White had arranged to rent was constructed from wood like many of the houses in Providence; it belonged to the novelist Robert Coover. Coover usually taught at Brown, but was away for the whole of 1990 in Berlin as the recipient of a writing grant from the city's DAAD Writers and Artists' Programme. Sorin was eventually able to move down from Montreal to Providence, and he and White were joined there by a young French friend of theirs named Christine Davenier, who worked as a children's book illustrator and had formed part of the circle of young people White had constructed around his relationship with Hubert Le Gall. She had been at a loose end in Paris and White had asked her to come and live with them for a while, in part so that she could provide a kind of 'cover' for Sorin if he felt the provincial environment in Providence to be too intrusive for him and White to live openly as a gay couple. In that case, it would appear that White simply shared his house with a young heterosexual couple. But Sorin was uninterested in White's subterfuge. He was pleased to have Christine Davenier there, but he forthrightly told every-one they encountered that he was White's lover and proud of the fact.

Soon after their arrival in Providence, White and Sorin decided to buy a basset hound. The decision was largely the result of Sorin's idiosyncratic and amused conception of how an American professor and his lover should behave. But White was eager that Sorin should feel at home in Providence. The city was a long train journey away from New York, and they were soon beginning to feel alienated from the introverted university society; Sorin viewed Providence as dull and full of absurdly conceited people. White and Sorin went out to a specialist kennels in the nearby state of Massachusetts, and Sorin chose one of the puppies immediately. They named the puppy Fred, from a resemblance Sorin perceived to a psy-chiatrist friend of theirs in Paris, Frédéric Pascal (the name was also that of a lust-crazed terrier in White's *Nocturnes for the King of Naples*). Fred, Christine, Sorin and White together formed an unruly and joyfully dysfunctional family. Although White and Sorin had endless fun with Fred, he was boisterous, always leaping at guests' legs and wildly slobbering at their faces. It was impossible to leave him alone in the house even for short periods of time without him exacting a terrible revenge for his abandonment. When White and Sorin did have to leave for a moment, they always returned to a scene of devastation. Within months, most of Coover's furniture and carpets had been destroyed.

Sorin investigated the potential for employment as an architect in Boston, but it appeared more difficult and daunting than he had anticipated. It was the worst possible moment to be looking for work as an architect: the North-East of the United States was experiencing an economic depression, and most building projects had come to a standstill. Sorin's health was starting to collapse: he was growing progressively weaker from the effects of his illness, and – even if he could have found architectural work in Boston – the demands of undertaking a full-time job and commuting each day from Providence would have been beyond him. He turned instead to working every day on his drawings, beginning with images composed simply of a few gestural strokes, but soon progressing to complete human figures. He started to produce caricatures of the people he and White met around Providence, at the cocktail parties and social gatherings which formed an integral part of university life; he also made notes to assist him with remembering particularly telling visual details. Sorin's work on his drawings elated him and he began to see it as an alternative career to architecture. His style of drawing was highly intricate but wayward and surreal, with a caustic edge; his American characters' speech bubbles contained the amiable inanities which Sorin was subjected to, and which he rendered in a mixture of English and French. The drawings formed narrative sequences that recounted the bizarre encounters of Sorin and White, who themselves appeared as heroic, elegant but slightly dishevelled figures, with heavy torsos and tiny heads, existing in a state of perpetual bafflement as they attempted to untangle the intricacies of the hierarchical university society. With White's encouragement, Sorin decided to give up his search for architectural work and to devote his time entirely to his drawings.

Brown University was a bastion of the then-current preoccupation with 'political correctness', which had become dominant in the second half of the 1980s in North American (and later in British) universities. This was the belief that issues of race, gender, sexuality and disability were sacrosanct territory and could only be discussed within rigidly determined limits. Political correctness had evolved in part from the innovative work of some American universities in promoting courses about minority literatures and oppositional cultures; this had led to a more over-arching concern with the personal behaviour and pronouncements of all members of society. Many prominent cultural figures in America – such as the opera director Peter Sellars – believed that the tenets of political correctness were entirely justified, and that everyone in their everyday life had the right to respect in the ways in which they were addressed, discussed or represented, irrespective of their sexuality or race. But in the rarefied university system, the doctrine of political correctness had gone haywire. White became a target for the righteous wrath of a number of his students because he had written approvingly of his friend Robert Mapplethorpe, who had photographed black men in works which were retrospectively judged racist, exploitative and offensive. Mapplethorpe had died of AIDS in the previous year. Walking around the university campus, White suffered taunts from students who associated his surname with male white racism (the word and colour 'white', certainly, have many other associations, such as the white heat of ecstasy and orgasm explored by Krzysztof Kieslowski in his film *Three Colours: White*). A group of White's students attended an event at which the black gay poet

Essex Hemphill denounced White for his association with Mapplethorpe. The doctrine of political correctness did not exist at all in France, not least because the impetus of most militant causes there had been lost following the election of the socialist government in 1981. And political correctness had hardly existed in the United States when White had left the country in 1983. As a result, he was unprepared now for the fanaticism and acrimony of his students, and was left bemused and hurt. For White, the intentions of Mapplethorpe's work (which at this time was under attack both from the politically correct and from right-wing religious fundamentalists disturbed by its sexual content) were never racist, and existed in an entirely different field from the social, religious and political oppression and negligence which constituted contemporary American racism. White saw an unquestioning naïveté in his students, and believed they were being manipulated into complicity with the politically reactionary elements of American society. He also viewed the media panic about AIDS as a major source for his students' attacks on Mapplethorpe. White grew discouraged when he felt that his students were impervious to being incited to ask questions about their sexuality and their relationship to the power of the dominant media. He found that being a male gay attempting to discuss lesbian culture was a proscribed area; when, in his seminars, he tried to explore the power structures determining the treatment of both male gays and lesbians, he watched some of his students get up and leave in a rage, slamming the door behind them.

Despite the prevailing rancour at Brown, White enjoyed working with many of his gay students, particularly in his creative writing class. There, the atmosphere was less fanatically heated than in his literature courses. He was on the university's admissions committee for his creative writing course, and so was able to determine which promising students should be admitted, having seen the extracts of their work which they attached to their applications to the university. He realized with a sense of shock that many of his gay writing students in their twenties had never before met a gay man in his early fifties like White: most of his generation of American gay men had been wiped out by AIDS. It became clear to White during his time at Brown that, even at the beginning of the 1990s, gay writing was still often considered a marginal literature in the United States, and that his gay students were finding it difficult to get their work published. With the death three years earlier of the editor Bill Whitehead, who had commissioned work from many gay writers (including White's biography of Genet) for the publishing houses he worked for, the situation had become still harder. White was particularly affected by the experience of one of his students at Brown, James Assatly, who had AIDS and was determined to complete a novel before his death. White found it heartbreaking that Assatly did manage to complete the novel, but then lived long enough to see it rejected by every publishing house he sent it to, before dying with the feeling that his precious last years had been wasted. White was disturbed too when he saw another of his students with AIDS, John Russell, who was in his early twenties, being cruelly taunted by the other students for having been lax enough to contract the disease when safe sex had already been a prominent issue for several years; White was well aware that even the most vigilant person could occasionally slip up. Russell was beginning to write plays and would eventually have one of his works staged in New York, in 1997; but, by then, he had already died. White remembered: 'It was shocking for me that a teacher's students should die before him.'

By the autumn of 1990, after spending a summer break with Sorin on the isolated island of Nantucket, off the Massachusetts coast, White was growing increasingly unhappy with his position at Brown. He was struggling to find moments in which

he could work on an anthology of gay fiction which had been
commissioned from him by the British publisher Faber and
Faber. He felt isolated from his friends in Paris and his
research there, and was making virtually no progress at all on
Genet; only the first three chapters of the book had been
drafted by this stage. He also had little time to travel around
America with Sorin, as he had hoped to do (they managed to
make just two long journeys, one of them to Mexico City,
where White did an assignment for *Vogue*, and the other to
Santa Fe in New Mexico, where White interviewed a woman
named Marianne de Pury who had been Genet's assistant
during his time in the United States with the Black Panthers).
In his first months teaching at Brown, White had had the
friendly company of the Sri Lankan-born novelist Michael
Ondaatje, who was just finishing a year's teaching there; White
was impressed with what he saw as Ondaatje's disorganized,
intermittent approach to his writing and his relatively low
number of writing hours on his novels, which paralleled
White's own approach. But, three months after White's arrival
at Brown, Ondaatje had left for his home in Canada. White
viewed the other literature professors at Brown as 'dismal and
dowdy – full of provincial paranoia'. It seemed to him that he
was spending most of his days correcting the spelling and
grammar of half-illiterate students. The need to be authoritarian with the often narcotically somnolent students and make
them hand in their essays on time was totally alien to White,
and filled him with a sense of deep futility. The students
continued to harass him with their Mapplethorpe taunts, and
the parochial atmosphere of Providence was becoming tedious
in the extreme.

At the end of the year, Coover returned from his stay in
Berlin and angrily reclaimed his dog-damaged house. White,
Sorin, Christine and Fred had to leave Angell Street and
relocate to a smaller house in Thayer Street. It was an old

three-storey house of white wood, with a garden at the side where Fred could play, situated between the town's central area of student bars and a hillside district of salubrious eighteenth-century mansions, including the one built for John Brown himself. After their move, it was clear to White that Sorin's health was now beginning to deteriorate seriously, and Sorin was keen to return to Paris. White was concerned that he might himself have only a limited time before the virus incapacitated him and prevented him from writing and travelling; if that were to be the case, his remaining time was a precious commodity, and he believed that it should not be squandered in the unrewarding atmosphere of the university, despite the financial security that a professor's salary offered. Although White had already agreed to return to Brown and teach there for several months during 1992, he and Sorin would be able to leave Providence in the spring of 1991. White commented: 'After I had been at Brown for about a year, someone asked me: "Why on earth did you exchange Paris for Providence?" I said: "Exactly!" – and I headed right back!'[63]

During their time in Providence, White and Sorin had experienced only one moment of complete respite from the university's oppressive atmosphere, when they made a hectic trip to England and France in November 1990. They travelled first to Leicester in the English Midlands, where White attended the first night of a production of a play he had written during the late 1970s, *Trios*, which shared the preoccupations with social initiation and resistance which he had explored in *Caracole*; although the play was met with largely hostile reviews, the interest generated by the provincial production – which lasted for three and a half hours – meant that it would eventually be given its first London production three years later. It was only the second of White's twenty-three theatre projects ever to be produced. After spending a day in London,

White and Sorin rushed to Paris, where they spent what White described as 'three perfect days'.

In May 1991, White and Sorin – accompanied by Fred – moved back to Paris with intense relief. In the same month, a major conference on Genet took place at the beautiful Odéon theatre in Paris, and White participated in it with relish. It was a largely dignified event and he was treated as a major Genet scholar. Among the participants were several people who had been key figures for Genet at the end of his life, such as the Moroccan novelist Tahar Ben Jelloun, Angela Davis, formerly associated with the Black Panthers but now an American university professor, and Leila Shahid, a Palestine Liberation Organization activist who had become one of the movement's official European representatives. White had met Leila Shahid before, at a talk he had given in Paris on Genet's last book, *Prisoner of Love*; he had then interviewed her over lunch at the Télégraphe restaurant, close to the IMEC archives, where she had spoken in vivid detail about the end of Genet's life. White had forgotten to bring along his dictaphone, and so had sat for several hours in her car after she had finished speaking, trying to note everything down. The Odéon event had been organized by Albert Dichy. As well as enabling White to make vital new contacts for interviews for his book, it also provided him with the opportunity to observe once again the arcane and often hilarious aspects of Parisian intellectual life which so fascinated him. The philosopher Philippe Sollers, so drunk that he oscillated from moment to moment between insane affability and guttural cursing, gave a performance of spectacular incoherence; by the end, the former revolutionary Maoist was in a barely conscious grunting stupor, and had to sweep his drink

to the floor to indicate to the audience that he had finished.
Pierre Guyotat, whose fiction was inspired by Genet, gave a
reading of such length and tortuous complexity that most of
the audience fled from the auditorium. Only the eminently
polite White and two or three others were left to applaud at
the end.

In June, the anthology of gay writing which White had been
working on in Providence was published in Britain. *The Faber
Book of Gay Fiction*, a richly idiosyncratic selection of short
stories and extracts, appeared as part of Faber and Faber's
series of literary anthologies. White's aim with the book was to
expand the area of gay writing by emphasizing in his selection
material 'that either had never been read in a gay context or
that had mysteriously remained unknown'.[64] The collection
was highly successful and received great acclaim; White and
Sorin travelled to London and Dublin for the publication, and
then took a short break on the western Irish coast at Galway.
In his Introduction to the book, written just before his return
to Paris, White had discussed the near-annihilation by AIDS
of the members of the Violet Quill group of gay writers in
New York, and the unexpected profile which AIDS had given
to gay fiction, manifested in media attention and in proliferating university courses. He noted: 'Curiously enough, AIDS,
which destroyed so many of these distinguished lives, made
homosexuality a much more familiar part of the American
landscape. It has also divided the gay community along ideo-
logical lines which have been reflected in gay literature.'[65] In
separating out the two main factions in this division of contemporary American gay writing – between the argument that gay
men, in the face of AIDS, should assimilate themselves with
heterosexual society, and the opposed argument that gay identity should be uniquely distinctive and militant – White placed
himself in the latter grouping. In Paris, he had absorbed the
influence of gay writers who were oblivious to such a division;

as he remarked, 'In France there is no Jewish novel, no black novel, no gay novel; Jews, blacks and gays, of course, write about their lives, but they would be offended if they were discussed with regard to their religion, ethnicity or gender.'[66] But White's time spent living in the United States once again had made him deeply sceptical about what he saw as a reactionary element of self-censorship operating within the endangered American gay culture; he saw the movement towards a kind of 'invisible' assimilation as part of that self-censorship. He declared: 'My own belief is that censorship of any sort is to be feared.'[67]

Since their return to Paris, White and Sorin had been staying at Sorin's apartment, but in early July they moved with Fred into a rented apartment which had been offered to White by its owner, an American novelist named Diane Johnson; it was in a beautiful seventeenth-century building in the Rue Frédéric-Sauton, a quiet street leading off the Boulevard Saint-Germain and ending on the banks of the Seine across from Notre Dame. When White opened the windows of the apartment and looked out to the right, he could see the southern side of the cathedral. The second-floor apartment was reached from the street entrance up a narrow, highly-polished wooden staircase, and was slightly smaller than the one in the Rue Poulletier, with, again, two rooms. A female prostitute lived on the floor above White and Sorin, and they would often be woken up at night – to Sorin's amusement and White's annoyance – by her drunken clients mistakenly ringing their doorbell. The apartment was furnished with eighteenth-century furniture; to White and Sorin's relief after their experience at Coover's house in Providence, the carpet was made of a sturdy jute material that resisted Fred's attempts to destroy it. Since White and Sorin had given away most of their possessions before leaving for Providence, they now had to replace everything. White began to haunt the flea-markets and antiques shops dotted around the edge of the city, picking up scores of objects that appealed to him; he did the same on his travels, and soon the apartment was packed to capacity with his purchases: elaborate bowls and vases of every style and period, nineteenth-century paintings of young men, and endless collections of cutlery and dinner services. He was anxious to impress on any visitor to the apartment the uniqueness and historical importance of every item. Sorin also happily contributed to the apartment's look of a heaving treasure house, though his selections were fewer and marginally more bizarre – he gathered together a collection of preserved spiders and other insects inspired by his time in Ethiopia. White and Sorin mercilessly ridiculed each other's purchases, but the apartment served as a perfect visual compendium of their life together as two radically dissimilar characters combined by their love. The sheer accumulation of objects also formed a tangible mooring for their precarious existence in Paris.

In the Rue Frédéric-Sauton apartment, a large round wooden table filled much of the floor space of the living-room, but White preferred to write sitting at a table in the kitchen or while in bed. Sorin often used a desk placed by one of the windows in the living-room to work on his drawings. Although Sorin thought the district was too snobbish (he preferred the other bank of the river and the anonymous districts on the outlying edges of the city), White loved the hectic atmosphere of the surrounding streets. The apartment was very close to the intricately stinking fish, cheese and vegetable market on the Place Maubert – where White did his food shopping – and a short walk away from the grand literary cafés of Saint-Germain-des-Prés which had become legendary during the 1950s, the Deux-Magots and the Flore. White had more of a feeling of being involved directly in the cultural heart of Paris than during his years on the Île Saint-Louis, with its strange community of islanders and absentee owners.

Apart from several months in the spring of 1992 – when White had to return to Providence, accompanied by Christine Davenier, and the ailing Sorin, who had no American health insurance, remained in Paris at his own apartment – White and Sorin would stay at the Rue Frédéric-Sauton apartment for a year and a half, until January 1993. During almost all of that time, White was trying to finish *Genet*, and spent most of his days working with Dichy either at the IMEC archives or at Le Télégraphe restaurant, a few doors down from the archives, going over interminable details and comparing contradictory interview materials. An American friend of White's named Harlan Lane gave White the use of his house in the countryside, a hundred miles or so from Paris in the lush Touraine region of central France, and White and Sorin would travel there together for periods of several months at a time in order for White to work on his book undisturbed; the house had no phone and was in a remote location. White had to carry huge cardboard boxes full of Genet's books and other research material with him to the countryside – 'It was just like being a packhorse', he remembered. Despite Sorin's constant support, he was often discouraged about finishing his book, and worried too about its reception, should he manage to resolve the complexities it presented and actually complete it. His mother had died in 1991, at the age of eighty-eight (in her last years, White had been struck by the way in which they were both losing all their closest friends, hers to age, his to AIDS); in their conversations during the final months of her life, she had urged White that it was above all essential that he should complete the book. But the final stages of the writing constituted tiresome and repetitive work. In a short story collected in *Skinned Alive*, in which he allocated events in his own life to a character modelled on Albert Dichy, White imagined with amusement the difficulty to be faced by a future biographer in describing his mundane duties at Brown University and his long months ensconced with his *Genet* manuscript at the IMEC archives: 'That winter he deliberated long and hard whether to give Suzy an A or a B . . . His step quickened that morning as he headed towards the archives.'[68]

Sorin was keen to move to a more cosmopolitan area than what he considered to be the stiff, haughty confines of the Rue Frédéric-Sauton; at first, White was reluctant to move, but in the face of Sorin's stubborn desire, he capitulated. He was soon used to the idea of another move, having become accustomed to an itinerant life with frequent changes of address. Throughout his decade in Europe, he had been moving between rented apartments and island houses that belonged to friends or acquaintances, and always liked the sensation of being an outsider arriving ephemerally in a new space which still bore the traces and presence of its last or usual occupants. But the new apartment would prove to have a much different rôle in his life. Sorin found the unfurnished apartment through the classified advertisements in the newspaper *Libération*. It was on the other side of the Seine, at the bottom end of a long pedestrianized street, the Rue Saint-Martin, that started from the bustling Rue de Rivoli, narrowed into an alley before forming part of the plaza in front of the colossal arts complex, the Centre Georges Pompidou, and finally tailed off in a sleazy garment district of sweatshops and street-walking prostitutes. The apartment was twice the size of the Rue Frédéric-Sauton apartment, but the rent was lower. The building had no elevator and the stairs up to the fourth-floor apartment were steep, but at that time Sorin was still well enough to manage the ascent without difficulty. The building was one of the few in Paris which still retained the services of a *concierge*. The *concierge* had long been a Parisian institution; charged with the maintenance of their buildings, these hawkish guardians – usually middle-aged widows – had been held in awe and terror by tenants during the earlier decades of the century, but had mostly been replaced by impersonal mobile cleaning services during the 1980s. The *concierge* in White and Sorin's building was unusually discreet and kind, and spent much of her time drinking in a nearby bar; when on duty, however, she would intently track the progress of any visitor to the building from her ancient glass-walled office in the hallway.

White was baffled that the new landlord appeared indifferent to his offer of references, and seemed eager for him and Sorin to move in immediately. White soon discovered the reason. The section of the street just under their window was being completely torn up to accommodate a multi-storey underground car park and new buildings, including a branch of Marks and Spencer at the junction with the Rue de Rivoli. Sorin was far from dispirited by the revelation: as a trained architect, the sight of the complex building work was compulsive viewing for him. But White knew that it would mean months if not years of noise (the building work would finally be completed in the summer of the following year). Cement dust often poured in through the windows, coating the furniture, and pneumatic drills shook the air. All day, crews of North African construction workers shouted urgent instructions to one another in a mixture of Arabic and French, and vast clanking cranes swung just feet from the apartment's windows – on one occasion, a crane accidentally struck the building's façade just below the living-room window, sending a scattering of debris down to the street below. The noise from the construction site initially made it hard for White to work, but over time he adapted to the cacophony, and learned not to expect anything approaching silence if he decided to take an afternoon nap.

White and Sorin were soon making new additions to their large collection of objects. They also had to buy items of furniture for the unfurnished apartment, and everything had to be arduously carried up the long flights of stairs. This time, it was Sorin who was chiefly responsible for the visual style of the apartment – he told White that he was designing the apartment as a space for White to inhabit after his own death. He gave it a sparser, more austere look than the Rue Frédéric-Sauton apartment: 'He liked a stripped-down look, while I like junk and piling things up as high as possible,' White commented. During his years in Ethiopia, Sorin had acquired two large paintings by a court artist of the dictatorial Communist régime, showing elaborately staged military parades. The vividly coloured paintings had an inept sense of perspective but a magisterial grip of the atmosphere of totalitarian power: they were an unintentional perversion of socialist realism, simultaneously chilling and hilarious. The paintings were hung on one wall of the beautiful, wood-beamed living-room, which was flooded with light in the mornings. On another wall, Sorin hung two of his large architectural drawings. For the bedroom walls, he assembled a vast collection of photographs of White, including the portrait which Robert Mapplethorpe had taken of White in 1981 in the act of screaming – a photograph which had shocked White so much at the time that he had sworn never to look at it again. Now it was part of his daily life. By the window in the bedroom looking out over the street, Sorin kept a black lacquered art deco desk which White had given him as a present to use as a working table for his drawings (after Sorin's death, White would use this as his own writing table). The only area which was completely under White's jurisdiction was his study, at the far end of the apartment, where he worked at a round wooden table. Soon, the room was bursting at the seams with White's prized objects, every surface completely filled except for a minute area reserved for his notebooks. On a trip to the Vanves flea-market in the summer of 1993, Sorin was furious when White blithely snapped up yet another collection of matching plates to add to the three sets he already owned (his mother had told him that you can never own too many plates). Sorin was only placated when White agreed to try and find room to pile up the plates in his study.

White quickly grew to be captivated by the atmosphere of the Rue Saint-Martin. On the Parisian social scale, it was far more down-market than his last address, but its sense of intense life was stunning – in many ways, it was more like the East Village district that White had inhabited in New York than the salubrious *quartiers* on the other side of the Seine. The local population was a mixture of manual workers, artists and prostitutes. The street had a raw edge to it, both visually and aurally, despite the close proximity of the luxurious shopping districts around the adjoining Rue de Rivoli. The streets beneath White's windows were alive at night with people out walking, going to bars and restaurants. Whereas the streets surrounding White's two previous addresses in Paris had been silent by ten or eleven in the evening, here the noise and shouts of night people continued into the early hours. During the daytime, the street was crowded with young tourists of every nationality on their way to the Centre Georges Pompidou. Once the building work was over, the sound of excited voices coming up from the street in the stillness of summer days would form a babel of different languages. Until Marks and Spencer opened in the summer of 1994, White had a long walk to the nearest street of food shops, the Rue Rambuteau, away on the other side of the Centre Georges Pompidou, but the streets around the Rue Saint-Martin itself held a vast array of restaurants, and the mixture of chic art cafés and gruff neighbourhood cafés gave White plenty of scope for breaks on his walks with Fred. He immersed himself into the street's vivid life. While Sorin was still well enough, he and White would frequently take a long walk from the Rue Saint-Martin to the Tuileries gardens, returning home through the Place des Victoires with its array of elegant shops and fashion designers' studios.

In February 1993, the British television arts documentary series produced by Melvyn Bragg, *The South Bank Show*, devoted a programme to Genet and White's research into his life. The documentary, entitled *The White World of Jean Genet*, had been filmed in August of the previous year, and White had hoped that it would be transmitted to coincide with his book's publication, but it was in fact screened four months before the book became available. The director of the film was an Englishman who lived in Normandy named Jack Bond; he had worked briefly with Genet himself during the 1970s on a project for a film adaptation of Genet's novel *Funeral Rites*. Bond had the idea of combining his abandoned material from that previous project together with a documentary portrait about White and his research, but was finding it hard to integrate the two strands. Finally, he asked White if he would write a scenario for the documentary. White then produced an outline dealing with the essential encounters and creative revelations in Genet's life, for which he was paid around £1,000. But when filming began, White realized that his scenario had been jettisoned. The director had decided to construct a whimsical portrait of White's daily life, randomly interspersed with voice-overs of extracts from Genet's novels and footage from productions of his plays. During the filming, the summer heat exhausted White as he was taken from one location to another around Paris. Bond had asked his friend Anthony Blond – who had been the first British publisher of Genet's novels in the 1960s and was now living in retirement in Bellac, a town in central France – to travel to Paris to be filmed in discussion with White. But Blond (who now dismissed Genet's novels as pornography) was an assiduous drinker who quickly entered a soporific and bewildered state, and the filmed encounter between him and White at the Train Bleu restaurant soon degenerated into incoherence. White commented: 'He dissolved in front of my eyes.' White was growing increasingly exasperated with Bond's demands, and was relieved when the filming was over. He provided the film's voice-over narration, describing Genet's incessant travelling and the many journeys he himself had taken in following Genet's life: 'I think writing this book turned me into something of a vagabond. I travelled all over in order to do my research for it. I found myself in Damascus where Genet was a young soldier at the age of nineteen. I went to Larache in Morocco where he's buried and looked at his tomb.'[69]

In the film, White is seen in Paris at a number of evocative but unconnected locations, often circled by an enigmatic young man on a bicycle (the young man was 'played' by an American gym instructor named Douglas Freeman, who regularly visited White to assist him in his efforts to stay at least minimally supple as he entered his fifties). White appears walking along the banks of the Seine with an unruly Fred tugging at his leash, having his naked body slapped and pounded at an old Turkish baths in the Barbès district, and visiting the extravagant tomb of the Egyptian pop singer Dalida at the Montmartre cemetery. The documentary also includes footage of White sitting by the window at the Rue Frédéric-Sauton apartment while reading extracts from his book into a dictaphone, and informally discussing Genet's work with friends in bars and restaurants. While White was largely indifferent about the inept end result of the project (which was also shown on American television), he noted caustically that the film's look of having been rapidly thrown-together accorded badly with his own long years of work on his book, and was likely to put viewers off both his and Genet's work. But the film comes to life at moments, particularly when White speaks about his own first readings of Genet's work, and about the formative impact it had on his gay identity, and on his open receptivity towards those on the wild margins even of gay sexuality: 'People often say that books don't change lives, that art has no real effect on your own life. In my own case – I started reading Genet in 1964, in English, and I read *Our Lady of the Flowers* first, and I was twenty-four years old. I think if I hadn't read Genet, I would have had a real *mépris* – a real scorn – for drag queens, because most middle-class homosexuals like me usually don't like drag queens. But Genet had such a wonderful feeling for the poetry of transvestites and the whole world of transvestite prostitutes, that came to seem to me to be terribly romantic and poetic, and I always had a soft spot in my heart after that for transvestites. I think that's what literature does really – it enlarges your sympathies, it allows you to feel what other people's lives must really be like. And so, for me, Genet was very much part of my own coming-out, part of my own coming-to-terms with being gay.'[70]

White took part in another television documentary at the end of 1992, again masterminded by Melvyn Bragg and entitled *Après le Deluge: Post War Paris*. This one featured Bragg expounding at length at a bar counter about his youthful enthusiasm for Camus and Sartre, writers who had long ceased to exert any influence in France itself. In *Après le Deluge*, Bragg interviewed White at the Petit Saint-Benoît restaurant, which had been one of the main gathering-places for Parisian intellectuals in the decade following the Second World War. Bragg had used his drink-fuelled interview technique to great effect in a documentary from 1985, when he had interviewed the painter Francis Bacon – equally drunk and garrulous – with raw and spontaneous results. But White never touched alcohol now, and he faced Bragg's questions with bemusement. They discussed the well-trodden history of American writers resident in Paris. White aligned his own time in Paris with that of the post-war writers and musicians, often blacks or exiles, who had wholeheartedly integrated themselves into the city's culture, rather than with pre-war figures such as Ernest Hemingway, who, for White, had no interest in French culture and had come to Paris simply to drink cheaply during the period of American Prohibition. He commented: 'The people who came after the war like Richard Wright and James Baldwin and Miles Davis were black Americans who came to stay. And they learned the language, and they came because they perceived – at least – a greater degree of racial equality here. I think now I'm closer to that generation of black Americans who came after the war than I am to the earlier generation of Hemingway and Fitzgerald.'[71] White also discussed his encounters in Paris, while writing *Genet*, with the surviving remnants of the intellectual circles that had animated the city in the 1940s and 1950s; he emphasized their work's preoccupation with exploring all deviant forms of sex, especially voyeurism, and with transforming the relationship between sexuality and society – a process that, for White, was still vitally ongoing in French culture. He viewed the seminal figure in those explorations as being the novelist Georges Bataille – rather than Genet (or, indeed, Camus) – and the key work inspiring the sexually transgressive mood of the post-war period as that of the Marquis de Sade: 'I think the real thing is that France is fascinated by a literature that represents transgression. That's been particularly true in this century. Maybe things were partly opened up by the Surrealists, who were interested in the unconscious and evil and forms of transgression. It came about too with the tremendous revival of Sade . . . And I think that Bataille is another figure who was interested in crime, transgression, evil: the dark side of human nature, a side that wasn't allowed to be expressed very often in conventional society.'[72]

The publication of *Genet* was finally set for June 1993, and White spent the preceding months endlessly putting the final touches to the book. He never had the sense of his work on the book being definitively over – a feeling he always experienced with liberating pleasure when his novels were finished – since new Genet manuscripts and letters were being constantly

discovered and had to be incorporated into the book. Friends
of Genet who were nearing the end of their lives, such as the
painter Leonor Fini, changed their minds about refusing to
meet White and Dichy and agreed to be interviewed at the last
moment, in the hope that they could have their final say on the
quarrels that had constellated Genet's life. And White had
realized that, in working on his chaotic hand-written manuscript of the book, he had often forgotten to keep a note of the
sources for many of the Genet writings he had quoted and
translated from, and he had to frantically go back over all the
material. Sections of the book – including its concluding pages
– had also been dictated by White into a hand-held dictaphone
directly from rough notes, and this too made locating sources
difficult. Working with Dichy to assemble all the sources for
the book had altogether taken up almost a year of White's time
to get absolutely right. It was only at the arbitrary moment
when the manuscript had to go off to the printer that an end
point in the writing of *Genet* was reached. In finishing the
book, White still had a strong sense of its incompletion – of
there being large sections in its vast expanse which he had
never been able fully to master. The book seemed finally
elusive. But writing it had proved to be an immensely challenging experience. White concluded that the process of writing
the book had transformed his personality as well as his views
on creative culture, on politics and on society. He now saw
himself as 'more severe, less charming as a person, more
uncompromising'.[73]

The scope of the book reflected that deep transformation in
White's personality and his view of the world. The book
charted the full complexity of a life that had moved from the
most peripheral social point – Genet had been brought up as a
discarded bastard by paid foster parents – to the pinnacle of
Parisian literary and aristocratic society, and back again to an
outsider's contempt for society, with Genet's espousal of a

succession of revolutionary movements. White had examined the huge range of revolutionary and political struggles with which Genet had engaged in his later years, such as those of the Black Panthers, the Palestinians, the Red Army Faction, and of groups campaigning for the rights of North African immigrant workers in France itself. White's work included re-evaluating moments which had been formative in his own development, such as the late 1960s American counterculture that was manifested in the violently suppressed demonstrations surrounding the Chicago Democratic Convention in August 1968; Genet had participated in and written about those demonstrations. In his questioning of the nature of political commitment and of the individual's rapport with society, Genet had moved in the last decades of his life from contradiction to contradiction and from extreme to extreme. He had both experienced fraternal solidarity with other revolutionaries, and been the isolated object of wide-spread derision. Notably, his support for the struggle of the Palestinians had allied him with a large number of fashionable Parisian intellectuals and politicians, but his support for the violent terrorism of the Red Army Faction had utterly isolated him. White's depiction of those decades of Genet's involvements meant that he had to find a means to present their contradictions in all their intricacy, but to avoid unifying them or simply explaining them away. White also had to discover a way to present the entire range of Genet's long search for a language in which to express his revolutionary concerns – a search that had extended from the polemic of newspaper journalism, to the fragmentary language of love and devotion for the Palestinians in his final book, *Prisoner of Love*. White's long exposure to Genet's revolutionary commitments – which had propelled Genet himself from suicidal depression to physical horror and acute elation – produced its inescapable impact on his own personality. It was both an exhausting and gruelling process of investigation, but also one that was salutary and creatively inspiring – it gave White the opportunity to construct an exact sociological and artistic account of one individual's revealing trajectory through the essential political and revolutionary events of the 1960s and 1970s.

In examining Genet's novels and plays of the 1940s and 1950s, White was faced with another set of dilemmas. He was dealing with material which, in the early novels, elaborated a myth of childhood, particularly in Genet's approach to his time at the harsh Mettray reformatory, which he retrospectively re-created as a unique paradise of desire and courage. White himself had produced a lucid account of childhood experience and its mythological potential in *A Boy's Own Story*, but with Genet's work he was confronting a reinvention of childhood to which secrecy and opacity were, for its creator, essential. Genet had always attempted to obscure his origins, refusing in his 1985 television interview with the BBC to disclose the name of the village where he had spent his early years. White reveals the name of the village in the very first sentence of his book: 'As a child in the village of Alligny-en-Morvan, southwest of Dijon, Genet liked to spend hours in the outhouse.'[74] Genet's own account of his crimes, and his suggestion of having committed a murder, formed another area in which he had attempted to cover up the more banal facts, in order to promote a self-mythology which he later came to detest, but which was indispensable for his early work. White was aware that he was writing a biography of a man for whom such exposure would be perceived as destructive to his work's carefully fabricated edifice of beauty and savagery. White wrote of how biography was anathema to Genet, that 'he was always hostile to biographers or researchers who might unmask him and establish the disparity between his poetic versions and the literal facts without recognizing the artistic purpose served by his distortions'.[75] White's book, then, had to overcome or overlook Genet's posthumous resistance. And White also believed that he was himself a man whom Genet might well have disliked personally, since Genet was attracted to ostensibly heterosexual men such as Sénémaud and Java, and had, during his time in the United States, expressed his curt dismissal of explicitly gay American men, such as White. In writing his book, White pursued a kind of work of revelation in an almost religious sense, illuminating Genet's work by documenting the encounters, situations and journeys through which it was created, but also demonstrating that the work of such an extraordinary writer – once it had been separated from the particular set of scattered moments in which it had first appeared – needed to be seen and understood in its entirety, as a set of interconnected elements, in order for its profound power to remain intact.

When it had become known that White was writing a biography of Genet, the response among the gay community of New York was sometimes hostile, particularly among those preoccupied with AIDS activism, for whom Genet's work now appeared irrelevant. The writer Larry Kramer rebuked White for wasting his time on Genet when he should have been campaigning for the rights of AIDS sufferers, or writing novels directly addressing the subject matter of AIDS. But, for White, those years at the end of the 1980s and the beginning of the 1990s formed a low point at which gay culture had been pitifully reduced to one medical issue, and he believed that part of his own work should be to expand that endangered culture. He saw Genet as an enduringly significant presence for gay men. Certainly, Genet had been a key figure in the process of gay liberation, not least through the way that his novels had – along with those of Burroughs – triggered a dematerialization of barriers on the gay imagination in the 1960s.

And, as White emphasized, one of Genet's glorious distinctions was that he had 'invented the drag queen for literature with Divine in *Our Lady of the Flowers*'.[76]

Genet had himself been closely involved in activism at the end of the 1960s, and his understanding of the repressive function of social power was exhaustive – as White noted, 'In a profound sense power is something he knew about in his very bones.'[77] While the main focus of Genet's activism had been racial – in his support for the Black Panthers – White highlighted in his book the rôle Genet had played in attempting to wipe out the Panthers' own homophobia and in encouraging collaboration between the Panthers and gay activists. This had resulted in a 'position paper' or manifesto issued by the Panthers' leader Huey Newton, in which he had called for revolutionary conferences between blacks and gays to discuss strategies to combat their shared oppression. White believed that this ability of Genet's to ally apparently disparate oppressed communities presented a valuable example for contemporary gay culture: 'In the recent past, there were these great gay figures like Genet, like Pasolini – and there's still one living, the Spanish novelist Juan Goytisolo – who are remarkable because they stand for a pre-ghetto culture, before homosexuality became such an important culture in and of itself. Though all three of these men were openly gay, they were interested in issues like the third world, workers' rights; they all had communist or leftist leanings. They felt that they were a kind of conscience for Europe in general, not just for the gay part of Europe. Although they occasionally spoke on gay issues, that was a minor part of their agenda. I think that that has completely vanished, partly the result of the ghettoization of gays *and* the emphasis upon gay culture, and typical of the whole American notion of identity politics.'[78] On an individual level, White encountered in Genet's work a conception of gay life which, in its style and preoccupations, was far removed

from the one he had experienced in the New York of the 1960s
and 1970s, but which still possessed parallels with the life he
had led there: Genet's work presented homosexuality as an
unbreakable alliance of courageous friendship, and as a refusal
to capitulate to the drudgery and oppression endemic to
society.

White locates the power of Genet's language in its cinematic
quality. This quality is present from the beginning to the very
end of Genet's work. White notes about the early novels:
'Genet always constructed his fiction like cinematic montage,
alternating one story with one or two others.'[79] He argues that
the same is true of Genet's final work, although here the
technique has become more intricate and challenging for the
reader: 'In *Prisoner of Love*, Genet's typical cinematic intercutting becomes rapid, constant, vertiginous – a formal device for
showing the correspondences between elements where no connection had been previously suspected.'[80] As White remarks,
Genet was preoccupied with cinema throughout his life and
began many film projects, though he only ever completed one.
But, for White, it is within Genet's written language itself that
the filmic construction of narrative and the pre-eminence
accorded to particular images comes most successfully into play
– cinematic techniques of construction and emphasis which are
also essential to White's own fiction. White even extends this
concern with film to Genet's life itself, which he constructs as
a kind of experimental montage of telling images, since, as he
remarks, 'no one could logically account for the extraordinary
leaps Genet made from the beginning to the end of his life'.[81]

White creates vivid portraits of Genet as an elegant young
dandy and as a shuffling old man, forever travelling from
revolution to revolution. Genet always remains a child, even in
his seventies, and White's book is a narrative of a life-long
childhood in which Genet tries to secure a succession of
surrogate mothers and erotic fathers for himself. That explora-

tion of childhood, which resonates with White's fiction on the same subject, exists alongside a preoccupation with death. The whole of the second half of the biography, especially after Genet befriends the sculptor Alberto Giacometti, is saturated in the aura of death – a medium White himself was living within during the years he was working on the book. White writes: 'Genet's writing is about dying, about anticipating death, about dedications to the dead, about feeling already dead, and he is complaining even at this point, "Life is what's missing."'[82] Even in his revolutionary engagements, Genet still intimately perceives the world around him as one of death, emptiness and loss. In an echo of the title of his most recent novel of the time, White writes about Genet's experience of inhabiting a new apartment: 'Genet recalled that when he was in one room he felt the other room was lonely and Genet would rush to its aid.'[83] Where the title of White's novel evokes the impossibility of shared happiness, Genet's life projects the impossibility of happiness even within the freedom of solitude.

In exploring Genet's language, White was especially fascinated and disturbed by Genet's obsession with the ideas of betrayal and treachery. He told Marina Warner that this was the sole aspect of Genet's life which shocked him. What White found most difficult to come to terms with was Genet's elevation of the idea of human betrayal, which existed in contradiction with his deeply sexual sense of solidarity with his fellow reformatory boys, convicts and revolutionaries. Genet viewed his capacity for betrayal as vital to his life. Over the years of writing his book, White tried to understand this determination to celebrate betrayal. He had himself evoked the elated sexual power of betrayal at the end of *A Boy's Own Story*, but Genet's attachment to betrayal was far more systematic and fundamental. White decided after a year or so of working on his book that Genet's idea of betrayal corresponded to his sense of independence from society. Genet had always resisted social assimilation and believed he could only subvert its action effectively through extremes of behaviour: cruelty, robbery, and treachery. In this sense, Genet's view of betrayal was close to his conception of language itself: that is, language as always ready to fail or betray the writer, who, in turn, seeks to corrupt or attack – and so also to betray – language, in order to seize its power. However, by the time White completed his book, he had gathered so much evidence of Genet's emotional torturing of his friends and lovers – driving a number of them, notably the acrobat Abdallah Bentaga, to suicide – that he now saw Genet's betrayal more as a perverse readiness to wound and alienate those close to him, in order to reinforce his own profoundly human isolation. But, for White, even these cruel betrayals formed poetic acts in Genet's world of contradiction and endless transformation. In speaking of Genet's novel *Funeral Rites*, in which the narrator praises the treacherous French militia who have killed his resistance-fighter lover during the Liberation of Paris in 1944, White remarked: 'Genet was returning to the roots of poetry, which is a kind of ritual; he was acting as cannibals do when they eat the noble organs of their enemies in order to steal their virtues. You eat the heart of your enemy in order to get his strength; you eat the sex of your enemy in order to get his virility. Just as cannibals understand that, in the same way Genet understood that you must eat your beloved and you must eat his enemy in order to embody within yourself the whole drama that has befallen you. It's a very passionate and savage kind of art that he practised.'[84]

The published book was a huge work of over seven hundred pages, with an additional seventy pages of notes, and White often wished he had produced something more streamlined. At the same time, he knew that the book's size had allowed him the freedom to experiment fully with using Genet's life to explore his concerns with the nature of language and the trajectory of social history. And the book was a unique achievement. White dedicated it both to Bill Whitehead and to Hubert Sorin. He made his own translations of all the extracts in French he had quoted from Genet's writings, and, as a kind of offshoot of the biography, he selected a number of short translations of Genet's writings for an anthology which appeared in the United States. Shortly after beginning work on the biography, he had also drafted an Introduction to Barbara Bray's translation of Genet's *Prisoner of Love*, which was eventually published in 1991. And White would later write an Introduction to a translation which his friend Neil Bartlett made – at White's suggestion – of Genet's long-lost play *Splendid's*, which Bartlett himself staged in 1995, at the Hammersmith Lyric Theatre in London.

For the publication of *Genet,* White travelled around Britain, together with Sorin, giving readings in bookshops. Many readers who attended the events knew White only as the author of *A Boy's Own Story*, and were bemused by his concern with the French writer. People called out: 'We don't want to hear about Genet – we want to hear about your work!' At this stage, White had been immersed in Genet's life for so long that he felt he had almost forgotten he had once written novels himself. As a result of the audiences' demands, his readings often extended out into fierce discussions of gay fiction, and of AIDS and its impact on gay culture in general. Sorin was surprised by the deep affection which the audiences showed White; in France, writers tended to be posthumously revered but not subject to personal adulation, and the enthusiasm with which White was received was deeply pleasurable to Sorin. He also enjoyed the freedom of being temporarily away from Paris and the round of interminable medical treatments he was enduring there. The key event to mark the publication of *Genet* took place in the Clore Auditorium at the Tate Gallery in London, which at the time was showing an exhibition of work from late 1940s Paris, including original editions of books by Genet and work by his friends and contemporaries such as Alberto Giacometti. The Tate event took the form of a dialogue between White and Jane Giles, whose book on Genet's cinema had appeared two years earlier. In the years since White had met her in Paris, Giles had become an infamous figure in British film culture for her promotion of gay and subversive cinema, and for having been put on trial for showing the banned film *A Clockwork Orange* at a cinema she had managed; her views on censorship and on politically engineered moral panics were coruscating. The dialogue between Giles and White had the reverse effect of the *South Bank Show* documentary, bringing out White's conception of Genet as a virulently anti-social figure, a deviant saboteur of oppressive languages and images. The event – attended by some of the foremost commentators on gay issues in London, such as Paul Burston – startled its audience with its urgency and its correspondences with the situation of contemporary British gay culture. Before the event, White had told Giles that he wanted to 'push things along', but hadn't said why. Once the dialogue was over, he confided in her that Sorin had suffered a sudden deterioration in his health; he had grown exhausted from their constant travelling, and they now had to rush to hospital in order for him to receive treatment. Giles understood why the event had been shot through with such a sense of urgency and immediacy.[85]

On his return to Paris, White was already experiencing nostalgia for the long years of researching and writing *Genet*, and began to contemplate taking on another non-fiction project. He had often wondered whether he would live long enough to finish *Genet*, and now that the project was suddenly over, he experienced a sense of loss for the dominant presence it had exerted over his life; he was also faced now with the creative and financial imperatives of life continuing. *Genet* appeared in French translation shortly after its British publication, and was met with an approval that was almost unknown for an English-language biographer of a French writer. The publication of *Genet* – by the publisher of Genet's own books, Gallimard – gave White far more of a public profile in France than he had previously had, since his fiction had received only erratic attention there (*Nocturnes for the King of Naples* had received the most acclaim of his novels). The largely positive reception of *Genet* in France, as well as in Britain and Germany, gave White a sense of dignity as a cultural figure that he seldom experienced in the United States, where he felt that he was always being assailed with questions about the financial profile of his books before any discussion could begin of their aims or preoccupations: 'The first questions there are always: "How many copies have you sold? How much money do you make? And are they going to make a movie out of it?" '[86] However, White did eventually win several American literary awards for *Genet*, and was gratified to receive positive responses to his book from Edward Saïd and William Burroughs.

White now formed the idea of following up *Genet* with a biography of Jean Cocteau, whose work had been important to White since the 1960s. In some ways, Cocteau appeared a better subject than Genet for White to work on. Cocteau's compulsion to immerse himself totally in his art had made him a scintillating but often detested figure among the acrimonious literary and political factions of 1920s Paris, which had parallels with those of New York in the 1970s. The Surrealists had particularly despised Cocteau and were notorious for making hoax telephone calls to his mother, announcing her son's death. Cocteau had been compromised during the German Occupation of Paris, but had weathered the resulting hostility with insouciance and defiance. He had an oblique and uniquely French way of manifesting his homosexuality, through his erotic fiction and his undisguised affairs with handsome actors such as Jean Marais. He had also written about his long-term opium addiction in anguished but loving terms. Like White, Cocteau had moved effortlessly between fiction, non-fiction and theatre; he had also produced a sequence of hallucinatory film works about his greatest obsession – his own death – which became a lasting inspiration for all European and American experimental cinema. And like White, Cocteau clearly conceived of his own personality, body and friendships as his ultimate art work.

White planned to work on the project once again in collaboration with Albert Dichy. The book would take several years to undertake, and White felt that launching into another long project would again help to keep him alive. The research on Cocteau promised to be far more pleasurable than the gruelling negotiations he and Dichy had often pursued with Genet's friends. Since Cocteau's death in 1963, his literary estate had been controlled by his lover (and unofficially adopted son) Édouard Dermit, who had appeared in Cocteau's 1950 film *Orphée* as the arrogant young poet who is killed at the beginning of the film, his body transported away by the Princess of Death. Dermit was now in his sixties, but still elegantly handsome; he lived in Cocteau's mansion at Milly-la-Forêt, in the wooded countryside south of Paris. His sense of control over the Cocteau estate was extremely tenuous at best, and he was happy to let any visitor who travelled to Milly-la-Forêt have unsupervised access to the priceless trunks of chaotically disordered manuscripts and documents. The Cocteau project would remain enticing for White during the next two years, but during that period it began to appear more and more difficult to realize: Dermit died, and Dichy became increasingly laden down with his work at the IMEC archives, which were forever receiving new consignments of manuscripts from the families of dead writers, such as Barthes, Barbedette and Guibert.

As the Cocteau project faded away, White became increasingly absorbed with an idea for a new fiction project, which he had begun to formulate in the period following the successful publication of *The Beautiful Room is Empty*. He had then been unable to pursue the idea since he was enveloped in working on *Genet*, although in 1992 – during the time when he was finally preparing the biography for publication and relocating all the sources he had mislaid – he had drafted out around fifty notebook pages towards the fiction project. His plan was for a novel that would form a trilogy with *A Boy's Own Story* and *The Beautiful Room is Empty*, and which would take his protagonist from the contemporary moment back into the two radically dissimilar decades separated by the onset of AIDS, the 1970s and 1980s. At first, in 1988, White had formed the idea of writing two separate volumes, dealing with each of the decades in isolation, but by 1992 he had decided that a novel purely about the sexual furore of the 1970s would be too upbeat, just as a novel about the human devastation of the 1980s would be too lacerating; a project which juxtaposed the two decades would provide a more authentic framework for exploring the gay life White had seen and experienced. The novel would be concerned with the nature of memory, and White was trying to develop a fluid structure for his book that would enable him to move from moment to moment, from decade to decade, and so articulate the movements of memory itself. He noted: 'I want to set up in the reader's mind that I can always break out of the chronology in order to enter another moment.' At an early stage, White chose the evocative title *The Farewell Symphony* for his novel, alluding to the alternative name for the composer Joseph Haydn's 45th Symphony of 1772, at the end of which the participating musicians gradually leave the stage, one by one, finally leaving only two violinists and the conductor; White had watched the same process happening with his dying friends and fellow writers, leaving him in solitude. The novel would be assembled only gradually, in fits and starts, over the next three years; during the eighteen months from the summer of 1993 until the end of 1994, while often preoccupied with its subject matter and structure, White wrote only a small part of the novel; it would only be in December 1994 that he began to devote his time assiduously to the project.

In the month following the publication of *Genet*, White's play *Trios* had its first London production at the Riverside Studios in Hammersmith. Fifteen years after he had written it, the play remained unpublished and White – still proud of his early work – hoped the production would create enough of a stir to make a British publisher decide to take it on. On the first night, he sat beside Sorin in the audience, intently concentrated on the play's elaborate layers of dialogue and complex constellations of relationships. The work's exploration of sexual identities still made it provocative contemporary material, though the audience's response was muted by a degree of bewilderment at its intricacy.

At the end of September 1993, White travelled with Sorin to the Italian town of Bellagio on Lake Como. He was there at the invitation of the Rockefeller Institute, which owned a sumptuous villa on the wooded hillside overlooking the lake. The villa provided a luxurious working retreat for groups of writers and scholars, and White spent his five weeks there working intermittently on *The Farewell Symphony*. He and Sorin were allocated a two-room apartment, with the study overlooking the granite mountains that surrounded the lake. White found the surroundings uninspiring and the self-absorbed resident scholars 'extremely odd'. It rained incessantly in Bellagio, the electricity blew out, and while they were there, White heard with sadness that Paule Thévenin had died of cancer. They were glad to return to Paris, but it quickly became clear that Sorin's illness was now entering its terminal stage. Throughout that winter, White and Sorin lived an isolated life in the Rue Saint-Martin. Sorin could barely manage the steep spiral stairway that led up to the fourth-floor apartment, and White – though over twenty years older than Sorin – had to help him up the stairs bodily. Every day, White scoured the local shops for delicacies which he hoped Sorin could digest, and almost to the end Sorin was obsessive and rigorous in the food he picked at. White found he was spending much of his day cooking both lunch and dinner for the demanding Sorin, with each meal comprising numerous small courses. 'I felt that I was running a real French household,' White remembered. But, while the meals made White increasingly put on weight, they almost invariably left Sorin vomiting in agony as a result of his chronic pancreatitis. The pancreatitis had been the side-effect from his short-term use of a then-experimental AIDS drug known as 'ddI'. White told the gay historian Thomas Avena: 'I'm going through all those stages that are so well-known to gay people: waking up five times a night to change the sheets, holding his hand while he's vomiting or shitting, plugging in the catheter, and all that stuff. Leading a very, very reduced life. We don't see anyone, we don't go out, we don't do anything . . . I suppose I was always holding myself in reserve for this; I always knew that it would come my way some day: first with him, and then later with me. So, now it's come.'[87]

White and Sorin were by now entirely centred on one another, to the exclusion of all other people; almost all face-to-face contact with their friends had ceased. White was writing very little now. The confinement he and Sorin suffered sometimes became exasperating, and Sorin could be scathing if he felt White was neglecting him. Although endlessly calm by temperament, White himself could occasionally snap in desperation at his lover's evident decline. Sorin viewed his disease with a certain clinical objectivity, and if White – ever candid when struck by a physical phenomenon – pointed out the striking difference in weight or complexion between Sorin and a guest of the same age, Sorin would be equally as absorbed in the contrast. His principal sadness was for the loss of his creative future: only thirty-two years old, he was deeply unhappy to be leaving his careers in architecture and drawing unfulfilled. Although Sorin preferred to deal with the bureaucracy of his illness alone – the French medical system demanded an endless filling-in of forms for refunds on medicines and for arranging treatment – he and White went together to see a number of doctors and specialists; but the consultations proved futile. On the recommendation of a friend of White's, they travelled to the southern French city of Montpellier to see an acupuncturist, who told them he could cure them of their homosexuality, but not of AIDS, which he saw as a symptom of racial degeneration. A Chinese doctor promised Sorin a series of miraculous injections, which it transpired he also administered to sick horses. The charlatans who proliferated in the treatment of AIDS in France left Sorin and White despondent and angry.

Over the last year or so of Sorin's life, he and White collaborated on a project that enabled Sorin to exercise his drawing ability with White's support, and at the same time allowed him to engage imaginatively with the surrounding district of Paris which he loved so much. After they had returned to Paris from the United States, Sorin had continued with the drawing work he had begun in Providence, and was now creating highly accomplished drawings; these were often biting caricatures of the people he and White met at Parisian literary events, and were accompanied by captions which caustically satirized the gatherings. Rachel Stella had exhibited a selection of the drawings at her gallery in 1992, accompanied by a limited-edition book. White believed that the satire articulated at a tangent Sorin's bitterness at the way his disease was limiting and curtailing his life. His proposal that they should work collaboratively – which Sorin accepted immediately – was intended as a way of giving Sorin a more satisfying focus for his work. The project which they undertook together was in fact far less rancorous in tone than Sorin's solo work, and it was intended for an audience, whereas Sorin's early drawings had been executed primarily for his own pleasure. The project celebrated their life together in Paris in the present instant. And it excluded the horror of the imminent future, negating the power which AIDS held to cut off both Sorin and White's future at any moment. Sorin kept drawing, even when he became temporarily blind in one eye from herpes sores. He made drawings depicting himself and White together on their adventures and excursions around Paris; he also drew their friends, and humorously catalogued the range of bizarre characters – the prostitutes, drunks and idlers – who haunted the Rue Saint-Martin. To counterpoint the new drawings, White wrote short, intensely evocative texts which he could complete very quickly. The project was perfect for him after the long years of often frustrating and labyrinthine work on *Genet*. Their work slowed as Sorin became more and more ill during the first months of 1994, but White held back from declaring the series of short chapters and drawings to be completed, despite Sorin's prompting: 'He was always pushing me to finish them, and I was always dragging my heels, because I thought if we finished, then he would die.' White insisted that they still had one more chapter to work on – a minute description and depiction of their apartment and its idiosyncratic collection of objects (in the end, White did write this text, but Sorin could never produce its visual counterpart).

White believed that the determined engagement of working on the book was vital in keeping Sorin alive. But by the beginning of March, Sorin was evidently too exhausted to work any more, even for short periods, and White conceded that the project was now finished.

Though a confirmed atheist, Sorin sometimes went in his final months to the nearby Saint-Merri church to light a candle, to mark his survival. But it was clear that he was nearing the end. Both he and White were reading again and again the extraordinary last novels of Hervé Guibert, in which the writer described the excruciating treatments and humiliations he was enduring in the final stages of his illness, and the desperate world-wide journeys he had made to try and momentarily escape his physical disintegration in Paris; like Sorin, Guibert had suffered interminable encounters with bogus doctors and faith healers, and he had entered a subterranean black-market world in order to obtain scarce or untried AIDS drugs. He had finally died in a Parisian clinic in December 1991, shortly after attempting suicide with an overdose of his medication. Guibert's novels – together with a film he himself had helped to make about his own terminal decline, *La Pudeur ou l'impudeur* (*Decency or Indecency*), which was screened on French television in January 1992 – prepared Sorin and White for what was to come, and helped instil in them a bleak courage. The demands of caring for Sorin now meant that White no longer had the time to take Fred for walks, and finally Sorin's brother Julien travelled from his home in Nice – where he ran a television repair shop with his gay lover – and took Fred to live there. Sorin knew that he would die soon, and wanted an end to his pain. He was talking increasingly about his time in Ethiopia, Tunisia and Morocco, and told White that he wanted to see the desert one more time before he died. White was aware that such a journey might kill Sorin in his exhausted, weakened state – several of their friends warned them not to make the journey, but as White said, 'I blinded myself to the danger of it.' And he knew that Sorin was reaching the end of his strength anyway, and that his overwhelming desire for the heat and vision of the desert – for a place that, with its immensity and purity, could give the event of death a certain dignity – took precedence over the inevitable mundanity of a drugged death in an impersonal Parisian clinic.

On 9 March, White and Sorin flew to Morocco (one of the countries Guibert had travelled to in his own final months). They had last been to Morocco together only a month before, for the first week of February. On that occasion, they had stayed in the city of Marrakesh. White had attempted to rent a large villa which he and Sorin had seen together there. They had planned to spend the spring months living at the villa, and to invite their friends to visit from France and Britain. Before they returned to Paris, White and Sorin drove out to the villa to finalize the arrangements with the owner; Sorin decided to stay in the car while White handled the rental details, but their driver insisted that Sorin too should meet the owner. White wrote a cheque for the deposit. But when he subsequently called the owner from Paris, he told White that he had changed his mind and would post him back his cheque. White realized that the owner, having seen Sorin's emaciated body, had assumed he was about to die, and had decided that it was too complicated to rent his villa to someone who might well die there.

For the journey to Morocco in March, White had made an arrangement with a Parisian travel agency whereby he and Sorin could move about the southern desert zones of the country by hired car and stay at luxury hotels in whatever towns they happened to pass through. Morocco was a good destination for a desert journey, since French was understood there, and health care was available and adequate, at least in the major towns. But despite the journey's aura of having been planned with White's usual meticulous care, he knew better than to invest any great rational preparation into the trip. He knew that it was likely to be Sorin's last journey. Sorin was too weak even to pack his own travel bag, and White had to do it for him.

White and Sorin flew from Paris to Agadir, on the Atlantic coast in the southern part of Morocco. The weather was warm but not oppressive. They picked up their hire car and made the forty-minute journey inland to the town of Taroudannt, a beautiful, sprawling array of markets and tiny houses enclosed within ochre-red walls, with the High Atlas mountains looming in the distance. White had last been to Taroudannt with David Stevenson, who had died of AIDS in the previous year, and he felt haunted by that last stay. For the next four nights, until 13 March, White and Sorin remained in Taroudannt at the Hôtel Palais Salam, a converted nineteenth-century palace built into the town's walls. At first, Sorin was alarmed when he saw their room, since it was on two levels linked by a flight of stairs, and he feared that he wouldn't be able to climb them. When White saw him in the shower one day, he realized that Sorin was 'Auschwitz-thin – he was just like one of the pictures from Auschwitz'. His pancreatitis meant that he could eat virtually nothing without painfully vomiting it out again. But Sorin was alertly interested in the architecture of the town, and in far better spirits than he had been in recent weeks in Paris. He began to wear a blue Arabic robe rather than his usual shirt and jeans, since his legs were so thin that the seams in the jeans hurt him. He and White hired a horse carriage and driver to take them around the town, and a Berber guide escorted them on 12 March to the settlement of Tioute, on the foothills of the High Atlas mountains, where they visited an ancient ruined stone palace, surrounded by palm trees and orange groves, which the American painter Philip Taaffe had told White not to miss. Huge peacocks strolled around in the grounds of the palace, which was slowly disintegrating. Only one person was now staying there – a decrepit old German doctor who had been the gay lover of the palace's long-dead last owner. Sorin loved the place; White took a series of photographs of him standing in the palace gardens, unshaven, wearing his almost biblical robe and breathing in the scent of a bunch of orange flowers which he held in his hands. The guide invited White and Sorin to drive up to his village in the mountains, but the track was too rutted for the car and they had to turn back to Taroudannt.

On the next day, 13 March, White and Sorin travelled on to Ouarzazate, an old garrison town built by the colonial French army on the edge of the Sahara. White was concerned that the travelling should not prove too exhausting for Sorin after their journey of the preceding day, but it took six or seven hours to reach the town by road from Taroudannt. On the next morning, 14 March, they looked out over the spectacular Drâa Valley, with its long ridge covered with date palms, stretching out to the south-east into the desert. As they travelled through the valley, the precipitous towers and spires of the village of Tamnougalt – made of a sculpted straw and mud mixture, in vivid white, blue and blood-red – reminded White of the buildings of Manhattan. They reached the oasis town of Zagora, on the edge of the desert. Sorin was disappointed that the desert at this point consisted only of a few windswept, scrubby dunes. White could see now that Sorin was becoming extremely exhausted and fragile. At their hotel in Zagora, Sorin decided to take a bath but was too weak to climb out again. White had to lift him up in his arms and carry him over to the bed: 'It was like holding an eighty-year-old man.'

The next morning, 15 March, Sorin wanted to continue through the desert, and head north-east, to the Saharan oasis town of Erfoud, around 200 miles away by a difficult track. Soon, the tarmac road they were following ran out, and they were driving through the 'piste' — two tracks in the sand into which the tyres of the car fitted. After several hours, they reached the settlement of Tazzarine which had the only hotel along the route, the Hôtel Bougaffer. White decided that they should make a break there for lunch. But, as he stopped the car, he suddenly saw that Sorin's condition had become much worse. Though he was still in good spirits, Sorin could no longer walk; White and the owner of the hotel had to take him by the arm on either side and support him up the steps to the hotel's veranda. Although the owner was eager to help and moved Sorin gently, he insistently wanted to know what was wrong with him. White knew that admitting Sorin had AIDS would terrify the owner, so he told him instead that he had liver cancer. The owner served them a *tajine* stew as White and Sorin looked out over the desert town, where the sand seemed to be inexorably submerging every building. Sorin tried to swallow a few mouthfuls of food. White remembered: 'His eyes were completely staring out of his head. He could barely hold himself up at the table any more. He looked bleached, a hundred and twenty years old.' They continued on through the desert, Sorin still contented but more and more exhausted, until they reached Erfoud, in the Tafilalt region. White saw camels wandering freely through the streets; both the men and women of the town wore veils.

They arrived at their hotel, but when Sorin began to get out of the car, he lost control of his bladder and began to urinate involuntarily over the ground. White was scared, since he could see the porter coming to take their bags and was concerned that they would be refused entry to the hotel. They went up to the reception desk, but the alarmed receptionist treated them aggressively. White tried to reassure the receptionist by telling him that Sorin had recently had surgery, but was now recovering. Finally, they were given a room, but its smell of sewage nauseated White. He helped Sorin to collapse down on to the bed: 'His arms were just two little sticks and his head was huge.' White now believed that Sorin was about to die, at the same time as he still refused to accept that it would actually happen: 'I was so in love with him and so determined that he would go on living for ever that I just couldn't accept the idea that death was imminent.' He called the airline Air France and booked seats on a morning flight from Marrakesh back to Paris on the next-but-one day. Then, while Sorin rested, White tried to distract himself by working on a short story; he began to read an extract to the smiling but now utterly depleted Sorin, who was too exhausted to listen. White decided that they should drive back to Ouarzazate on the following day, and then up through the High Atlas mountains to Marrakesh, where he hoped they would find a suitable hospital at which Sorin's condition could be stabilized before they returned to Paris.

The next day, 16 March, they took the two-lane tarmac road that ran between Erfoud and Ouarzazate. It was an immensely long journey, but Sorin was happy again and engaged with everything he saw. He could only whisper, but told White again and again how beautiful he found the landscape. Camels passed by as they drove. It was the end of the religious festival of Ramadan – the men in the oasis villages they went through wore white robes; the women wore sequinned black robes, tied with red or gold belts. Sometimes, the car's progress would be stopped altogether by crowds of festive villagers with their donkeys. At other times, they would have to drive with excruciating slowness through villages clogged with stalls for market day. As they finally neared Ouarzazate, the road ran between two sheer mountain ranges of black volcanic rock, the Djebel Sarhro and the High Atlas; the fields on either side of the road were covered with small pink roses. White now felt an urgent responsibility for Sorin, and was anxious to get him to a doctor as soon as possible. At one point, Sorin wanted

White to stop the car so that he could walk around in the open air, but once out of the door, he began to slide down a slope and White had to steady him; even being touched was now too painful for Sorin in his fleshless, dehydrated state. White stretched him out on the back seat of the car. Sorin, still totally lucid, told White that he didn't want to return to Ouarzazate and then to France; he demanded that they head north instead, up through the Middle Atlas mountains to the city of Fes, many hundreds of miles away, which he had once visited as a student of architecture.

Once they had arrived back at the same hotel in Ouarzazate which they had left two days earlier, White left Sorin in the car while he went inside to register. The hotel was made up of an arrangement of small pavilions spead out through a park. When he returned, he saw that Sorin was covered in excrement. Sorin asked White to drive the car all the way up to the door of the pavilion, but White was reluctant; Sorin was growing angry and frustrated, and hissed at White: 'I hate you!' As they struggled over from the car to the pavilion, Sorin suddenly fainted. White stretched him out on the grass. A passerby saw what was happening, panicked and called an ambulance. White was dismayed since he knew that – instead of returning to Paris – they would now be taken straight to a Moroccan hospital where any treatment for AIDS would be unknown. The ambulance arrived, siren screaming, and transported them to the town's basic hospital. When White spoke the word 'AIDS', the nurses ran from the room. After trying to clean the excrement from Sorin's body, White left the hospital to return to the hotel, to call the insurance company in Paris whose responsibility it was to repatriate Sorin should he fall ill abroad. White looked desperately for a taxi, and finally found a large shared taxi; he squeezed in next to the driver. Then, to his horror, he felt the driver's hand trying to stroke his penis. Back at the hotel, White called the insurance company, which arranged for an ambulance to carry Sorin and White to a clinic in Marrakesh; from there, a private plane would fly them back to Paris. White returned to the hospital, and the ambulance arrived to collect Sorin. White sat in the back of the ambulance with Sorin as it began the long journey through the High Atlas mountains to Marrakesh. From the heat of the desert, they suddenly entered the freezing air of the snow-covered mountains. The ambulance was unheated, and White and Sorin grew colder and colder while the driver muttered to himself, predicting Sorin's imminent death. Halfway through the journey, the ambulance abruptly stopped, high up in the mountains. The driver explained that Sorin now had to be transferred to another ambulance, which was waiting to take them the rest of the way to Marrakesh. Sorin and White staggered through the glacial night air into the other ambulance. White wanted above all to have a final moment of tenderness with Sorin and to exchange a few last words about what they had meant to each other, but Sorin either maintained an angry silence or murmured anxiously about his medicines and the process of being repatriated.

After a journey of around six hours, the second ambulance was approaching the city limits of Marrakesh when one of its tyres burst. Finally, at two o'clock in the morning of 17 March, they reached the clinic and Sorin was taken into the emergency room. The doctors and the ambulance driver surrounded him in baffled consternation, never having seen an AIDS patient before. Sorin, still completely lucid, shouted out in English: 'I can't bear this!' After being given a chest X-ray, he was allocated a room in the clinic. A nurse attempted without success to locate a suitable vein in Sorin's arm in order to connect him to an intravenous drip of minerals and salt; the ambulance driver, who had followed them, seized the needle and stuck it brutally into Sorin's arm. Sorin screamed in pain. White remembered: 'To me, it was really like a crucifixion scene.' Sorin believed they were giving him a lethal dose of morphine to end his agony. When White explained what the intravenous solution in fact consisted of, Sorin began to switch from moment to moment between wanting to be saved and wanting to die. Exhausted, White lay down on the bed alongside Sorin's own bed, and slept.

At seven that morning, White awoke and looked over at Sorin's face. It appeared startled, his eyes wide open, as though he were about to sit up in alarm. He had died from a heart attack around an hour before; his body was still warm. White remembered hearing a noise while he had been dreaming: a whispering, or the sound of air escaping from lungs. The nurse came in and confirmed that Sorin was dead. White dressed, then sat by Sorin's body and wept. The clinic's mortuary attendants entered the room to take Sorin's body away. The representative of the insurance company arrived and told White coldly: 'You can go now.' White remembered that he still had the original reservation he had made in Erfoud for the flight that morning to Paris. He rushed out of the clinic, searching for a taxi to take him to the airport. By now it was nine in the morning, and the plane was to depart at ten thirty. But all he could find was a shared taxi which took a circuitous route, dropping people off in different parts of the city, and he missed the plane. The next available flight to Paris was not until two o'clock that afternoon. He found he was shaking uncontrollably. He called Marie-Claude de Brunhoff to ask her to meet him that evening in Paris. Then he decided to write, hoping to calm himself enough to stop the shaking before he boarded his plane. After searching through the entire airport building, he finally found a stall with a photocopying machine and was able to buy paper from its owner. For the next few hours, he sat alone in the airport restaurant and wrote the final text for his collaborative book with Sorin, continuing it after he had boarded the plane. White was always proud of being able to write anywhere, at any time, and this was the ultimate test of that ability. Using Sorin's favourite drawing pen, White wrote the Introduction to the book, describing the circumstances under which it had been produced, and Sorin's courage and tenacity in his last days. He wrote: 'Hubert Sorin, my lover, who died just two hours ago in the Polyclinique du Sud in Marrakesh, was an architect who turned himself into an illustrator with a remarkable patience and diligence and above all a flair for capitalizing on his talents and pictorial discoveries . . .'[88] In the evening, with the book's Introduction completed, White landed back in Paris, where Marie-Claude de Brunhoff and Albert Dichy were waiting for him at the Rue Saint-Martin.

White was bewildered by his own response to Sorin's death, which was not one of conventional mourning. At first he felt shocked and numb; then he became aware of a huge encompassing silence and absence around himself, with the sudden withdrawal of the immense presence Sorin had exerted on every part of his existence for the last five years; all of the objects in his silent apartment now seemed imbued with particular moments from Sorin's lost life. But then, White felt the greatest sense of exhilaration he had ever experienced. When friends called with their condolences, he was keen to move the conversation rapidly on to what they had been doing during the past few months when he had been isolated by Sorin's illness. His mood became increasingly manic in the weeks that followed. He took new lovers, and started a hectic round of travels and dinner parties. In April, he travelled to Cork in Ireland to give a lecture – or, as he put it, a 'comedy routine' – based on the more bizarre aspects of Genet's life. In May, he gave a reading in the luxuriant surroundings of the

Music Room at Brighton's Royal Pavilion, accompanied by the gay novelist Alan Hollinghurst, whose novel *The Folding Star* had recently appeared. White then went on from Brighton to a symposium on Genet's work in London; there, he delightedly showed Jane Giles photographs of a handsome new lover. The experience of once again forming part of a vibrant human community made White ecstatic. In time, though, Sorin's death took him to the other extreme of sensation, with a numbing depression. He began to feel that he wanted to die as soon as possible, to follow Sorin into death. He was also perplexed to discover – from the accounts of the range of people who contacted him in the wake of Sorin's death – that Sorin had led a more promiscuous life in Paris, in the years prior to their meeting, than he had been aware of, and that Sorin's family background had been more mundane than the semi-aristocratic and adventurous milieu which White had been presented with in Sorin's account. White suspected that Sorin had constructed an idealized identity for himself which had in part been designed to mislead and captivate White.

Still, White believed that Sorin had been the love of his life, and though he was elated to have had the opportunity of experiencing an all-consuming great love, he grew despondent that it had lasted for such a short time, and had ended senselessly as a result of a futile and physically humiliating disease. By the summer of 1994, he was profoundly dispirited, preoccupied with Sorin's death and with his own oscillating emotions and fears. He often took the same long walk to the Tuileries gardens which he had made many times with Sorin, and every day he would visit the Saint-Merri church and light a candle there for Sorin. A month before Sorin's death, he had begun to see a young American psychotherapist who lived in Paris and specialized in treating patients who were HIV-Positive, or who had friends or lovers with the virus. White had seen his services advertised in an English-language magazine. Initially, the therapist had told White that he should 'rebel against' Sorin, and, to White's regret, he had started acting more briskly towards Sorin in the weeks before their journey to Morocco, not realizing then that he would die quite so soon. After Sorin's death, the therapist recommended that White should start taking Prozac; Marie-Claude de Brunhoff was strongly against the treatment, and White took the drug only very briefly. But White felt the therapist was doing him some good, since his attitude was the reverse of the psychiatrists from White's youth, with their prohibitions and manipulative strategies. White even felt that he himself had almost too much authority over the therapist, who was gay and had read all of White's books. White was now receiving 'advice your grandmother could give you', as he put it. The therapist simply asserted that it was fine to feel elation after a lover's death, that it was natural to experience extreme emotions in an extreme situation. That objective reassurance was exactly what White needed at that moment. After travelling to Büyükada for the end of the summer, he was ready to continue with his life.

White was now concerned that his collaboration with Sorin, for which he chose the title *Sketches from Memory: People and Places in the Heart of Our Paris*, should be published as soon as possible. It would mark both a living and creative memorial to Sorin, and a tangible limit from which White's own life could start again. White's two British publishers agreed to issue a joint paperback edition (rather than the usual hardback followed by a paperback), and the book appeared in December of that year. The American edition, with the shorter title *Our Paris*, was published at the end of the following year. In its published form, the slim book of just over a hundred pages looked frail alongside the brick-like solidity of *Genet*, but in many ways, it was *Sketches from Memory* that, of all White's writings, most essentially caught his central preoccupations.

Where Genet's life had been elusive and contradictory, and had taken many years to pin down, *Sketches from Memory* momentarily seized a joint life which was one of courage edged by despairing exhilaration. The book captured the intense pleasures of existing on a precipice alongside the abysmal horror of imminent death. The power of the book was that its capturing of sensation had been undertaken instantaneously, in a headlong rush of language and image that tried to keep its moment intact. It was a book about the joy of survival.

The book forms a compendium of gestures and pleasures. White's short texts construct fragments of experiences that hold an evocative and atmospheric substance, as in the book's opening sentence: 'We were lying in bed one evening after dinner, digesting, idle as ever, the windows thrown wide open on the pulsing sky.'[89] White's texts have a luxurious and suggestive visual feel to them. Their own quality of slightly indolent construction blurs their visual focus to a degree, so that Sorin's more rigorous accompanying drawings work to snap White's language into focus. The writings and drawings are placed in intimate juxtaposition. The book is a dialogue between White and Sorin, from lover to lover, and from language to image and back again; the position allocated to the reader in this oscillating process is more that of an accidental onlooker and observer, rather than the highly implicated participant of White's novels. Occasionally, though, White becomes carried away in his enthusiasm to narrate and leaves Sorin's drawings behind – as, for example, when he spends three pages describing his misadventures with the visiting German boy which he had previously recounted in the film *The Day the Shit Happened*. Although, this time, the story of the German boy is narrated largely through an invocation of place rather than through comedy – in a sequence of venues such as Goldenberg's restaurant in the Parisian Jewish quarter of the Marais – it is clear, as the unillustrated pages pass by, that this is not a sequence of text for which Sorin is concerned to imagine a visual counterpart. At other points, such as the sequences of drawings depicting characters in White and Sorin's neighbourhood, it is the extravagance of the drawings which takes the upper hand.

White includes numerous recipes in the book, always emphasizing the sonorous French names for each ingredient in the dish he is describing. The highlighted names in French acquire their own identity within White's language, possessing a resonance of beauty and meaning which exists independently of the items of food they signify, but then rejoins those items through the parallel distinctiveness accorded by White to words and to food. White evokes recipes formed out of ' "a tear of wine" (*une larme de vin*), "a suspicion of ginger" (*un soupçon de gingembre*) or "a cloud of milk" (*un nuage de lait*) or "a nut of butter" (*une noix de beurre*)'.[90] The emphasis on food is so vivid as to be almost hallucinatory, like the obsessive lists of food compiled by the starving principal character in one of White's favourite novels, Knut Hamsun's *Hunger*. White is tangibly evoking food for Sorin, whose physical condition makes it impossible for him to eat, except in fantasy. In addition to this emphasis on a rhythmic vocabulary of food, the book is also propelled by its rhythm of anecdotes, which often recount the visits of friends. The fragmentary anecdotes come thick and fast, the language of each one working to build on the momentum of the last one, despite the dissimilarity of their contents and the sudden abandonment of each short narrative. The resulting language of the book has a hypnotic and mythical quality, almost biblical in its genealogy of visiting friends and big dinners.

The book is a fabulous transformation of Paris – a city readily amenable to such transformation from a long history of artistic and literary reinvention – into an arena especially designed for White and Sorin to fulfil their desires. White constructs his portrait of the Châtelet district of Paris as one which meets his demands for a mythical but human backdrop for his account of love. It is a place of magnificent buildings and quirky, provocative people. Extending out from its account of the Châtelet area, *Sketches from Memory* also portrays a largely gay community in Paris that – through a kind of emphatic omission – is not presented as a gay community, unlike those White describes in *States of Desire*; these are figures with a wide-open social sphere. It is a community in which the Parisian artists and writers encountered by White and Sorin are always the possessors of a defining obsession or totem which, however bizarre, serves to accord them their legendary status and character. The writer Pierre Guyotat, for example, is depicted with his obsession with testicles: 'As he spoke, he created a vision of a foul dog writhing in the filth of primeval slime, belly huge and erotically bulging, the trade-mark testicles much dwelled on.'[91] The designer Azzedine Alaïa has a more endearing and nostalgic obsession with the great Egyptian singer Oom Kalsoum, recalling how as a child in Tunisia he had regularly rushed to reserve a café seat for his grandfather to sit and listen to her monthly radio concerts: 'There his grandfather would install himself with a jasmine flower behind his ear and sigh and weep as Oom Kalsoum improvised verse after verse, hour after hour, of her lovesick ballads.'[92] In White and Sorin's Paris, all social and religious values have been mercifully dissipated: a priest visits White not to discuss religion with him, but to trade literary gossip. One chapter of the book has been created explicitly to name-drop outrageously, and forms a listing of all the illustrious names – such as Picasso and Hemingway – which White has encountered in Paris, embodied in their idiosyncratic human forms (usually those of the children or grandchildren of more celebrated ancestors). This community of independent eccentrics, brought together only through White's perspective as an outsider, appears not to be an endangered community (White does not, for example, describe his encounters with Guibert or Foucault). It exists in a zone beyond the dangers of time. The book also depicts the lesser-known but equally mythically presented inhabitants of the Parisian district that White and Sorin inhabit, such as the *concierge* of their building. White describes the warmth of his deeply disabused *concierge*: 'She knows we're gay, of course, and says nothing but does not resort to the polite fiction used by the restaurateur on the corner of referring to Hubert as my "son" (*votre fiston*), a lie particularly difficult to sustain given my American accent.'[93]

In addition to the book's transformation of Paris, White's aim in *Sketches from Memory* was to transform a doomed situation into one of joy, even ephemerally, through the power of his language. That language wilfully suspends time. As White notes in his Introduction, this work of metamorphosis was assisted by a kind of transformation-in-reverse carried by Sorin's accompanying images: 'Hubert came to despise his emaciated body, but in his drawings he remains as dapper and handsome and *élancé* as he was the day I met him, five years ago.'[94] In those drawings, White and Sorin live their everyday life within a protective medium of insolence towards the eroding passage of time – giving their dinner parties, meeting their friends, and standing together in the shadow of the fifteenth-century tower (from the '*gothique flamboyant*' era) which marks their territory.

The book is a portrait of two gay men, surviving. It tails off abruptly, on a note of sadness and anticipated loss, with an account of White and Sorin's antique collecting. In the Introduction to the book, written in Marrakesh airport and on the plane back to France on the day of Sorin's death, White steps back from his gloriously concocted fragments and more objectively narrates the origins of the project; he inserts the element of AIDS which – like the gay aura of *Caracole* –

permeates the rest of the book through its enforced absence. *Sketches from Memory* is a book about AIDS in its refusal or insouciance towards (rather than a denial of) the subject. In his Introduction, White adopts the tone of direct address to his reader – and of transparency towards his book – which he was developing in the same period in his novel, *The Farewell Symphony*. But even here, the element of a dialogue – now suddenly one-sided – between White and Sorin remains. He writes: 'I'm writing with his beautiful Art Pen which he always forbade me to touch; today I couldn't find anything else to write with and I wanted to – needed to – give a form to my grief that he would have approved of. That's why I'm daring to use your pen, Hubert.'[95]

In the spring of 1994, soon after Sorin's death, a volume of White's non-fiction writings entitled *The Burning Library* was published. It was compiled from essays and articles dating from the late 1960s to the present, on the trajectory of gay culture, and on sexuality, politics and literature in general. White had in the past been sceptical about the then-fashionable practice of writers publishing compilations of their old pieces of work – he had himself criticized Martin Amis for this – but felt that his individual history now imparted a sense of urgency to his scattered and often unavailable essays. After seeing a volume of essays by the poet John Ashbery that had been edited by an American scholar, David Bergman, he conceived of his own volume as one that would evade what he saw as the over-egotistical trappings of such compilations, by using the strategy of its being edited by someone other than himself. David Bergman, who was also researching the context of New York gay fiction of the 1970s and 1980s, was happy to serve as White's editor. Since White was in Paris, it was impossible for him in any case to locate copies of the original publications where the essays had appeared. White chose around two-thirds of the volume's contents, and Bergman proposed the remainder of the material. Much of this material was taken from White's journalism, which he always wrote at high speed. Especially after he acquired a laptop computer in 1994, White would work at an astonishing rate. Characteristically, he would take a nap after a long lunch, then wake up in mid-afternoon and clear his backlog of journalism, producing several articles in the space of an hour or two. He commented: 'I write them just as though I were writing someone a letter.' Marina Warner was always amazed at the ease and fluency with which White polished off writings which were direct in address but highly intricate in structure, encompassing a vast field of interconnected cultural references. She commented: 'There's absolutely none of the painfulness and laboriousness of writing there — he's an effortless and commanding writer. It's a great mystery to me.'[96] But this ease existed in sharp contrast to White's fiction, which — though assembled in short writing days — often stalled for many months on end, and proceeded in fragments by odd fits and bursts.

It was Marina Warner who had suggested the title for White's volume. During her research into Caribbean culture, she had come across the phrase 'the burning library', used to describe the death of someone who had lived through an extraordinary time and held a vast archive of memories of it; before their extinguishment, those memories needed to be passed on, orally or as writings. In White's case, those memories were themselves already inflammatory through their sexual, passionate content, and through their raw anger at the social oppression and the threat of AIDS which together endangered White and all gay men. The book concerned in part the work of a number of White's friends who had, already, died of AIDS without having created all the work they had envisaged or without that work having achieved a public profile. White adopted the phrase – which he had also heard in a number of other forms, all with different implications, over the preceding years – as the title for his volume. He chose two photographs by Robert Mapplethorpe – who had died of AIDS, but whose exhibitions continued to incite a huge furore after his death – for the book's cover: an image of two juxtaposed male heads, one black and one white, for the paperback edition, and a close-up portrait of White's own face for the hardback. White dedicated the book to his mother's memory.

With White's approval, Bergman had decided to arrange the book on a strictly chronological basis. This structure meant that the subject matters and styles of the essays fluctuated constantly – a nuanced essay about a poet, for example, would be located next to a polemic about masochistic sex. The advantage of the structure was that it gave a clear trajectory of the principal running themes of White's work and their development over the course of twenty-five years. The book tracked the history of gay culture, changing approaches to sex and sexual culture, and White's engagement with other writers, both in the form of intricate readings of their work and of interview profiles. In particular, the book mapped the evolution of White's views on the rôle of the individual in relation to society. For White, this relationship always held a political content. He saw politics operating in the creative work of the individual aimed against – or else representing the tensions of – social power. These struggles and tensions, he argued, had been the main preoccupation of his own work: 'The power dynamics between populations, the jousting for position within a group, the struggle for dominance in a couple, even the empowering awareness of individual oppression – by all these definitions, politics has been a constant theme in my work, even or especially in my novels of pure fantasy, *Forgetting Elena* and *Caracole*.'[97.] While a book such as *States of Desire* had explicitly political themes such as wealth inequality and repressive legislation, White now recast his imaginative novels as political in another sense: with their rarefied distance from the chaotic detail of everyday life, they possessed a pure, wild concentration on the nature of power.

Alongside these sustained themes of the book, *The Burning Library* also constituted a statement from more than two decades of White's commitment to his own concept of multi-culturalism. Even as a child, he had voraciously absorbed material from every world culture through his extensive readings. He now conceived of multi-culturalism as a commitment to the idea of all-inclusiveness: a passion for all of the deviant, marginalized, hybrid, perverse, crazy, oppressed, extravagant, and bizarre elements of humanity, and for their creative combination. This aspect of his work had recently generated anger among sections of White's audience, since it clashed with the then-current preoccupation with political correctness. In opposition to the sprawling creativity and vitality which he ascribed to multi-culturalism — with works made up of intersections of ideas and images from disparate and seemingly contradictory sources — White saw the threat of enforced categorization and limitation posed by the doctrine of political correctness, with its strategy of isolating and insulating away each element of a society's dissident culture. What White viewed as the stultifying power of political correctness had been brought home to him by his time at the beginning of the 1990s at Brown University, where he had been reviled as a friend and collaborator of Robert Mapplethorpe — one of whose provocatively inter-racial images he now deliberately used as the book's cover. White conceived of political correctness as integrally censorial, and therefore opposed to human creativity — which, he believed, required the freedom to be as dangerous, subversive or aberrant as its expression demanded. He noted: 'There's no way that a sensibility can be disciplined into an uplifting social programme.'[98]

White included in *The Burning Library* an essay he had written at the end of his time at Brown University on the exiled Spanish novelist Juan Goytisolo, whom he had met several times in Paris while doing his research on Genet, whom Goytisolo had known well. Goytisolo, while gay, scorned the notion of his work being defined uniquely as that of a 'gay writer' as a useless and limiting categorization of its multiple concerns and experiments. In his essay on Goytisolo, 'The Wanderer', White articulated his anger about political correctness, especially the way he saw it cancelling out the concept of the 'revolutionary body', which had been fundamental to the development of gay culture. The concept of the 'revolutionary body' referred literally to the body's capacity to overturn social forms through street protests or sexual acts, and also to the idea that the human body held its own essentially insurgent force, in that it was impossible to fully represent, subdue, or control. Goytisolo's work was preoccupied with precisely the kind of receptive human sensibility which White associated with multi-culturalism, and he wrote in defence of Goytisolo's concerns that: 'The idea that "the body is always revolutionary" is outmoded in a society where feminist puritans join hands with Christians to ban pornography, where authorities (even certain gay authorities) urge gays to practice abstinence or monogamy, where inter-racial coupling is branded "sleeping with the enemy", where "political correctness" of the most banal but rigid sort is used to paralyze sexual spontaneity, artistic and intellectual expression, compress individual differences into a few "acceptable" scenarios.'[99] Once White had moved back to Paris, where American political correctness was viewed with bafflement, this strain of anger in his work lessened. But he continued to believe that culture, in defiance of political correctness, always irresistibly mutates beyond prescribed limits. At the time of the publication of *The Burning Library* in 1994, a new and widespread cultural preoccupation with masochism (and with the representation of sexuality and violence in general) meant that the book was seen as offering a seminal and valuable perspective from the late 1970s on sexual masochism and its creative portrayal – precisely in work such as Mapplethorpe's.

The Burning Library also demonstrated White's enduring concern with the nature of language itself, and with its transforming rôle in structures of power and in the development of culture. He sited his investigation of language within the context of his own work and its history, viewing the moment of gay liberation at the end of the 1960s as the point of expansion for a new vocabulary with allied political and individual concerns. He wrote: 'What I want to emphasize is that before 1969 only a small (though courageous and articulate) number of gays had much pride in their homosexuality or a conviction that their predilections were legitimate. The rest of us defined our homosexuality in negative terms, and those terms isolated us from one another.'[100] The subsequent years had witnessed the rapid development of a collaborative vocabulary to encompass the changing situation, and White saw a new, vital language of human and sexual experience emerging from this transformation. He was also concerned with the way in which the influential work of contemporary French philosophers such as Roland Barthes had questioned the rigidity of a language in which the word and object were identical, experimenting instead with a language which was more multiply resonant in its textures, and more focused on the body and its sensations. White believed that his own work had absorbed and embodied both of these upheavals in language.

The Burning Library explored many of the resulting strategies of language used by White in his fiction. He noted that his construction of his characters involved adopting an element of raw material from the world around him, and then imaginatively building on and transforming that source: 'I pattern a lot of my characters on people I know, but there is a strictly imaginary element which creeps in after I start writing. I begin by writing a fairly close portrait of somebody I know, but then the character begins to seem real to me in his own right.'[101] White's language sought to have an open quality, accessible to the reader's own imaginative intervention. He gave his language its sense of focus not through narrative or character, but by the use of a sequence of vividly revealing images. This eminence accorded to a particularly expressive image appeared even in White's non-fiction, as in his description of watching the behaviour of the playwright Tennessee Williams, his lover and his sister at a party: 'I noticed right away that all three of them had a wad of yellowed cotton in their right ears and that when they separated they still kept communicating with each other through little eerie grins.'[102]

Along with White's preoccupation with the expression of a visual image through language, *The Burning Library* also presented his engagement with other media forms, especially that of cinema. White was fascinated with cinema's ability to seize the beauty of the physical form, and also with its capacity to exert power – either for ends of revolutionary liberation (as in the work of the 1960s and 1970s political film-makers such as Pasolini and Godard, and of contemporary gay film-makers), or, conversely, as an instrument for maintaining oppression through its representations. For White, cinema possessed an aura of being forbidden and daring, partly because he had not been allowed by his parents to see films as a young child, as he noted, 'on the strange theory that they were corrupting to the young'.[103] On the very few occasions when he had been taken to the cinema as a child, the experience's impact was concentrated: scenes of violence had excited him intensely and given him prolonged bouts of nightmares. Instead of going to the cinema, he had listened to radio soap operas and imagined his own visual counterpart for the soundtrack of words. When he was in his mid-teens and allowed to go to the cinema more frequently, he had been particularly impressed by Hollywood musicals – then in their glorious heyday – and with the almost hallucinatory richness of Technicolor. He was also captivated by the way in which Hollywood narratives elevated moments of what he called 'burningly expressed romance' – embodied for White in the half-naked figures of Marlon Brando and William Holden – and disdained to represent the linear mundanity of everyday life.

In his fiction, White adopted what he saw as cinematic techniques of montage, flashback and ellipsis in the construction of his novels' narratives. Cinema inspired him to develop a strategy of going straight to the essential matter of a situation and its sense of movement, taking the reader with him. He commented: 'It is precisely film that has promoted the use and understanding of ellipsis. In the nineteenth century novel, the reader was oriented for a full chapter before the action began. A film, however, will begin with one man chasing another and they're desperately racing over rooftops, and then they're suddenly speeding away in cars and – who are these people? You don't care; you're suddenly seized by the action.'[104] In the mid-1990s, White was especially struck by such visceral experiments in rendering time and space in the films of Quentin Tarantino, whom he spent several evenings with while serving as a judge at the 1994 Locarno film festival in Switzerland. Although this was the time of a frenzied moral outcry over Tarantino's work, he and White were more keen to discuss the technique of constructing images and writing that would exert an intense impact on their audience. White himself still always experienced the extreme emotional responses to films which he had had as a child – he described his regular visits to the

Cannes film festival as being like the life of a Japanese geisha: 'You're always in a dark room, weeping.' But despite his fascination with cinema, White believed that his own novels were intentionally impossible to film – 'movie-proof', as he described them – because of their underpinning emphasis on layers of memory and perception, rather than on plot. Certainly, attempts to make films of his novels and stories – including a project by the director Louis Malle to film *Caracole* as a narrative about a child's experience of inhabiting a city occupied by an inferior foreign power – invariably foundered, to White's wry satisfaction.

White also developed his ideas about the nature of the visual image in the writings about art and the rôle of the artist which he undertook during the mid-1990s, following on from the publication of *The Burning Library*. These writings reflected different preoccupations from his art writings of the mid-1980s, when he had been concerned with the urgent necessity for an art that could angrily combat and interrogate AIDS. Now, White was more concerned with the mass of radically dissimilar but intersecting cultures he found himself living within in Paris, and the ways in which contemporary art could evoke the dissolution of national identity which was resulting from that cultural furnace. He saw something potentially very positive and attractive emerging from the breakdown of French identity into a new, hybrid and multi-cultural form. In 1994, he wrote an essay for *Artforum* magazine about the American painter Philip Taaffe – one of White's favourite artists – who had spent time in Europe and North Africa, and whose work explored his own status as an outsider with a distinctly individual and independent view on the rapidly transforming cultures he was observing and experiencing, particularly the results of the collision between European and Islamic cultures. White had met Taaffe while he was living in a villa on the bay in Naples, a city White knew from his time in Italy in 1970 and which he considered to be the supreme multi-cultural city in Europe. Like Taaffe, White felt that – while he himself was happily absorbed into an alien culture – he desired at the same time a strong sense of creative and sensorial independence in the way in which he reformulated that culture through his work (this was a central element also of Genet's attitude to culture). White declared that: 'my decade in Europe is something I want to make my own, just as I hope to turn "France" into a region of my mind'.[105]

White's writing on art also served as one of his main sources of income. Between 1994 and 1996, he wrote a series of profiles for *Vanity Fair* magazine of the three most prominent American gay artists: Jasper Johns, Cy Twombly and Ross Bleckner. Of the three, only Bleckner – whose work White had previously written about in his essay on art and AIDS, 'Aesthetics and Loss', and also in an article for the Swiss art magazine *Parkett* – was openly gay. White was curious to discover whether, with his other two subjects, the experience of being a closeted celebrity (an experience he had never had himself) actually enhanced or impaired the artists' creative powers; he would come to no definite conclusions about the matter, although he commented about Johns: 'I certainly wouldn't want to live his life.' And partly as a result of his intensive research into French society while working on *Genet*, White was also interested in exploring the sociology of an artist who possessed immense wealth – as was the case with all three of the artists he profiled – and the impact of this on their creative work and its reception. The profiles were all accompanied by lavish photographs of the artists and their work, by eminent photographers such as Bruce Weber. White was extremely well paid for his work: for the profile of Johns, he received $10,000. (Even so, a running feature of the profiles is the moment when the artists look White in the eye with boundless pity and remark on the huge difference between their earnings and his.)

White approached his work for *Vanity Fair* in a completely different way from his writings for magazines such as *Artforum*. For one thing, he was writing for a readership often more interested in the artists' personalities and status, and in their living environments, rather than in their work. He noted: 'You can't assume the reader is already interested in the artist – you have to create the interest and then approach the work.' White devoted extensive amounts of time to the profiles; for the article on Johns, he flew to the United States and met the uncommunicative artist – whom he had first written about for *Horizon* magazine in 1977 – at his vast and newly acquired estate in Connecticut, where White stayed overnight. Johns was receptive and friendly to White, whose work he had known since the time of the publication of *Forgetting Elena*; but his inarticulacy made it difficult for White to portray him with the vividness which the assignment demanded: 'There was never a tougher interview,' he commented.

For his interview with Twombly, White travelled to Italy, where Twombly had been living since the late 1950s, to visit him at his house on the Lazio coast at Gaeta. White had to wander around the streets of Gaeta, together with an Italian friend named Beatrice Monte who had arranged the interview, trying to locate Twombly's house; none of the locals had ever heard of the reclusive painter. White had met Twombly several times before – they had spent an evening together on Crete in the spring of 1984, during the first of White's two stays in the town of Xania, and they had met up again in November of that year while White was travelling in Egypt with Matthias Brunner; Twombly had told White that he was uninterested in the monuments of the ancient Egyptian civilization, but loved the contemporary landscape of the country. Despite these encounters of the previous decade, Twombly was remote during the interview in Gaeta and seemed to White not to fully recognize his interviewer. With both Twombly and Johns, White was dealing with introverted painters whose elevated status had made them very defensive and touchy, particularly about their sexuality (Johns' private life was under particular scrutiny in the United States at the time); the profiles White was writing had to be circumspect. His physical descriptions of all his subjects, though, were intimately detailed, and executed with extreme precision. He wrote of Twombly: 'He's tall, with a big Founding Father nose and a hazy elegance of sketched-in gesture. He has a sloppy, shuffling way of walking. He dresses in high-Wasp thrift-store chic (shapeless old white linen trousers, a moth-eaten blue pullover). And he speaks with a mouth of corn pone, for he was brought up in Lexington, Virginia, by an African-American nanny to whom he remains fiercely attached.'[106] White was particularly fascinated by the bizarre stories Twombly told him about his Italian wife's aristocratic family, and the article formed a series of short interlocking narratives about power and eccentricity. But Twombly detested White's profile of him, even though White had managed to skirt around the sensitive subjects of his gay lovers and his depression.

White had met up with Ross Bleckner both in New York and Paris. Bleckner was a rich socialite painter more renowned for his lavish parties and dispiriting wisecracks than for his art, which used a multiplicity of different styles. Extending the theme of 'Aesthetics and Loss', White now wrote that Bleckner 'has become the great memorialist of our day, the primary painter to bear witness to the constant losses occasioned by AIDS'.[107] He was eager for Bleckner to present his own views of his work's potential impact on the discourses and imageries of AIDS; however, to White's exasperation, Bleckner avoided being drawn by the questions about the preoccupation with AIDS in his art, preferring instead to highlight his rôle as an AIDS activist hosting celebrity fund-raising galas, and insisting that his work itself dealt only with 'metaphysical' themes such as mortality and the presence of angels.

Although he never wrote at length about his work, one of White's favourite artists since the mid-1980s had been Anselm Kiefer, a German born at the end of the Second World War on the banks of the Rhine, who was obsessed with the wounds on Europe inflicted by his country's history. Kiefer painted immense canvases of fire-scorched terrains, scrawled across in black with what looked like the terminal gestures of human language and memory; he also built monumental archives of books and film reels that were constructed in lead in order to survive a nuclear holocaust. For White, Kiefer's haunting work – itself a burning library – embodied the deepest scars of contemporary Europe.

White spent two weeks of January 1995 on the island of Key West with John Purcell, who was now entering the final stages of his illness; in March, he would be hospitalized back in New York in a state of terminal dementia. On Key West with Purcell, White was haunted by memories of visits he had made to the island with Hubert Sorin, who had particularly liked its atmosphere: 'He loved it more than any other place on earth.' White felt that Purcell and Sorin had always been 'bitter rivals': Sorin had been scathing towards Purcell on every occasion they had met, although Purcell was too amiable by temperament to respond in kind. Since Sorin had died before Purcell, White was relieved that he was now able to achieve a strong sense of reconciliation with Purcell in the intervening months before he, too, was to die. After a brief stay back in Paris, White travelled on to Australia to give the opening speech for an exhibition of Robert Mapplethorpe's work at

Sydney's Museum of Contemporary Art. He had previously visited Australia on a lengthy reading tour with Julian Barnes; White had had misgivings about spending an extended period of time with the British novelist, but it transpired that they thoroughly enjoyed each other's company, despite a deep uninterest in one another's work. For White, the thriving gay culture of Sydney was as sophisticated and materialistic as that he had experienced on the American West Coast at the moment before the onset of AIDS, fifteen years earlier. His visit to Sydney coincided with the time of its wild Mardi Gras festival, which had the reputation of being the biggest gay event in the world. White took Ecstasy for the first time there in order to participate in the entirety of the main carnival celebration, which lasted from midnight until ten the next morning.

On White's return from Australia, his collected short stories were published in Britain under the title *Skinned Alive*. The book's cover, in both its British and American editions, used black-and-white photographs showing fragments of male bodies by the German gay photographer Herbert List, whose key work dated from the 1930s; White had first grown attached to List's work in the mid-1980s, when one of List's old lovers had visited him on the Île Saint-Louis to ask him to write an essay for a catalogue of the photographs. White asked the novelist Michael Ondaatje, whom he knew from the short time when they were both professors at Brown University, to write a text for the cover of *Skinned Alive* – he had admired the evocative power of place in Ondaatje's *The English Patient* (a novel which he had favourably reviewed on its publication), and the stories in *Skinned Alive* had the same infatuation with constructing a human incident within a tangibly visualized location; Ondaatje called White's collection 'a series of new maps'. In fact, the terrain of the short story had been one which White had been attempting to master since his mid-teens. The form of the short story was not one he ever felt particularly at ease with; in addition to the stories collected in *Skinned Alive*, he had in all written twenty-one short stories which had never been published, along with a small handful which had appeared in magazines over the years. The volume of stories constituted close to the entirety of his life's published work in the form. The earliest of the stories was *An Oracle*, written in 1985, and the volume included all three of the stories around the theme of AIDS which had been collected seven years earlier in *The Darker Proof*. One of those stories, *Palace Days*, now appeared in a different form; White had shortened the long story by several pages, cutting two episodes set on the island of Büyükada, as a delayed response to the criticism in Britain of his stories' supposedly over-exotic settings when they had first appeared in *The Darker Proof*.

White regarded his short stories as having the form of radically abbreviated novels. He commented: 'I found that my short stories were like mini-novels. They were like speeded-up novels or compressed novels rather than traditional short stories, which explore a very small space. Because I'm only really a novelist, I wanted to tell a whole long story, but speeded-up and condensed.'[108] White saw a parallel with his stories in the work of Hervé Guibert, who had written at a furious pace in his final two or three years, when he was dying of AIDS, determined to write all the novels he would have written if he had lived to old age, rather than only until his mid-thirties. The resulting novels were often very short, completed in a matter of weeks, and – even if they often appeared raw or botched – Guibert was satisfied to have made them exist. White himself experienced that sense of having death itself as an imminent deadline, inciting him to explore all the subject matters that had ever attracted him, immediately. A number of the stories had been written while White was engaged in the vast process of writing *Genet*, and there the speed of composition was largely the result of being able to snatch only short periods of time away from his research. The sense of being temporarily liberated from his work on *Genet* had combined with the stories' qualities of intensity and condensation to give White an extraordinary feeling of elation during their composition: 'I wrote almost all of them in a hallucinatory state, in a state of great excitement of a kind which I hadn't really known since adolescence as a writer.' Even with the stories written after the publication of *Genet*, that sense of elation remained compelling. Whereas he always found it hard to hold the entire, intricate form of one of his novels in his head as he worked on it, White was able to perceive the miniature form of his short stories with a far greater clarity, like a painted image to which he was adding new gestures and figures as he went along. Then, at the right moment, he loved to end his stories with startling abruptness.

The volume's title-story, *Skinned Alive*, was the first of White's stories to be written after those included in *The Darker Proof*. The story had been commissioned in 1989 by a friend of White's named Lucretia Stewart, who had recently become one of the editors of the British literary magazine *Granta*. White remembered her saying to him at a cocktail party in London: 'I want to commission you to write a story about a boy's bum.' White was happy to accept, and set to work. The title of the story carried the urgent emotional turmoil of White's life in that period, with both the threat of AIDS, and the sexual violence of his then-current relationships with Hubert Le Gall and David Stevenson, on whom the characters of Jean-Loup and Paul were based. The story's scene of an actual flaying appears in a mythological form, in a fragment of writing given to the narrator by Paul, his young American lover; the lovers can only confront each other sexually in a single encounter of explosive physical violence which takes place in a hotel on the edge of the Moroccan desert. Paul's fragment – a story within a story that serves to open out the multiple implications of the characters' power rôles – concerns the flaying alive of the satyr Marsyas after a battle in music with the god Apollo. White had to fight hard to retain this section of his story when Bill Buford at *Granta* decided to cut it. The narrative of the story proceeds through intersecting sequences, each one suddenly abandoned and superseded by the next. The narrator complains about the 'wet sand' of his writing, which endlessly but impossibly tries to capture the bodies of his lovers. Sexually, too, his relationships are impossible. Finally, though, he achieves the physical form he is searching for in his writing with a long, exact description of Jean-Loup's anus: 'If he spreads his cheeks – which feel cool, firm and plump – for the kneeling admirer, he reveals an anus that makes one think of a Leica lens, shut now but with many possible F-stops. An expensive aperture, but also a closed morning-glory bud.'[109]

White had written another of the stories in 1992, while he was engaged in the tortuous final stages of his work on *Genet*. This story, *Reprise*, was inspired by an encounter four years previously between White and a figure from his past. During his years in Paris, White would often encounter in their woeful aged state the youths on whose ephemeral beauty or desire he had based his fictional characters, as they now passed through Paris on family holidays or business trips. In 1996, he met again the boy named Steve Turner on whom he had based the character of the beautiful Tommy in *A Boy's Own Story*, now an overweight, balding businessman (though, for White, still warm and attractive). And his encounter in August 1988 with Bob Hamilton, the decrepit old man who, over thirty years before, had briefly been his suave, Perry Como-obsessed lover, gave rise to the nostalgia for nervous youthful ecstasy which White recorded in *Reprise*. White had spent the intervening four years 'hovering over' the incident, as he put it, allowing time for his memory to sieve the encounter and transform elements of it into the raw material for fiction. The narrator of the story meets his old lover, and they have sex again; the passage of time has ruined their bodies, but an element of pure passion has survived: 'Now each time I touched him I could hear music, as though a jolt had started the clockwork after so many years.'[110] The story was first published in Britain in the *Guardian*, and then in the American literary magazine *Grand Street*.

All of the remaining stories in the collection had been written during 1994. White had begun the story entitled *His Biographer* in Morocco in March of that year, while on his final journey through the desert with Hubert Sorin. The story conveyed the sense of fascinated intimacy that had resulted from White's collaboration with Albert Dichy on *Genet*. While White's natural human curiosity had become absorbed in the compelling narratives of Dichy's tumultuous life of war and exile, Dichy too found himself becoming intensely curious about White's own life and celebrity.[111] The story concerns a hapless professional biographer who himself becomes the subject of an equally hapless biographer. To Dichy's flattered bemusement, White had drawn on his collaborator's personal history and his relentless heterosexual conquests for the story's main character, Charles, and on his own exasperating experiences at Brown University for the story's politically correct academic setting.

The other stories in *Skinned Alive* had been written later in 1994, after both the publication of *Genet* and Hubert Sorin's death, and they carried a more languorous and detailed sense of evocation than the stories from earlier periods. The story *Watermarked* evokes the provincial gay scene of late 1950s America. A group of ambitious young dramatists chide one another scathingly as they discuss each other's work. Though their gay sexuality makes them feel alien figures everywhere else, they create a sense of freedom for themselves through their meetings at the 'Pancake Palazzo' café, assembling their own language of gestures and affectionate abuse. That pre-Stonewall gay language is one that is still tentatively in the making: 'We could roll our eyes, do double takes, coo and murmur like powder pigeons, but still silences would creep into our dialogue and our snappy comebacks would go soggy.'[112] The narrator falls in love with an actor he meets through the group, Randall; in the concluding pages of the story, as the narrator looks back on the years of their relation-ship and the following decades, almost forty years shoot by in four dense pages. The story *Pyrography* captures another 1950s American world. Three boys make a canoeing journey together through a silent world of vast lakes and forests. One of the boys, Howard, is attracted to Danny, a wild and unpredictable boy whom he hardly knows; Danny defies the other two boys and shoots dead a bird on the lake. The narrative of the story traces the mute yearning Howard feels as he stares at the other boy's naked body in the deep solitude of the hot forest at night. *Pyrography* (whose title refers to the art of making designs on wood or bone with a heated metallic point) delineates a world of exquisite frustration, in which the boy's incipient passion is just beginning to shape his self-awareness as a gay man.

The American paperback edition of *Skinned Alive* contained an additional story which had been written after the others, and which White forgot to include in the British edition. This story, entitled *Cinnamon Skin*, had already appeared in the *New Yorker* magazine (where the editor Bill Buford – who had previously edited the story *Skinned Alive* while at *Granta* magazine in England – had 'flattened it out', as White put it). Although it appeared both there and in *Skinned Alive* as fiction, White also gave the story in its original version to his former colleague from the early 1970s, Patrick Merla – who had commissioned it in the first place – for a collection he was editing of factual coming-out accounts, entitled *Boys Like Us*.

The complex publication history of *Cinnamon Skin* mirrored the intricacy of the story itself – together with the entirety of White's work – in its ricochets between imaginative fiction and fiction based on memories of actual events in his life. The story evokes a journey made by the narrator's childhood self, together with his father and step-mother, Kay, to Mexico. Despite his father's dour wisecracks, the boy experiences everything about the journey as a thrilling concoction of sex and glamour, encapsulated by his step-mother's lapis-lazuli brooch. The story charts a process of initiation, and – in an echo of the title of the volume of stories – the boy's bout of sunburn is depicted as a kind of revealing excoriation, both painful and lividly beautiful in what it momentarily uncovers: 'My skin was peeling in strips, like long white gauze, revealing patches of a cooked-shrimp pink underneath.'[113] In the resort of Acapulco, the boy has an encounter with a sullen hotel pianist; they meet up on a pier, and while arranging their sexual assignation for later that night, the boy's father drunkenly appears and interrupts them. This was an incident from his life which White had evoked twice before. It appeared as part of a delirious sequence in *Nocturnes for the King of Naples*, where the pianist is rendered as the romantically willing accomplice in a youth's desire to escape his father's power. And in *States of Desire*, White noted the incident bluntly as something which had factually happened to him at the age of thirteen. *Cinnamon Skin* uses the incident in an entirely different way from either delirium or reportage. Here, the brutally short sex act between the boy and the pianist shows the abyss between the boy's captivating youthful desires and the desultory squalor of having those desires realized. The story seizes that transformation of ecstasy into adult loss, and the narrative is driven by its atmosphere of memory and nostalgia, visualized in a series of images of sexual desire and pain. In a concluding coda to the story, in which the now-suicidal narrator returns to

Mexico City decades later, the dense atmosphere becomes almost overpowering in its nostalgic poignancy. Everything in human experience is lost and dead, including the narrator's father and step-mother: 'Now they were both dead, and the city was dirty and crumbling, and the man I was travelling with was sero-positive, and so was I. Mexico's hopes seemed as dashed as mine, and all the goofy innocence of that first thrilling trip abroad had died, my boyhood hopes for love and romance faded, just as the blue in Kay's lapis had lost its intensity year after year, until it ended up as white and small as a blind eye.'[114] White, as he said, had conceived of *Skinned Alive* as a sequence of condensed novels; *Cinnamon Skin* embodies this sense of fatal urgency, using the vivid instrument of memory to distil the entirety of human experience, from the sexual exhilaration of youth to the desperate physical betrayal of age and death.

White spent several weeks in London during the summer of 1995, staying with the publisher Jonathan Burnham, who had edited *Genet*. He met up with Jane Giles, and they travelled together to Brighton at the end of July, where White was to act as a witness at a friend's wedding. Giles was impressed as ever by White's spectacular running commentary on every beautiful – or even remotely beautiful – man who passed by their seats in the train. White had recently attended the Cannes film festival with Matthias Brunner, and told Giles about his misadventures there. He had met up with an old friend, the American film director John Waters, renowned for his obsession with all kinds of social deviance and for his friendships with serial killers. White, Brunner, Waters and his film producer ate all their meals together. White became increasingly desperate since both Waters and his producer were fanatical dieters, and White was obliged to subsist on a severe régime of carrot salads. When he rebelliously ordered fish one day, Waters insisted that he remove all the skin before even thinking about taking a bite. Finally, White slipped off to the seafront, with its esplanade of palm trees, and bought the biggest ice-cream he could find. Just as he was about to take his first lick, he heard a shout of 'Edmund! Busted!' and Waters emerged grim-faced from the palm trees to admonish him. When he and Giles arrived in Brighton, White told the taxi driver that he was there for a wedding, and had to wryly deflate the taxi driver's assumption that it was going to be White's own wedding.[115]

While in London, White had formed the idea for a non-fiction project which he hoped to undertake after completing *The Farewell Symphony*. In his travels around Europe, he had met many young people whose sexuality seemed far more flexible and multiple than the clearcut distinctions of the 1970s and 1980s between homosexual and heterosexual identity had indicated. Young men and women told White that they were equally as happy to have sex with either men or with women: if someone attracted them, they saw little difference in the sensations and the experience of sex with men or with women. He believed too that the emphasis in the 1970s and 1980s on matters of race – both as an enduring site of oppression and as a source of sexual excitement – had now largely dissolved away in an increasingly hybrid and multi-cultural Europe. In terms of sex, what White felt he could see emerging were signs not so much of an increasingly pervasive bisexuality as of a kind of ultimately undifferentiated sexuality. He wondered whether, in the wake of the upheaval of AIDS, homosexual identity would become meshed – willingly or not – into some new form of open and gender-less sexuality, which would necessarily detonate the existing social structures that prioritized the heterosexual couple or family and segregated other forms of sexuality.

White wanted to explore the implications of that new sexuality and discover whether they were liberatory. He viewed the project as a kind of contemporary sequel to *States of Desire* (where he had already written about the resistance to gender distinctions in his male and female students at the university where he was teaching at the time) – but set this time in Europe rather than the United States. His idea was to travel around many of the European capitals, including the Eastern European cities such as Prague and Budapest where the fall of Communism had in some ways marked a completely new beginning for sexual experience, and to interview young people about their transforming sexuality. He noted: 'International boundaries, racial boundaries, gender boundaries are all breaking down, and something new is being formed.'

One creative inspiration for the project was the work of the young New Orleans-based writer Poppy Z. Brite, whose short stories deeply impressed White in this period. He said that she was one of the very few new American writers to really seize his imagination. Brite's stories were extravagantly baroque creations, full of decadent and death-obsessed boys who oscillate endlessly between gay and heterosexual sex in order to experiment with the extremes of human experience and of beauty: 'When we had exhausted the possibilities of women we sought those of our own sex, craving the androgynous curve of a boy's cheekbone, the molten flood of ejaculation invading our mouths. Eventually we turned to each other, seeking the thresholds of pain and ecstasy no one else had been able to help us attain. Louis asked me to grow my nails long and file them into needle-sharp points. When I raked them down his back, tiny beads of blood welled up in the angry tracks they left.'[116]

That summer of 1995, White invited an American writer, Michael Carroll, to live with him at the Rue Saint-Martin apartment. Carroll, who was from Memphis, had been teaching in colleges in Yemen and the Czech Republic as part of an American Peace Corps programme. After corresponding with White, he travelled to Paris, where White fell in love with him: Carroll was thirty-one years old and beautiful, moody and unruly, his hair cut short at the sides and longer on top. Like White, he had a deep sense of politeness and tact, shot through with an unpredictable wildness. Carroll was working on his first novel, and White gave him the study at the far end of the apartment to write in. At first, Carroll felt unsettled in Paris and wandered around the alien city, not understanding the language and finding the rituals of the city deeply arcane. He was absolutely devoted to White, and had told him that his side of their relationship would be monogamous. Carroll often felt intimidated by White's long-term Parisian friends, who had deeply different interests from his own and could be arrogantly off-hand with him. At first, he and White discussed the possibility of moving back to the United States, to Los Angeles, where neither of them had lived before and where contemporary art and performance were thriving. A financial factor was also in play: the French franc had become extremely strong, and cut into White's income in dollars to the extent that the mid-1980s now seemed like a long-gone era of lavish-ness. Now, White found it hard just to pay the rent in Paris, and would sometimes spend sleepless nights worrying about money and the precarious financial future he faced, even as a celebrated writer in continuing good health. But Carroll was reluctant to influence White's thinking on the matter. He knew that Paris was essential for White and that his attachment to the city remained intense. White finally gave up his New York apartment after John Purcell's death in that year, and he had even arranged for an after-life in Paris, stipulating in his will that his ashes should be housed – together with those of Hubert Sorin – in the Columbarium at the Père Lachaise cemetery, a vast and chaotic park of tombs where Oscar Wilde and Marcel Proust were buried. By the final months of 1995, Carroll was feeling more confidently at home in Paris, though he spent his days absorbed in his study while White – having usually completed his writing for the day by mid-morning – sped around the city.

In November, White and Carroll travelled around all the major cities on the East Coast of the United States, where White gave readings from the newly published American edition of *Sketches from Memory*. Carroll was amazed to see people shaking with fear as they approached White to ask him to sign their books. White commented: 'They must have mistaken me for Armistead Maupin.' One of his trembling readers told him: 'I'm so nervous – I kept vomiting all day long and I kept hoping a truck would run you over so I wouldn't have to come to this.' After returning from the United States, he and Carroll flew on to Barcelona, where *A Boy's Own Story* and *The Beautiful Room is Empty* were being published in Spanish and Catalan translations; White read extracts from the books to enthusiastic audiences of university students, for whom a gay literature was almost unknown. After spending much of December in London, where they stayed at the home of the architect Richard Rogers in Chelsea, White and Carroll travelled to Key West for three weeks in January.

After returning from Key West to Paris, White went on to Rome to record a radio programme about his time spent living there in 1970, for the BBC's series *Sentimental Journey*. The BBC had arranged for him to be accompanied in Rome – in a bizarre mismatch of companions – by a morose British comedian named Arthur Smith. The programme revolved around Smith's attempts to persuade a nonplussed White to attend a football match at the Stadio Olimpico in Rome. White commented: 'One of the ways in which the British media responds to a gay man is to have a kind of hardy heterosexual man indulgently deal with this strange bird.' White and Smith

walked together through the city's streets and markets, searching out the building where White had lived over twenty-five
years earlier, and paying unexpected visits on people he had
known then. White was struck by how empty the streets of
Rome had become at night – in 1970, they had been the vivid
focus of all of the city's life, but now it seemed to him that
everyone was staying in their apartments at night to watch
television. The district where he had lived, Trastevere, had
become much more up-market and quiet. He visited his former
Italian teacher, now old and infirm, who told him that Rome
had changed for the worse, and she would now often go for six
months without seeing a friend. But an American gay novelist
living in Rome, David Leavitt, told White that his own
perception as an outsider inhabiting the Rome of the mid-
1990s exactly matched that of White in 1970. White had
experienced his time spent living in Rome as one of estrange-
ment and erotic hallucination; being in the city again twenty-
five years later brought back vivid memories of that time, and
newly consolidated those responses to the city. He remembered: 'At other times in my life I've drank harder, took more
drugs and had more sex than I did while living in Rome, but
in the sense of day-by-day pleasure-seeking, dissipation and
non-productivity, it was my most sustained performance.'[117]

Despite his extensive travelling away from Paris, White was
looking for a temporary change of scene from the city during
those first few months of 1996. He had decided that *The
Farewell Symphony* finally had to be finished by the summer,
and the intricate negotiations of dividing his time between his
friends in Paris – though deeply pleasurable – meant that he
was making little progress with the book. White was usually
happy to see his books assemble themselves in their own time,
sprawling over years or even decades, but *The Farewell Symphony* – as the final part of the trilogy that had begun with
A Boy's Own Story and continued with *The Beautiful Room is*

Empty – was one project that he particularly wanted to see completed. He had amassed what seemed to him to be a huge accumulation of hand-written notebook pages over the previous year, and could see that the eventual book was going to be far longer than any of his previous novels. As he wrote, he glanced at the preceding volumes of the trilogy and was struck by how the language of his new book was being driven along by its narrative of urgent sex and sudden death, in contrast to the other books' dense, more static texture. The language of *The Farewell Symphony* seemed to him freer, and a more fluent medium for his preoccupations as a result. To escape from Paris to work on the novel, White contemplated a stay in Berlin or in Prague – a city which Carroll knew well – but then settled on London. He arranged to exchange his Paris apartment for most of the spring for a vast house in Gloucester Crescent, between Camden Town and Regent's Park. The street was quiet and salubrious, but the vivid life of Camden Town was only a moment's walk away. The area epitomized London's strange 1990s mixture of wealth and dirt – the street behind Gloucester Crescent, Arlington Road, housed a drying-out centre, and drunks spent their days veering crazily around the rubbish-strewn pavements.

For the first few days in Gloucester Crescent, the telephone hardly rang. White got down to work on *The Farewell Symphony*, while Carroll worked on his own novel. Then the house starting filling up. Friends from Paris began to arrive. An old friend of White's from London, ill with AIDS and weak from a haemorrhage, came to stay. White began planning a party in a local hall in an effort to see all his friends in London in one go, but had to abandon the plan when the guest list soared into the hundreds. A relentless schedule of dinner parties filled the evenings. White was enjoying seeing Martin Amis, who lived nearby; the fact that the two writers had very ambivalent feelings about each other's work only enhanced the pleasure of the evenings. White also saw a friend from New York, the novelist and film-maker Lynne Tillman, who was over in London for a book launch. By now, the house in Gloucester Crescent was teeming with people and White – though accustomed to writing in odd corners and for short snatches of time – was having to move from room to room with his notebook on his lap, making only very sporadic progress with his novel. He was also worried about Marie-Claude de Brunhoff, who was having an operation for cancer in Paris. Finally, he and Carroll took a train to Scotland for a few days' social remission – stopping off *en route* in Leeds to see an exhibition of Jasper Johns' sculpture – before returning to Gloucester Crescent. Then their spring in London was suddenly over, and they returned to Paris.

In the wake of the publication of *The Burning Library*, White's growing reputation in the United States as a cultural commentator as well as a novelist led to his nomination for membership of the American Academy and Institute of Arts and Letters. A number of writers White revered, such as William Burroughs, were also members. The gay composer and diarist Ned Rorem (who had himself lived in Paris, during the 1950s) had proposed White to the Academy. White greatly appreciated the honour, which had no British parallel whatsoever and came long after the French had accorded him their own cultural honour, the Chevalier de l'Ordre des Arts et Lettres, in 1993 (the French had an open and international approach to this cultural award – distinctly different from membership of their own staid Academy – and bestowed it to figures such as the outrageous Spanish film-maker Pedro Almodóvar). The French award to White had been one of the socialist Arts Minister Jack Lang's last acts before leaving power, and White proudly kept the medal on his mantelpiece in the Rue Saint-Martin apartment. At the beginning of June 1996, White travelled to New York for his induction ceremony, which took place at the Academy's grand, Italian Renaissance-style building on the Upper West Side and lasted for an entire day. White had often visited the building as a young, unpublished writer in the early 1970s with David Kalstone, to hear talks by the Academy's members. For the ceremony, White wore a dark Italian suit that he had had specially made for him by a tailor in the Tuscan town of Lucca, which he had visited in the previous month with Michael Carroll. In the morning, he was photographed; then, he was given a cocktail party; then, he was given lunch; then, he was officially inducted – and presented with the Academy's rosette – and himself delivered a speech of acceptance; and finally, in the evening, he was given a big party in a tent erected in the Academy's grounds. White was delighted with the day, although he was initially nonplussed that the induction address – which had been written by Ned Rorem, although it was actually read out by the novelist John Updike – was 'barbed', as he put it, with mischievous and ironic comments about his prose style. But he soon decided that this was Rorem's characteristic way of showing his regard, and that it was better to be discussed in a vivid rather than a banal way.

White was the first member of the American Academy to have been known as a gay writer virtually throughout his career. He was aware of the way in which contemporary gay fiction – which he had feared ten years earlier would be obliterated by AIDS – was now in the process of acquiring an institutionalized status; AIDS, he believed, had partly backfired in its obliterating intent, making gay culture in general a publicly prominent and essential part of American life. Though White felt some pride at the idea that the work produced by gay writers of his own age group had rapidly acquired the aura of consecrated literature – as a kind of living document of America's upheavals – he had witnessed too much social duplicity and transmutation not to regard the process of institutional approval without a degree of ambivalence. In the 1991 Introduction to his anthology of gay short stories, he had noted: 'Not long ago I wrote that gay culture seemed to be following a rapid trajectory – oppressed in the 1950s, liberated in the 1960s, exalted in the 1970s and wiped out in the 1980s. Perhaps I was too hasty. The 1990s may be the decade when gay fiction will be institutionalized.'[118] Now, five years on, the process of becoming an institution in himself was a source of contradictory feelings for White, since it made his deviance and idiosyncrasy appear mainstream. But that contradiction was overridden by the enduring facts of survival and creativity, and the will to keep experimenting with life and language. Beyond the concerns which were specific to White's work as a celebrated gay writer who had experienced both the gay liberation movement and the impact of AIDS at close range, he was determined too to explore subject matters which he saw as being crucial to contemporary human life, and to discover new forms of language in which to do so. His time in Paris – and particularly his contact with writers such as Juan Goytisolo – had given him the capacity to disregard external limits arbitrarily or intentionally placed upon him. White declared: 'There is no way I could give up the transgression of my work.'

By the mid-1990s, White's physical appearance and manner had lent him a certain invisibility in the streets of Paris. He was completely absorbed into the city's contemporary look as well as into its history and culture. His now fluent French retained a markedly individual accent, but Paris was a city largely populated by people from the provinces with innumerable regional accents which native Parisians had grown to indulge. Tourists regularly asked White for directions, assuming he was a native of the city. The years in Paris had

given him an elegance of dress – his preferred designer being
Kenzo – and he dressed in greys and blacks which accorded
with the colours of central Paris. The last vestiges of his
American college-boy style had gone. Like all Parisians, he
moved through the streets rapidly, from assignation to assignation. The centre of Paris encompassing the apartments of
White's friends and his favourite meeting places was a very
small sphere, easily covered on foot. If pressed for time, White
took taxis, preferring the brusque slang of the taxi-drivers to
the labyrinthine métro stations.

His walks around the districts bordering his home were also
geared to working off the relentless impact of rich lunches and
dinners. Over his first decade in Paris, White had gradually
put on weight and moved from the still boyish figure of his
mid-forties to the appearance of a suave patrician, jowled but
wryly amused by the transformation, with lined eyes and grey
hair, cut short and brutal in the Parisian style. He apprecia-
tively grew a formidable stomach and joked about his weight
gain to friends. He was conscious that where so many of his
friends and lovers – especially Hubert Sorin – had grown
emaciated with their disease and had found eating a torture, he
continued to wolf down whatever was placed in front of him
and saw his waistline expand accordingly. His physical appearance was the antithesis of that often associated with someone
whose body had held the virus for a decade or more. In 1993,
White had detailed his superstitions in avoiding the onset of
AIDS: 'Mine are that I'm fat, which protects me, that I sleep
a lot, which protects me, and that I'm very calm.'[119] He
particularly haunted the restaurant Le Grizzli, close to his
apartment in the Rue Saint-Martin, and on most days had one
of his meals at the Café Beaubourg, on the plaza in front of the
Centre Georges Pompidou, where the handsome young waiters
were sure to flirt with him. The Café Beaubourg was also a
place where he found he could write easily in the mornings,

with an unobtrusive buzz of people around him. Most evenings, he either attended or gave a dinner party, often spending almost the entirety of the day preparing multiple courses. At times, it seemed that White was more vulnerable to the excesses of his rich diet than to AIDS. On one occasion, after spending a month on holiday in the Périgord region of South-Western France, intensively sampling the region's celebrated pâtés and other rich dishes, he noted: 'I'll have to be carried back to Paris in a wheelbarrow.' On another occasion in October 1994, after an evening at a Saint-Germain-des-Prés restaurant renowned for the extravagance of its pâtés (the owner had recently died of heart failure after over-indulging on his own dishes), White experienced severe heart pain and had to call out the emergency medical services, who, having taken an electro-cardiogram, diagnosed the problem as 'gas'.

In August 1996, White met and befriended the young French gay novelist Guillaume Dustan, whose first novel *Dans ma chambre* (*In My Room*) created a sensation in Paris on its publication in that autumn. Dustan was a provocative pseudonym – the novelist was thinking of Saint Dunstan, who tweaked the Devil's nose with a pair of pincers – adopted in order to safeguard a professional career. Dustan led a double life, working for most of the year as a lawyer on the island of Tahiti, but was spending the summer in Paris and had visited White at the Rue Saint-Martin. For White, Dustan was writing a kind of rawly explicit semi-autobiographical fiction about contemporary Parisian gay life that was revelatory, especially when set aside his discreet compatriots' evasions and the more baroque narration of English-language gay writing. The novel's first-person, present-tense narrative had a remorseless honesty about sex and drugs that White admired as something almost unique in contemporary European writing. Dustan hilariously mixed meticulous accounts of intensive fist-fucking and disco brawling with lengthy shopping lists of his narrator's purchases at the Parisian branch of Marks and Spencer.

Dustan's novel demonstrated to White that the essential preoccupations of Parisian gay life had remained the same in the decade or so since his arrival in the city; indeed, they stretched far back into the sexual history of the city. Dustan's characters, like those of Genet fifty years earlier in the original edition of his novel *Our Lady of the Flowers*, are often introduced with the exact dimensions of their penis size (in centimetres), and they are far more concerned with latex hoods, Prozac and the London club scene than with their HIV-Positive status. In Dustan's Paris, the necessity for safe sex has been overruled by his characters' need for immediate pleasure in a situation with an unknowable future: 'He tells me that his new guy loves to be fucked by him but that he hasn't yet fisted him. I ask him if all this is with or without a condom. He tells me, "You know that nobody uses condoms anymore, not even the Americans, now everybody is HIV-Positive, I don't know anybody who's still HIV-Negative" – that's true, I think, neither do I, except for Quentin, and he was last tested six months ago – "and you know me, I just go crazy, I love to drink sperm." '[120] At the end of the novel, the narrator comes close to suicide, but miraculously escapes Paris to begin a new life abroad – a striking parallel with the first-person narrator of a novel which had been inspirational for White in the 1960s, Knut Hamsun's *Hunger*, who escapes near-fatal starvation in 1890s Oslo at the last moment, by talking his way on board a freighter bound for Leeds. For White, Dustan was brilliant evidence of innovation in the Parisian gay writing that had been largely dormant since Hervé Guibert's death.

White was aware that the perception of AIDS had shifted in the mid-1990s, particularly among young gay men in their twenties. This new media-conscious generation of gay men had been aware right from childhood of the dangers of AIDS and of its evolving impact upon the gay community, and had decided to respond to the disease in their own ways. AIDS no longer held its mid-1980s aura of mercilessly certain death, and it had long been far from certain that those who carried the virus would develop full-blown AIDS. Many people had now been HIV-Positive for a decade or more, White included. With the development of effective new drug therapies, the virus was beginning for many to appear more as a threatening but potentially manageable condition than as a death sentence. White initially viewed that relegation of the dangers of AIDS with deep scepticism: the deaths of John Purcell in 1995, after an agonizing period of dementia, and of James Merrill in the same year, confirmed for him that the disease was potentially as lethal and unpredictable as ever. However, the sudden foreshortening of time which he had experienced with his diagnosis in 1985, with its attendant compulsion to experience life as intensively as possible and to rapidly fulfil all personal ambitions, had leaked into a future which was now conceivably that of a normal life-span. White's poignant belief of the period following his diagnosis that he was always seeing every friend and city for the last time had now completely gone. He commented: 'When I first discovered I was HIV-Positive, I lived in an elegiac twilight. Then I got bored with that. I thought I was saying farewell in my most melancholic way to things which I then found I came back and did again the next year.'[121] By the beginning of 1997, American news magazines were beginning to run headlines announcing that 'AIDS is over' (although the British and French media remained in general slightly more cautious). As advances in AIDS drug treatments accelerated – particularly with the lauded 'triple combination therapies' – White finally became convinced that, at least for Europeans and North Americans who could afford the treatments, it appeared that the epidemic had been largely defeated. For the first time since 1985, he could now expect to survive. The response among HIV-Positive gay men to that cancellation of imminent death was wide-ranging. Dustan's characters displayed an elated, defiant indifference towards AIDS and built their lives around an all-consuming sexual culture. Other gay men saw the opportunity to form a stronger and more resistant gay community through activism and art.

White had always felt a certain distance from the visible Parisian gay scene – which Dustan referred to with pride as a 'ghetto' – despite its proximity to his apartment in the Rue Saint-Martin. His lovers in Paris had tended either to be North Americans, or else to form part of the large but less overt community of Parisian gay men who conducted their affairs well away from the inhabitants of the brash gay bars and nightclubs around the Rue de la Ferronnerie and the Rue des Lombards, just south of the immense subterranean shopping complex of Les Halles. The visible Parisian gay scene was highly insular, structured around youth, dress code and house music, and though it fascinated White as a variant on the many other codified gay communities he had observed or participated in, it was firmly sealed from him. The focus of the more discreet gay community in Paris was a bookshop, Les Mots à la Bouche (the only gay bookshop in France), in the Marais district, and – as in the mid-1980s – its primary means of communication was still the Minitel. Much of the discourse about AIDS in Paris took the form of state-funded poster campaigns in the streets and métro stations, emphasizing the disease's hold on all sections of society. The main focus of attention of that discourse about AIDS during the early 1990s had been the French government's alleged culpable responsibility for the widespread infection with the virus – through contaminated blood transfusions – of a large number of haemophiliacs. Even from its outset, AIDS had never been represented in Paris as a 'gay disease'. In contrast to London or New York, the level of debate about AIDS among gay men was muted, in part because many of the emerging gay militant groups of the early 1980s in France had dissolved on Mitterrand's election, believing their objectives to have been fulfilled. Older gay men were often concerned not to highlight the contradiction between a candid gay identity and a respectable place in Parisian society.

Although White made occasional appearances on French television and radio to discuss gay issues, it was in London and the United States that he was able to contribute to the vitally developing debate about AIDS. In March 1996, he spoke at a conference at the Institute of Contemporary Arts in London, which explored the cultural representation of AIDS and the ways in which the new advances in treating the virus were being only selectively disseminated to the gay community. White was close to those in London who were the most influential figures in the sustained interrogation of the disease's impact there: the cultural commentator Simon Watney had tracked the homophobic distortions of AIDS in the media, while White's former lover Neil Bartlett was undertaking crucial creative work around AIDS, in the form of performances and writing projects that pointed out incisive historical parallels to the sensations and dilemmas of the present moment.

In the United States, the cultural response to AIDS was also undergoing considerable upheaval. The despondency of the mid-1980s had mutated both into a creative fury, and into a calm desire to track the history of gay life and to place AIDS legibly, without hysteria, into that history. In literature, one manifestation of this latter project was the publication in 1995 of the vast and evocative novel, *Like People in History*, by Felice Picano, White's friend from the Violet Quill days in New York; White had donated to Picano the title of his own unpublished novel of the mid-1970s. Picano's *Like People in*

History spanned the decades from 1954 to 1991, documenting the colliding trajectories of gay life and of AIDS. White, too, emphasized the necessity of producing histories of gay life that pointed out all that had been lost through AIDS – for White, the act of inscribing names was in itself a precious act of memory: 'I understand the imperative need to record names, to keep lists of the dead, to inscribe something about them on a quilt or on the page or on a gravestone.'[122] On his visits back to New York in the mid-1990s, White would walk the streets of Greenwich Village and see how it had been almost depopulated by AIDS of its dynamic 1960s and 1970s community of gay men; for him, that time was now a unique and painfully lost moment that was hard to sustain in its intensity in memory alone, so the remaining visual traces and languages of the gay life of the time were all the more essential. After years of its site serving as a bagel shop, the Stonewall Inn had reopened as a gay bar – with a clientèle mainly of tourists, and specializing in bingo sessions – and it bore a plaque commemorating the riots of the night of 27 June 1969. The section of Christopher Street around Sheridan Square that had seen the police charges and violence of that night had now been renamed 'Stonewall Place' on its street signs. But the community of Christopher Street had irreversibly changed, becoming a mixture of the street's new and more wealthy inhabitants, together with a street population at night of Puerto Ricans who used the street as a stopping-off point on the subway journey from central Manhattan to the city's outlying districts. The gay population of Christopher Street had been largely supplanted, just as its many previous layers of populations, such as its Italian shopkeeper families, had disappeared over time.

The Los Angeles-based performance artist Ron Athey was at the experimental forefront of the North American response to AIDS, and he embodied the creative fury against the disease and its manipulation by the media. In 1995, White met the

HIV-Positive Athey; the legendary rock singer Patti Smith had instructed him to go and see White, with the message: 'Patti sent me.' Patti Smith – a former lover of Robert Mapplethorpe, who had photographed her fragile but ferocious body for her record sleeves – had found White's biography of Genet inspirational. Athey was a striking figure with his imposing dress and shaven head – a 'scuzzy faggot with a tattooed face',[123] as he liked to describe himself. He was notorious for impaling himself with hooks in mid-performance, but his most powerful stage persona was one based on the fundamentalist faith healer Miss Velda, whose spectacular church services Athey had witnessed in Los Angeles in childhood. White admired the way in which Athey probed the explosive ground between AIDS and fundamentalism with his imagery of a violent, hard-won healing. Athey's work also mirrored the exasperation which many gays, including White, felt towards the stagnating political situation in the United States. Although Bill Clinton's pro-gay promises and his election as President in 1992 had been greeted with delight by American gays – anyone had to be better than his war-crazed predecessors of the supposedly affluent 1980s, Reagan and Bush – they found that little essential change took place in subsequent years. Clinton's promises about terminating anti-gay discrimination in the military faded into air; he was constrained by the Republican-dominated Congress, and many gays feared he had veered to the right under the pressure of the vast religious fundamentalist influence in American society. His re-election in November 1996 was greeted with little enthusiasm by White, who viewed him as a bogus figure on a par with John F. Kennedy. On many levels, America remained deeply reactionary and hostile to gay culture, and White was exhilarated by work such as Athey's which exposed the lethal workings of conservatism and fundamentalism in American society.

An increasing conservatism was also exerting its power on

French society, and White watched with unease the changes which took place in the racial climate of the country in the wake of Jacques Chirac's election as President in 1995. With his preoccupation with the workings of memory, White had been acutely aware throughout his years in Paris of how selectively memory operated in France, from the collective forgetting of the French administration's collaboration with the Nazi régime during the 1940s Occupation, to the more recent oblivion among contemporary French writers and philosophers about their now-unfashionable allegiance to Communist ideals during the late 1960s and early 1970s. He also viewed with alarm the increasing polarization of wealth and poverty in contemporary France, and the entrenchment of social strata through a rigid system of power privileges. Above all, the racism of France shocked him. Now, the influence of Chirac's government of patriotic right-wingers, with their determination to curb North African immigration and place tighter surveillance on Africans resident in Paris, increasingly began to take its toll on the city's multi-cultural life. In August 1996, the Parisian police stormed a church in the Barbès district of Montmartre, the Église Saint-Bernard, to expel a group of Africans who had barricaded themselves in to avoid forcible deportation. A huge protest from cultural figures and celebrities, led by the young actress Emmanuelle Béart – who was expelled from the church alongside the Africans – was given saturation coverage in the media and exposed chronic divisions in French society. Many in France believed that Chirac's government had appropriated the essential substance of the National Front leader Jean-Marie Le Pen's racist agenda. White was horrified by the expulsions, which seemed to negate the idea of the open and racially plural country which Mitterrand's government had been espousing at the time he had arrived in Paris. For the first time, White's Parisian friends were telling him outright that they were ashamed to be French.

White spent much of the summer of 1996 travelling with Michael Carroll. They first spent two weeks in Venice. White no longer rented the floor of the Palazzo Barbaro where he had spent many summers with David Kalstone; on this occasion, he stayed in the apartment of a friend named John Hohnsbeen, an American expatriate art curator whom he had known since the early 1970s. Though still attached to the beauty of the city, White now had few surviving human links with Venice, and its atmosphere had become irreparably sad for him; so many of the close friends and lovers he had spent his summers with there were now dead. 'Venice was full of ghosts,' he commented. He and Carroll went next to Perpignan, on the border between France and Spain, to visit the Giacometti scholar James Lord at his home in the countryside, a large mansion surrounded by fields of peach trees. Lord also spent much of the year living in Saint-Germain-des-Prés in Paris, and formed part of a circle of gay men who staged highly ritualized dinner parties with an archaic and elegant style that reminded White of the virtually disappeared world of Proust's novels. He and Carroll then drove across rural South-Western France to the Île de Ré off the Atlantic coast, where Marie-Claude de Brunhoff – by then recovered from her cancer – had her summer home in the fishing village of Ars-en-Ré. White had visited the island, with its strange landscape of small white-washed fishermen's cottages and bicycle tracks lined by enormous hollyhocks, on many occasions over the past decade. The uncanny atmosphere of the island was in some ways close to that of Büyükada, and White always found it an ideal environment to write in; but the Île de Ré was also intensely fashionable with Parisian cultural figures such as Kristeva and Sollers, and the community became dense with intellectual intrigue in the summer months.

White had often expected *The Farewell Symphony* to be his final novel. In 1993, when he had just started working on it, he had said: 'First I had to finish the Genet book, and now I have to finish this novel. I think when I finish that, then I'll die. Maybe it's one reason I have trouble writing it, because I feel it's almost like a curse. It's like some fairy tale; when the princess finally finishes weaving the cloth, then she must die.'[124] Now, as at the moment when he had completed *Genet*, White was faced with the creative and human imperatives of life continuing in full flood, with new dilemmas and new pleasures. Rather than leading a posthumous existence, White found his life still expanding in intensity, demanding a more and more intricate creative response as he grew older. After completing *The Farewell Symphony* in July 1996, he spent much of the following autumn and winter contemplating future fiction projects. He had the idea for a novel that would explore the transforming European sexuality he had witnessed on his recent travels, and which had preoccupied him in London the previous year with the non-fiction project he had formulated there. His idea for the novel focused on the liaisons of a young Texan man living in contemporary Paris, in particular his relationship with an older American woman. White was convinced that he would be looking at the heart of upheavals in contemporary sexuality with his Paris novel, and was hurt when one of his American friends told him dismissively that Americans weren't interested in Paris any more. White was still deeply haunted by his relationship with Hubert Sorin and by Sorin's death, and he was contemplating the idea of writing a novel that would take as its starting point his experiences with Sorin; the project would form a kind of postscript to the trilogy that ended with *The Farewell Symphony*.

White had also formulated a new non-fiction project and began work on it almost immediately. In part, the project came out of his recent experiences of interviewing Jasper Johns and Cy Twombly for *Vanity Fair*. He was now planning a book of around twenty interviews with seminally influential gay men in every cultural area, aiming to probe the border between their fame and sexual identity. In October 1996 he travelled to London to interview the musician Elton John; he then flew to the United States for an interview with the gay music tycoon David Geffen at his house beside the Pacific Ocean in Malibu. Although Geffen was openly gay, he was coming under heated media scrutiny at this time as speculation intensified about a relationship and gay marriage between himself and the actor Keanu Reeves. White – who was accustomed to writing about other writers or artists – felt intimidated by the powerful businessman, who was preoccupied with the same arcane consciousness-raising therapies which White had encountered at the end of the 1970s among Los Angeles' rich gays, while he was researching *States of Desire* there. During his stay in the United States, White also travelled to New Haven on the East Coast, to give a reading at Yale University's Beinecke Library, which had acquired a large collection of his manuscripts and of photographs he had taken on his travels. The squares of white marble which formed the walls of the library's ground floor – where White gave his reading – had been designed to be so thin as to be partially translucent, allowing in natural light and giving the interior's atmosphere a strangely subaqueous quality. The reading marked the publication of the volume of coming-out stories edited by White's former magazine colleague, Patrick Merla, to which White had contributed his story *Cinnamon Skin*. It was a dignified occasion, but the day also made White aware once again how fragile a sense of dignity could be in New York. Merla had intended to accompany White to New Haven in a chauffeured car, but changed his mind at the last minute, distraught at the prospect of leaving New York even for an afternoon. Once the car had set off on the two-hour journey towards New Haven, White grew increasingly anxious: 'The driver was a real thug with killer's hands.' The driver demanded to be paid in cash for both the

outward and return journeys when they arrived at the Beinecke, and then immediately disappeared, leaving White
stranded. When his hosts called the car hire agency in New
York to complain, they were met with vicious abuse and heard
the phone slammed down. White commented wryly: 'It was a
real New York experience.'

At the beginning of January 1997, White and Carroll travelled to Key West, where White had often spent part of
January each year since the late 1970s. As well as writing the
first chapter of *A Boy's Own Story* on Key West, he had also
visited the island in 1979 to report on the situation there for
States of Desire, at a time when the vast expansion of gay life
on the island was just taking off. Then, White had evoked an
island still visibly in the process of being turned from a decrepit
redneck outpost – whose houses were 'almost audibly dilapi-
dating into the rank soil'[125] – into an upmarket gay resort with
astronomical property prices; by the mid-1980s, the island's
metamorphosis into a tourist industry product had been complete, and much of its distinctive character and isolation –
which had attracted notorious residents such as Ernest Hemingway – had disappeared. But over the next decade, the island
became less fashionable through the ascendancy of nearby
Miami Beach, and the ramshackle atmosphere of Key West
began to reassert itself again. Its gay population had dwindled
too from the losses through AIDS. The island had a long
history of prominent gay writers spending the winter months
there; its most celebrated gay resident had been Tennessee
Williams, who had lived there for over thirty years. With its
Caribbean climate, Key West's atmosphere had always been far
more indolent than its northern counterpart, Fire Island, but
its high season was marked by extravagant celebrations. An
informal gay writers' conference had taken place during each
year's season since 1982, around a particular current issue; in
January 1997, the theme was the changing perception of AIDS

and the range of responses from gay literature to those changes. White delivered the main address at the conference, but its rancorous atmosphere demonstrated to him that the many polarized factions in American gay literature – which the Violet Quill club had attempted to reconcile in 1980 – remained as strong and divisive as ever. From Key West, White and Carroll travelled on to Mexico City, and then headed south to Oaxaca, an elegant eighteenth-century city of white-walled mansions and markets, where they stayed for three weeks. After returning to Paris at the beginning of February, White spent the spring months at the Rue Saint-Martin, working on his new projects, particularly a plan for a book on Proust.

The Farewell Symphony was finally published in Britain in May 1997. It brought to an end the trilogy which had encompassed eighteen years of work for White, from its origins in the first chapter of *A Boy's Own Story*, written on the island of Key West in the autumn of 1979. For the book's cover, White had chosen a photograph taken by Louis Stettner in New York in the 1950s, of a young man sitting on a bench with his back to the camera, his eyes looking up to the sky, with a stark, exhilarating backdrop of the Manhattan skyscrapers and the East River. The novel was dedicated to Michael Carroll, who had been living with White throughout the latter stages of his work on it. The book was longer than the previous two volumes of the trilogy, *A Boy's Own Story* and *The Beautiful Room is Empty*, put together; writing *Genet* had convinced White of his ability to sustain and intensify his preoccupations over the span of a long book. He had been impressed while writing *The Farewell Symphony* with Felice Picano's 1995 novel of the same length, *Like People in History*, which also used an intricate flashback structure (though Picano's novel was modelled far more on a pre-existent saga format, intercutting sequences from one night in 1991 back to points over nearly four decades, in order to construct its historical panorama of gay culture as a glamorous continuity, only momentarily torn by AIDS). Picano had visited White in Paris in June 1996, while White was completing *The Farewell Symphony*, and White had introduced a bookshop reading given by Picano in Paris from his novel. In the final stages of his work on *The Farewell Symphony*, the other English-language novel which had most struck White was Neil Bartlett's intricate piecing-together of London's secretive gay life of the 1920s and 1950s, *Mr Clive and Mr Page*. This was a very different kind of reconstruction of gay history, both in style and preoccupation, to Picano's artless approach (Bartlett commented: 'I wouldn't line my budgie's cage with *Like People in History*').[126] Like White's narrator, Bartlett's Mr Page moves fluidly and intimately from decade to decade through the fragile medium of memory, uncovering and connecting together moments of violent ecstasy and painful loss. But in contrast to the work of both Picano and Bartlett, White gave the narrative of *The Farewell Symphony* an accumulating power, developed through its lengthy depiction of the unique sexual culture of the 1970s, then explosively unleashed in its account of the devastation of the years of AIDS. As the novel's title suggested, it was also a work of someone still creating and communicating while surrounded by silence and loss. It explored the necessity and vitality of surviving through memory, existing through the life language creates.

In *The Farewell Symphony*, the narrator of *A Boy's Own Story* is more identifiably White himself, older now and ready to reveal himself in his contemporary life. Characters from the previous two novels of the trilogy reappear in the narrative, together with figures from the stories collected in *Skinned Alive*, such as the film producer Hajo. Events which had previously only appeared in White's non-fiction, notably the episode involving his Texan step-grandfather which had been recounted in *States of Desire*, now cross into the terrain of fiction. But the language of the novel is delirious, like that of *Nocturnes for the King of Naples*, and every incident and character becomes the product of that articulate delirium. The resulting book is a novel about what it means to reveal the self, and about how human experience can be transformed into a material so vivid that it is absorbed intact by its reader. White believed that the novel's narrative structure returned to the intricacy of *A Boy's Own Story* – after the more streamlined, spare structure of *The Beautiful Room is Empty* – in its sensual and intimate placing together of the narrator with his character. But the central element of the narrative of *The Farewell Symphony* is a story never told, although it is occasionally intimated in fragments, and its telling is once attempted and soon abandoned. That story – the death of the narrator's lover, Brice – is the loss around which all of the other stories of loss that make up the novel revolve.

The novel begins with a visit to the cemetery where Brice's ashes are kept. As with the two previous novels of the trilogy, the narrative begins in immediacy, in the presence of memory: 'I'm beginning this book on All Saints' Day in Paris, six months after Brice's death. This morning I went with Brice's brother and his brother's lover to the Père Lachaise cemetery to leave some flowers before the white marble plaque that marks the niche where Brice's ashes are stored in an urn.'[127] The narrative abruptly flashes back to the first visit to Paris made by the narrator's younger self in the late 1960s, and the bout of hepatitis he suffers in his hotel room. Paris is deeply unsettling and alienating, but also irresistibly attractive. Momentary sensations and incidents from the narrator's contemporary life in Paris occasionally seep into the central narrative of the early 1970s in New York, with sudden, hallucinatory force, then abruptly recede again; images from the narrator's dreams, too, make sudden apparitions that flash into the reader's eyes and then disappear. The narrator's character perceives his experiences in New York as essentially filmic – with time condensing, expanding, or suddenly leaping forwards or backwards – especially when his perception is disrupted by drugs or drink or sex. His life is driven by sex. He meets a new lover, Craig: 'Our bodies were immense, geographical, ideal as those elemental gods, dispersed to the flowing elements except where touch quarried out a rich, juicy intricacy of shape and feelings – shame, bliss, sluttishness, awe.'[128] This combination of monumental transformation and intimate sensation is extended out to the entire gay sexual culture of the 1970s, with its experiments into opposing social structures and recreating them from zero.

After a stay in Rome, the nameless character begins to meet a world of New York intellectuals, such as the poet, Max, and the professor, Joshua, who help him with his writing career. He simultaneously inhabits two mutually exclusive spheres: that of the cerebral and seductive rituals of his intellectual friends, and that of the raw sexual rituals of the bath-houses and the marginal piers and docks of Greenwich Village. One evening, at the docks, the character meets an immense retarded man named 'the Doofus' who, to the narrator's astonishment, manages to service six men at once: 'I knew that I was capable of jerking off for years to come thinking about him; now that the years have come and gone I can swear to the accuracy of my prediction.'[129] The character begins to share an apartment with a young actor named Kevin, with whom he falls in unreciprocated love. The character's family is in turmoil: his father dies, his divorced mother develops cancer, and his alcoholic sister is placed in a psychiatric hospital. He looks at a family photograph of his ancestors: 'The family picture of all twelve children and the parents on the porch looked like roadkill caught in the headlights.'[130] By the beginning of the

1980s, the New York worlds he has inhabited are beginning to disintegrate with the onset of AIDS, and he moves to Paris, where he meets a new lover, Brice. But Brice also has AIDS: 'I was no longer afraid of intimacy, since I knew that I'd finally arrived at the end of all feeling, all experience, and that the moments that remained to him and to me might as well be as intense as possible.'[131] By the final pages of the novel, virtually everyone who has figured in it has now died, and the narrative breaks off in Venice in the mid-1980s as the character discards his dead friend Joshua's possessions.

The Farewell Symphony is a book absorbed with the nature of time, and with the power of language and art to make time accelerate or slow down, in order to render the transformation of time by memory and perception. In the narrative of the novel, this power is humorously embodied in the work of the New York theatre director Ross Stubbins. A lover of Stubbins describes his obsession with time: 'Maurice had told Kevin that Stubbins didn't despise the commercial theatre but had just found that everything on stage happened too fast. "Everyone was speeding around in such a brisk, artificial way, making entrances and exits like birds in an overwound cuckoo clock, and Stubbins thought any five minutes would be good if it was slowed down to five hours." In a Stubbins play a woman could take an hour to peel and slice an onion.'[132] The entirety of *The Farewell Symphony* is itself an experiment with time: in the first part of the book, sexual experiences and sensations are ecstatically sustained, minutely probed and explored; but, when the book passes on to depict the coming of AIDS, it accelerates with thunderous immediacy.

The novel, like all of White's books, is concerned with the ephemerality of memory, as something which corrodes with age and has to be induced to transmit the past with all the lucidity and precision of a filmic image. The book constantly catches the matter of memory in the form of images, as when the narrator remembers the body of one of his lovers: 'His biceps looked like veined gooseberries packed in snow.'[133] In writing *The Farewell Symphony*, White was also conscious that, like a kind of subjective ethnographer, he was using elements of memory to re-create a recent but already lost reality – that of the 1970s New York gay culture that had been decimated by AIDS. Whereas with *A Boy's Own Story* he had been reconstructing the universal terrain of individual childhood through memory, he was now acting to document a community in which he himself had been intimately involved. While writing the novel, he commented: 'I have had to become anthropologist, historian and novelist rolled into one, re-creating the smallest details of dress and behaviour that once might have been taken as read. It's the weirdest thing, as if you were Marcel Proust writing in the 1920s about the 1890s.'[134]

In its evocation of the gay community of 1970s New York, *The Farewell Symphony* presents a compelling portrait of the city itself, as well as of its venues for sex, with their dark, hallucinatory interiors. The novel's character visits the Mine Shaft sex club (a venue familiar from *States of Desire*), which is located in the city's meat-packing district. White evokes the surrounding city as one made of danger and sexual meat: 'The whole area was badly lit except for a sudden flare of flame in an oil drum on the curb where the butchers warmed their hands before heaving a side of beef onto moving overhead hooks that lurched and dangled the carcass out of a truck and into a warehouse. The pavement was gummy with dried blood and the air thick with the rich, gamy smell of fresh blood. The men in their blood-stained white aprons shouted orders and jokes – commands, anger, humour all sounded equally hostile.'[135] The novel's dense texture of sex is integrally linked to its preoccupation with death. One of the novel's key scenes is the death of the father who had been so crucial to the two preceding books of the trilogy, as a source both of oppression and of sexual, incestuous desire. When the character goes to see his father's corpse, he is aware that it has a stench of meat – the same stench the character experiences when he then sees a group of brash, drunken men on the plane as he returns to New York from his father's funeral. In the scene of the father's sudden death, observed by his second wife, his life leaves him by slow but relentless physical stages, just as his power over his son has gradually evanesced as his son has explored his own gay identity: 'He'd been sitting, watching TV and, as he was lighting his cigar, he'd suddenly stood up and said, "I can't feel anything in my feet. My God, it's moving up my legs. It's all over me." She said he should sit down. He did and he was dead, the lit match falling from his hand.'[136]

In representing the sexual and social experiments of the 1970s – and their unexpected suspension by AIDS in the 1980s – the novel holds no regrets. The narrator defiantly remembers that 'I assumed there was going to be a future and that it would get more and more extravagant. We saw gay men as a vanguard that society would inevitably follow. I thought that the couple would disappear and be replaced by new, polyvalent molecules of affection.'[137] White's own aim with the novel was to offer a kind of retrospective vindication of the decade's elevation of sex, and to highlight the incendiary and idealistic position of gay culture in its relationship with the dominant power of family and social structures. In 1993, shortly after he began work on *The Farewell Symphony*, he noted: 'The seventies were a period that had its own direction and would have developed in quite a different way without AIDS. I feel it wasn't a mistake, that it was a noble experiment – people were trying to get away from the traditional couple towards a community of sexual partners, lovers, friends. An American utopian experiment.'[138] White believed that he possessed a lucid view of the 1970s in New York since he had then abruptly left the city for Paris, leaving his memories of that decade intact and vivid. He was especially concerned to write about the decade's experiments in masochistic sex (as he had in some of the non-fiction pieces collected three years earlier in *The Burning Library*), since he was aware how urgent and productive a cultural interest had developed around masochism and its representation in the mid-1990s. *The Farewell Symphony* accords far more emphasis to the insurgent gay culture of the 1970s than to the massive devastation subsequently wrought by AIDS – though, with the concentrated impact of the concluding pages of the novel, that final curtailment is visceral in its force.

The Farewell Symphony confronts the desire for a revealing transparency about the presences in the novel of its own writer and narrator, its reader, and about the story being told. In 1993, after his years of being saturated in the constant self-revelations (and self-concealments) of Jean Genet's writings, White declared that his 'new goal' with *The Farewell Symphony* was 'to confide everything, including the drudgery, the fear of failure. I believe in a total transparence now.'[139] For White, achieving an ultimate candidness would be an authentic way of exploring the creative process of art – unveiling the writer's means of representing memory and experience, and, at the same time, resulting in a complete revelation of the writer's own self. This idea of transparency also had another meaning – it referred too to the ghostly transparency White felt in being a writer who was HIV-Positive. He noted: 'Something about being sero-positive gives you this slightly ghostlike feeling toward the world and toward the reader, and toward your own experience even.'[140] And, finally, the idea of transparency is conceived by White in *The Farewell Symphony* as the necessity to transform life through language, through the creation of a kind of beautiful emptiness or void – a void which is then to be filled by the reader. As Jean Genet declared in the very last sentence of his final book: 'This last page of my book is transparent.'[141]

But, even with the desire for all the layers of the book and the self to be peeled off, there can be no final transparency in language or the image or the self for a living writer. There remains the ongoing search for that ultimate transparency in the art of writing, and for the next book.

Coda

The Burning World

Edmund White's writing is about the burning necessity to transmit sensations, histories, cultures from a life that has encompassed some of the most extreme upheavals of the contemporary world. In White's work, with its urgent desire to communicate, there is always the presence of the reader, who may be appalled by his work, seduced by his work, but whose position within it is essential and determining. As White has noted: 'A book exists only when a living mind re-creates it and that re-creation comes into being only through the full imaginative participation of a particular sensibility.'[1] It is through this imaginative rôle of the reader – inflecting the book individually and making it the reader's own story – that the book becomes lost from the writer to the reader. In White's work, with its absolute intimacy, that loss is both an exposure and a vital release. This sense of release – integral to White's desire for transparency – is what then compels the writer to move on to create the next book. All of White's work is a kind of survival through language.

White's life has been shaped by memory. His life has, alongside it and throughout its course, the power of memory enveloping the present. His work is saturated in the imageries of memory. In 1977 – even before his books had helped to form gay life, and even before AIDS had decimated that gay life – he had described his memories of his life as 'complex, fragmentary and far from logical'.[2] Equally, his life, accompanied and transformed by memory, is vivid, extraordinary and immediate – a contemporary life all the more prescient for its intricacy and illogicality.

White's life is bound up with the trajectory of AIDS. He watched the first manifestations of the disease as it began to exert its influence in the gay community of New York at the beginning of the 1980s. White responded initially with disbelief, and then through his work in the founding of the Gay Men's Health Crisis group. By the end of the 1990s, he had seen the indications that AIDS was finally on the way out, at least as far as America and Europe were concerned. Although AIDS became the dominant feature of gay culture in the last two decades of the twentieth century, White himself treated it with great familiarity as a constant companion to his life – responding to it like a writer engaged with a particularly fickle kind of reader, who is sometimes sharp and even inspiring, sometimes dull and uninteresting, but who, at any moment, has the ability to capriciously throw the book away across the room. Much of White's work during those decades sought to place AIDS – which, by its murderous, random profile had first appeared to be entirely irrational – within the history of gay culture: not as something which had over-ridden that culture, but as something which had interrupted that culture and had to be dealt with on that basis.

For White, AIDS and America eventually formed a strangely gelling concoction. Certainly, much of conservative America had been repelled by AIDS, and the religious fundamentalists saw it as providing the ideal opportunity to overturn the degree of political power which gays were beginning to acquire at the end of the 1970s, while White was travelling around the country to write *States of Desire*. But there was also in America a compelling human fascination with AIDS – mirrored in the countries of Europe to diverse degrees – which allowed America a channel into gay culture. In the 1970s, by the swimming-pool at the Continental Baths on the Upper West Side of New York, White had experienced gay culture as something which was becoming highly attractive and inspirational to young heterosexual Americans. The first years of AIDS brought an end to that fascination with the revolutionary forms of gay sex, fashion and art. But the media profile of AIDS (with all its excesses) then joined together with the persistent vitality of gay culture to result in a degree of eminence accorded to that culture. White came to believe that he had seen gay life liberated, exalted, devastated and, finally, given an institutional status over the last three decades of the twentieth century. His own life formed a sensitized embodiment of all those transformations.

White's life is divided by his experiences in two cities – New York and Paris – and it is marked by the conflicting impacts of those cities upon it. The New York island of Manhattan – and White's other American islands, Fire Island and Key West – were replaced by the Île Saint-Louis in Paris and by a collection of other European islands whose cultures fed into his work, most notably Crete and Büyükada. For White, arriving in 1962 from the Mid-West to live in New York, the city was a revelation in its sexual and creative potential, epitomized by the night streets of Greenwich Village. But by the time he left the city, twenty-one years later, New York was beginning to take on the contours of a damaged, emptied city for White: almost all of his closest friends and lovers from his years there – David Kalstone, James Merrill, Bill Whitehead, Christopher Cox, John Purcell, among very many others – would die of AIDS over the decade or so following his departure. With his move to Paris in 1983, White encountered another city in which he was to see many of his friends and lovers again die from AIDS: Gilles Barbedette, Michel Foucault and Hervé Guibert among them. He himself learned after his move to Paris that he was HIV-Positive. But Paris remained a deeply sustaining and pleasurable city for White – one that vitally opened out his preoccupations as well as provoking and exasperating him. His move to Paris also led him to what he experienced as his great love affair, with Hubert Sorin – a relationship whose brevity and final tragedy in the desert towns of Morocco failed to dissolve its intensity.

White's writings look forward to a future of culture as one unlimited by either the rigidity of political correctness, or by the persecution of individuals for their race or sexuality (for White, the power structures behind those two forms of repression have a resemblance). In large part, his experiences as an outsider in Paris – and his contacts with other expatriate writers and artists there – gave to White his view of the future of culture as hybrid and proliferating, impossible to pin down to a national or political or social formula, and finally, joyfully elusive.

White's work explores what it is to experience life fully. His work has dealt with everything from the minutely nuanced moods of gay childhood to the sudden desolation resulting from AIDS. His compelling fascination is for the beauty of the male human body, for sex and for death, and for the impulses behind creativity. In White's world, these preoccupations and values move irrepressibly and provocatively between one another. He has said: 'I do think that sex is something worth dying for. I believe what art is primarily about is beauty, and what beauty is about is death.'[3] So White's world burns.

Notes

Unless otherwise noted, all quotations from Edmund White are from interviews with the author, recorded in Paris and London between July 1993 and June 1997.

Part 1: Terrains of Memory – Cincinnati to New York

1. Edmund White, *States of Desire*, Picador, London, 1986, p. 180.
2. ibid., pp. 135–6.
3. 'The Gay Philosopher' (written in 1969, but unpublished at the time), in Edmund White, *The Burning Library*, ed. by David Bergman, Picador, London, 1995, p. 4.
4. Edmund White, *Genet*, Picador, London, 1994, p. 669.
5. 'The *Paris Review* Interview' (1988), in *The Burning Library*, p. 242.
6. Edmund White and Dale Brown, *The First Men*, Time-Life International Books, The Netherlands, 1974 edition, p. 9.
7. Juan A. Suárez, *Bike Boys, Drag Queens and Superstars*,

Indiana University Press, Bloomington and Indianapolis, 1996, p. 137.

8. 'The *Paris Review* Interview', in *The Burning Library*, p. 242.

9. Edmund White, 'Edmund White Speaks with Edmund White' (a 'self-interview' from 1994), *Review of Contemporary Fiction*, Normal, Volume XVI, Number 3, Fall 1996, p. 16.

10. 'The Gay Philosopher', in *The Burning Library*, p. 11.

11. ibid., pp. 18–19.

12. Edmund White, contribution to BBC Radio 4 programme *Sentimental Journey* (recorded in Rome, January 1996), transmitted on 4 February 1996.

13. Brian Boyd, *Vladimir Nabokov: The American Years*, Princeton University Press, Princeton, 1991, p. 608.

14. Edmund White, *Forgetting Elena*, Picador, London, 1984, p. 57.

15. ibid., p. 11.

16. ibid., p. 25.

17. ibid., p. 53.

18. ibid., p. 69.

19. ibid., pp. 29–30.

20. ibid., p. 18.

21. 'The *Paris Review* Interview', in *The Burning Library*, pp. 251–2.

22. Derek Jarman, *Kicking the Pricks*, Vintage, London, pp. 63–5.

23. ibid., pp. 60–62.

24. *States of Desire*, pp. 282–3.

25. *Kicking the Pricks*, p. 63.

26. ibid., p. 62.

27. Edmund White, 'Remembrances of a Gay Old Time', *Harvard Gay and Lesbian Review*, Boston, Volume III, Number 3, Summer 1996, pp. 8–9.

28. Robert Wilson, *Mr Bojangles' Memory*, Centre Georges Pompidou, Paris, 1991, p. 3.
29. Edmund White, 'Two Princes', in *The Burning Library*, pp. 328–9.
30. Edmund White, 'Two Eulogies', in *The Burning Library*, p. 342.
31. ibid., p. 343.
32. Edmund White, 'The Personal is Political' (1993), in *The Burning Library*, p. 370.
33. Edmund White, *Nocturnes for the King of Naples*, Picador, London, 1984, pp. 135–6.
34. ibid., p. 162.
35. ibid., p. 202.
36. ibid., p. 147.
37. ibid., pp. 185–6.
38. ibid., p. 165.
39. 'The *Paris Review* Interview', in *The Burning Library*, p. 262.
40. 'Remembrances of a Gay Old Time', p. 9.
41. Edmund White, Introduction (February 1994) to *A Boy's Own Story*, Picador, London, 1994, p. vii.
42. Edmund White, 'Sweating Mirrors', in *The Burning Library*, p. 101.
43. Edmund White, 'This is Not a Mammal', in *The Burning Library*, p. 109.
44. ibid., pp. 108–10.
45. *States of Desire*, p. 156.
46. ibid., p. 40.
47. ibid., p. 52.
48. ibid., pp. 86–7.
49. ibid., p. 37.
50. ibid., p. 282.
51. ibid., p. 26.
52. ibid., p. 334.

53. ibid., p. 13.
54. ibid., p. 40.
55. Afterword (1986) to *States of Desire*, p. 337.
56. James Miller, *The Passion of Michel Foucault*, Flamingo, London, 1994, p. 264.
57. Interview with Marina Warner, London, July 1996.
58. Edmund White, Introduction (March 1991) to *The Faber Book of Gay Fiction*, ed. Edmund White, Faber and Faber, London, 1991, pp. xiv–xv.
59. Felice Picano, *Like People in History*, Abacus, London, 1996, p. 416.
60. Oscar Moore, 'Rites of Fatality', *Guardian Weekend*, London, 21 September 1996, p. 16.
61. Thomas Avena, 'Interview with Edmund White' (1992), in *Life Sentences: Writers, Artists, and AIDS*, Mercury House, San Francisco, 1994, p. 222.
62. *A Boy's Own Story*, p. 5.
63. ibid., p. 124.
64. ibid., p. 31.
65. ibid., p. 217.
66. ibid., p. 83.
67. ibid., p. 1.
68. ibid., p. 9.
69. ibid., p. 17.
70. ibid., p. 107.
71. ibid., p. 134.
72. ibid., p. 175.
73. ibid., p. 84.
74. Avena, p. 237.
75. ibid., p. 217.
76. 'Sweating Mirrors', in *The Burning Library*, pp. 104–5.

Part 2: Edmund White in Paris

1. Edmund White, '1983', in *21: 21 Years of International Writing*, Picador, London, 1993, p. 128.
2. Simon Clarke, 'Three Cheers for Pornography', *The Independent*, London, 28 April 1995, p. 25.
3. Interview with Pierre Guyotat, Paris, August 1996.
4. Edmund White, *Sketches from Memory: People and Places in the Heart of Our Paris*, Picador/Chatto & Windus, London, 1994, p. 48.
5. Edmund White, contribution to BBC Radio 3 programme 'Speaking Volumes' (recorded in Paris, 10 December 1996), transmitted on 14 December 1996.
6. Susan Sontag, *AIDS and its Metaphors*, Penguin, London, 1989, p. 79.
7. Interview with Neil Bartlett, Brighton, April 1997.
8. Neil Bartlett, *Dressing Up* production documents, July 1983.
9. Interview with Neil Bartlett, Brighton, April 1997.
10. Neil Bartlett, *The Uses of Monotony in the Language of Oscar Wilde, Jean Genet, Edmund White and Juan Goytisolo*, Birkbeck College Publications, London, 1994, p. 9.
11. Interview with Neil Bartlett, Brighton, April 1997.
12. Introduction to *A Boy's Own Story*, p. xiv.
13. Adam Mars-Jones, Introduction to *Monopolies of Loss*, Faber and Faber, London, 1992, p. 3.
14. Susannah Clapp, *With Chatwin*, Jonathan Cape, London, 1997, p. 162.
15. James Morris, *Cities*, Faber and Faber, London, 1963, p. 357.
16. 'The *Paris Review* Interview', in *The Burning Library*, p. 251.
17. ibid., p. 252.
18. Introduction to *A Boy's Own Story*, p. vii.

19. Edmund White, *Caracole*, Picador, London, 1986, pp. 14–15.
20. ibid., p. 105.
21. ibid., p. 178.
22. ibid., p. 125.
23. ibid., p. 37.
24. ibid., p. 128.
25. 'The *Paris Review* Interview', in *The Burning Library*, p. 252.
26. Interview with Marina Warner, London, July 1996.
27. 'The *Paris Review* Interview', in *The Burning Library*, p. 252.
28. Edmund White, 'Aesthetics and Loss', in *The Burning Library*, p. 212.
29. ibid., p. 216.
30. Edmund White, *An Oracle*, in *Skinned Alive*, Picador, London, 1995, p. 144.
31. ibid., p. 159.
32. Interviews with Salomé (Wolfgang Cilharz), Berlin, February 1991, and with Rainer Fetting, Berlin, July 1991.
33. Edmund White, *His Biographer*, in *Skinned Alive*, p. 103.
34. Interview with Adam Mars-Jones, London, April 1997.
35. Edmund White, *Palace Days*, in *Skinned Alive*, p. 181.
36. ibid., p. 200.
37. Interview with Adam Mars-Jones, London, April 1997.
38. Edmund White, *Running on Empty*, in *Skinned Alive*, p. 34.
39. ibid., p. 44.
40. 'The Personal is Political', in *The Burning Library*, p. 372.
41. Edmund White, *The Beautiful Room is Empty*, Picador, London, 1988, p. 1.
42. ibid., p. 7.
43. ibid., p. 10.
44. ibid., p. 38.

45. ibid., p. 90.

46. ibid., p. 84.

47. ibid., p. 102.

48. ibid., p. 183.

49. Martin Duberman, *Stonewall*, Plume, New York/London, 1994, p. 202. In my description of the Stonewall riots, I've drawn partly on the eye-witness accounts offered of them in Duberman's book, together with Edmund White's own accounts.

50. *The Beautiful Room is Empty*, p. 143.

51. ibid., p. 110.

52. 'The Personal is Political', in *The Burning Library*, p. 372.

53. Interview with Pierre Guyotat, Paris, August 1996.

54. Interview with Albert Dichy, Paris, September 1994.

55. Interview with Paule Thévenin, Paris, March 1987.

56. Interview with Jane Giles, London, November 1996.

57. ibid.

58. ibid.

59. ibid.

60. Interview with Marina Warner, London, July 1996.

61. ibid.

62. Interview with Adam Mars-Jones, London, April 1997.

63. 'Speaking Volumes', 14 December 1996.

64. 'Remembrances of a Gay Old Time', p. 8.

65. Introduction to *The Faber Book of Gay Fiction*, p. xvi.

66. '1983', in *21: 21 Years of International Writing*, p. 127.

67. Introduction to *The Faber Book of Gay Fiction*, p. xvii.

68. *His Biographer*, in *Skinned Alive*, p. 105.

69. *The White World of Jean Genet*, directed by Jack Bond, a documentary transmitted by London Weekend Television in its series *The South Bank Show*, on 28 February 1993.

70. ibid.

71. *Après le Deluge: Post War Paris*, directed by David

Thomas, a documentary transmitted by Channel 4 Television in its series *Without Walls*, on 15 December 1992.

72. ibid.
73. Avena, p. 236.
74. *Genet*, p. 3.
75. ibid., p. 208.
76. 'The Personal is Political', in *The Burning Library*, p. 374.
77. Edmund White, Introduction (1995) to Jean Genet, *Splendid's* (trans. Neil Bartlett), Faber and Faber, London, 1995, p. xi.
78. Avena, p. 233.
79. Edmund White, 'Genet's *Prisoner of Love*', in *The Burning Library*, p. 308.
80. *Genet*, p. 723.
81. Introduction to *Genet*, p. xxxix.
82. *Genet*, p. 115.
83. ibid., p. 512.
84. Avena, p. 235.
85. Interview with Jane Giles, London, November 1996.
86. 'Speaking Volumes', 14 December 1996.
87. Avena, p. 223.
88. Introduction to *Sketches from Memory*, p. 1.
89. *Sketches from Memory*, p. 11.
90. ibid., p. 15.
91. ibid., p. 51.
92. ibid., p. 23.
93. ibid., p. 34.
94. Introduction to *Sketches from Memory*, p. 8.
95. ibid., p. 2.
96. Interview with Marina Warner, London, July 1996.
97. 'The Personal is Political', in *The Burning Library*, p. 367.
98. Avena, p. 239.
99. Edmund White, 'The Wanderer: Juan Goytisolo's Border Crossings' (1991), in *The Burning Library*, p. 294.

100. Edmund White, 'The Political Vocabulary of Homosexuality', in *The Burning Library*, p. 70.
101. 'The *Paris Review* Interview', in *The Burning Library*, p. 260.
102. Edmund White, 'Writer on a Hot Tin Roof: Tennessee Williams', in *The Burning Library*, p. 193.
103. Edmund White, 'On Reading: An Exaltation of Dreams', in *The Burning Library*, p. xxvi.
104. 'The *Paris Review* Interview', in *The Burning Library*, p. 262.
105. Edmund White, 'Philip Taaffe's *Al Quasbah*', *Artforum*, New York, Summer 1994, p. 67.
106. Edmund White, 'Twombly's Rebel Vision', *Vanity Fair*, New York, September 1994, p. 171.
107. Edmund White, 'Brightness Visible', *Vanity Fair*, New York, March 1995, p. 84.
108. Avena, p. 236.
109. Edmund White, *Skinned Alive*, in *Skinned Alive*, p. 88.
110. Edmund White, *Reprise*, in *Skinned Alive*, p. 177.
111. Interview with Albert Dichy, Paris, September 1994.
112. Edmund White, *Watermarked*, in *Skinned Alive*, p. 221.
113. Edmund White, *Cinnamon Skin*, in *Skinned Alive* (American edition), Vintage, New York, 1995, p. 269.
114. ibid., p. 273. (The term 'Sero-positive' – an Anglicization of the French term – means 'HIV-Positive'.)
115. Interview with Jane Giles, London, November 1996.
116. Poppy Z. Brite, 'His Mouth will Taste of Wormwood', in *Swamp Foetus*, Penguin, London, 1995, p. 46.
117. *Sentimental Journey*, 4 February 1996.
118. Introduction to *The Faber Book of Gay Fiction*, p. xvii.
119. Avena, p. 243.
120. Guillaume Dustan, *Dans ma chambre* (translation of this quotation by the author), P.O.L., Paris, 1996, pp. 46–7.
121. *Sentimental Journey*, 4 February 1996.

122. 'Remembrances of a Gay Old Time', p. 7.
123. Ron Athey, 'Raised in the Lord', *LA Weekly*, Los Angeles, 30 June–6 July 1995, p. 21.
124. Avena, p. 243.
125. *States of Desire*, p. 213.
126. Interview with Neil Bartlett, Brighton, April 1997.
127. Edmund White, *The Farewell Symphony*, Chatto & Windus, London, 1997, p. 1.
128. ibid., p. 20.
129. ibid., p. 220.
130. ibid., p. 326.
131. ibid., p. 420.
132. ibid., p. 312.
133. ibid., p. 301.
134. 'The Diarist of a Doomed Generation: an Interview with Edmund White' by E. Jane Dickson, *Daily Telegraph* (Arts Supplement), London, 3 December 1994, p. 14.
135. *The Farewell Symphony*, p. 399.
136. ibid., p. 438.
137. ibid., pp. 413–14.
138. 'The Charmer and the Thug: an Interview with Edmund White' by Philip Hensher, *Guardian* (Second Section), London, 15 June 1993, pp. 12–13.
139. Avena, p. 217.
140. ibid., p. 214.
141. Jean Genet, *Prisoner of Love* (translated by Barbara Bray), Picador, London, 1991, p. 375.

Coda: The Burning World

1. 'The Personal is Political', in *The Burning Library*, p. 376.
2. Edmund White, 'The Joys of Gay Life', in *The Burning Library*, p. 31.
3. Avena, p. 238.